Housing Markets &
Planning Policy

To Doris and Harry Jones
and to John and Isabel Watkins

Housing Markets & Planning Policy

Colin Jones

Professor of Estate Management
School of Built Environment
Heriot-Watt University

Craig Watkins

Reader in Property
Department of Town and Regional Planning
University of Sheffield

WILEY-BLACKWELL

A John Wiley & Sons, Ltd., Publication

This edition first published 2009
© 2009 Colin Jones & Craig Watkins

Wiley-Blackwell is an imprint of John Wiley & Sons, formed by the merger of Wiley's global
Scientific, Technical and Medical business with Blackwell Publishing.

Registered office
John Wiley & Sons Ltd, The Atrium, Southern Gate, Chichester, West Sussex,
PO19 8SQ, United Kingdom

Editorial offices
9600 Garsington Road, Oxford, OX4 2DQ, United Kingdom
2121 State Avenue, Ames, Iowa 50014-8300, USA

For details of our global editorial offices, for customer services and for information about
how to apply for permission to reuse the copyright material in this book please see our
website at www.wiley.com/wiley-blackwell.

Library of Congress Cataloging-in-Publication Data

Jones, Colin, 1949 Jan. 13-
  Housing markets and planning policy / Colin Jones, Craig Watkins.
    p. cm. – (Real estate issues)
  Includes bibliographical references and index.
  ISBN 978-1-4051-7520-3 (pbk. : alk. paper)
  1. Housing policy–Great Britain. 2. City planning–Great Britain. I. Watkins, Craig. II. Title.

  HD7333.A3J66 2009
  333.33′80941–dc22

                                                                              2009016435

A catalogue record for this book is available from the British Library.

Set in 10/13pt TrumpMediaeval by Newgen Imaging Systems (P) Ltd, Chennai, India
Printed and bound in Malaysia by Vivar Printing Sdn Bhd

1   2009

The Royal Institution of Chartered Surveyors is the mark of property professionalism worldwide, promoting best practice, regulation and consumer protection for business and the community. It is the home of property related knowledge and is an impartial advisor to governments and global organisations. It is committed to the promotion of research in support of the efficient and effective operation of land and property markets worldwide.

Real Estate Issues

Series Managing Editors

Stephen Brown   Head of Research, Royal Institution of Chartered Surveyors
John Henneberry   Department of Town & Regional Planning, University of Sheffield
K.W. Chau   Chair Professor, Department of Real Estate and Construction, The University of Hong Kong
Elaine Worzala   Professor, Director of the Center for Real Estate Development, Clemson University

Real Estate Issues is an international book series presenting the latest thinking into how real estate markets operate. The books have a strong theoretical basis – providing the underpinning for the development of new ideas.

The books are inclusive in nature, drawing both upon established techniques for real estate market analysis and on those from other academic disciplines as appropriate. The series embraces a comparative approach, allowing theory and practice to be put forward and tested for their applicability and relevance to the understanding of new situations. It does not seek to impose solutions, but rather provides a more effective means by which solutions can be found. It will not make any presumptions as to the importance of real estate markets but will uncover and present, through the clarity of the thinking, the real significance of the operation of real estate markets.

Books in the series

Greenfields, Brownfields & Housing
Development
Adams & Watkins
9780632063871

Planning, Public Policy & Property Markets
Edited by Adams, Watkins & White
9781405124300

Housing & Welfare in Southern Europe
Allen, Barlow, Léal, Maloutas & Padovani
9781405103077

Markets and Institutions in Real Estate &
Construction
Ball
9781405110990

Building Cycles & Urban Development
Barras
9781405130011

Neighbourhood Renewal and Housing
Markets
Edited by Beider
9781405134101

Mortgage Markets Worldwide
Ben-Shahar, Leung & Ong
9781405132107

The Cost of Land Use Decisions
Buitelaar
9781405151238

Urban Regeneration in Europe
Couch, Fraser & Percy
9780632058412

Urban Sprawl
Couch, Leontidou & Petschel-Held
9781405151238

Real Estate & the New Economy
Dixon, McAllister, Marston & Snow
9781405117784

Economics & Land Use Planning
Evans
9781405118613

Economics, Real Estate & the Supply
of Land
Evans
9781405118620

Development & Developers
Guy & Henneberry
9780632058426

The Right to Buy
Jones & Murie
9781405131971

Mass Appraisal Methods
Kauko & d'Amato
9781405180979

Economics of the Mortgage Market
Leece
9781405114615

Towers of Capital – office markets & international financial services
Lizieri
9781405156721

Housing Economics & Public Policy
O'Sullivan & Gibb
9780632064618

International Real Estate
Seabrooke, Kent & How
9781405103084

British Housebuilders
Wellings
9781405149181

Forthcoming

Transforming the Private Landlord
Crook & Kemp
9781405184151

Affordable Housing & the Property Market
Monk & Whitehead
9781405147149

Property Investment & Finance
Newell & Sieracki
9781405151283

Housing Stock Transfer
Taylor
9781405170321

Real Estate Finance in the New
Economic World
Tiwari & White
9781405158718

Contents

Acknowledgements

We would like to thank all those who helped bring about this book. The thoughts contained in this book developed over a long period of time and several of the core ideas about analysing and planning for housing markets have appeared in previous publications (Jones and Watkins, 1999; Jones, 2002; Adams and Watkins, 2002; Watkins, 2001, 2008; Jones and Maclennan, 1991; Jones and Brown, 2002; Jones and Leishman, 2006). Clearly the book has benefited from collaboration with numerous accomplished researchers. We would hope this book develops our thinking and reflects the comments that colleagues have offered on this work over time.

We would like to acknowledge the considerable debt we owe to Chris Leishman (University of Glasgow) who worked with us in developing a series of papers about the structure and dynamics of the Glasgow housing market (Jones *et al.*, 2003, 2004, 2005a). We would also like to thank Berna Keskin (University of Sheffield) for providing research and editorial assistance during this project.

We are grateful to the following for permission to reproduce copyright and illustrative material: Office for Public Sector Information for the use of data and Figure 6.1; Wiley Blackwell for the use of material from Chapter 8 of Adams and Watkins (2002); Taylor and Francis for the use of Tables 5.1 and 5.2 published originally in Jones *et al.* (2004); and Ed Ferrari (University of Sheffield) for the use of Figure 6.2.

Finally, we would like to thank Madeleine Metcalfe and Lucy Alexander at Blackwell Publishing for encouraging us to write the book and for giving us the 'nudges' required to ensure that the project reached completion.

Colin Jones
Craig Watkins
October 2008

1

Introduction

At the time of writing this book, the international authorities were engaged in coordinated action to shore up the international financial system and to avoid an unprecedented global economic recession. International housing markets had already seen significant adjustments to property values and numerous developers had been plunged into serious financial difficulty. The rate at which housing markets entered recession took many by surprise and has kick-started a process of adjustment in the perceptions and expectations of consumers and investors and in the rhetoric and priorities of policy makers.

Real house prices had risen very strongly in the vast majority of OECD (Organisation for Economic Co-operation and Development) countries since the mid-1990s. The rate of inflation had been particularly high in the UK, Ireland, Spain, the Netherlands, Belgium and Australia. This housing boom was notable for the size and duration of the market upturn and for the extent to which there has been convergence in price trends across countries. Significantly, housing market trends – it is argued – have become disconnected from economic fundamentals and had moved out of step with the business cycle (Girouard *et al.*, 2006). In fact, the International Monetary Fund (IMF) suggested that house prices in the UK, Ireland and Australia were 20–30% higher than could be justified by rising incomes or population growth (IMF, 2008). The explanation for this is, of course, complex and partly reflects mortgage lending practices, and non-rational investment behaviour. The weak response of new housing supply to price signals has also been a widespread problem. This low level of responsiveness reflects the high construction costs in some countries, such as the Netherlands and Sweden. Importantly, however, it also reflects the fact that most countries have imposed tight policy constraints to limit land supply (Ball, 2006).

These governmental constraints on land supply are to some extent understandable. Spatial economic restructuring and population growth have underpinned rapid urbanisation and urban sprawl around the globe. Urban sprawl is often accompanied by a host of negative outcomes including the loss of open space and environmentally valuable land, greater car usage and traffic congestion, and the abandonment and/or disinvestment in older neighbourhoods. The response has often been to introduce and expand planning policies to control urban development and mitigate these outcomes, even if this does limit the capacity of the housing market to respond to changes in demand.

These supply constraints make less sense when viewed in a context where owner occupation is the dominant tenure, the population is growing and housing demand is rising rapidly (e.g. in USA, Australia, Spain, Iceland, Greece). In these circumstances large (and growing) segments of the population will be unable to afford access to decent quality homes. Simple (mainstream) economics principles suggest that this can be remedied by increasing the supply of units by such an extent that the price of all new and existing housing is reduced. This can be politically unacceptable. Despite the obvious benefits to households on low incomes there may not be a widespread appetite for lower house prices. In fact, most voters like rising house prices and so do many powerful business interest groups including the development industry, financial institutions, real estate agents, valuers and lawyers. As a result, affordability problems tend to be addressed in three ways: offering lower quality (and cheaper) units; lowering construction costs through grants or subsidies to producers; or lowering real occupancy costs by raising incomes (Downs, 2004). Even though planning policies often explicitly emphasise social equity in the context of housing provision, this tension between controlling sprawl by limiting development and tackling affordability problems by encouraging new building and/or propping up demand continues to pose a conundrum for policy-makers and academics worldwide. This book seeks to explore these issues. It is hoped that, while we acknowledge that the arguments developed in the book are grounded within the context of planning for housing markets in the United Kingdom, there are important lessons that reach beyond this national context. There are, however, no simple solutions.

One housing market or many housing markets?

In the light of the trends discussed above, the performance of *the* housing market has become a national obsession in the UK. In the upturn, new stories about house price trends appeared in the popular press and media with relentless regularity. Even now, the appetite for housing market news remains undiminished, even though tales of significant prices rises and acute affordability problems have recently been replaced by stories of double-digit price decreases and record levels of repossessions and mortgage arrears. These stories have been and continue to be fuelled by a never-ending supply of market reports produced by mortgage lenders, including HBOS and Nationwide, who have an interest in supporting the profile of their brand; by professional organisations, such as the RICS, who seek to be seen as mature commentators on the property market; and by an ever-increasing number of firms who provide HM Land Registry house price data online and have businesses to promote. Although they are used in the press in a relatively indiscriminate manner, and there is almost never any veracity warning attached, the price indices published by these organisations vary greatly in terms of the methods used in their construction, their technical reliability and their accuracy. Very often each tells a marginally different story but this only serves to fuel the interest.

Significantly, these market indicators tend to be at their least meaningful when highly aggregated (at the national or regional level) and their least reliable when disaggregated to the local level. At the highest levels, the indices suffer from aggregation bias associated with pooling prices from different markets. At the local level, where sample sizes are smaller, prices changes are often a result of differences in what has been sold between reporting periods rather than any substantive change in underlying market conditions. This information offers little basis for an authoritative discussion about house prices in the UK, the South East or even the Sheffield or Edinburgh housing markets. This practice also exemplifies a more general problem in housing market analysis.

A key theme in this book is that the tendency to talk about *the* housing market is actually rather unhelpful. This masks the fact that, even in a buoyant market, there are some neighbourhoods where prices have remained flat or have fallen and that, despite the overwhelmingly gloomy media coverage in recent months, *some* homeowners in *some* neighbourhoods in *some* parts of the country have continued to experience price rises. The reality is that there are many markets for housing and that the geography of the housing market (or should that be markets) is extremely complex. These broad housing market indicators might be helpful in very general terms but one of the central arguments in this book is that it is important that the complex spatiality of the housing system (and the markets and submarkets that are its component parts) is properly understood. Planning policy decisions, in particular, need to be informed by highly detailed and relatively sophisticated analyses of the system.

Housing markets and planning policy

This brings us to a second important theme: the role of planning in the housing market. The UK housing system has, in recent, years been characterised by strong household growth and acute housing affordability problems. As a result, the government plans to deliver three million new homes in England by 2010. The planning system has increasingly become central to securing the delivery of this large increase in supply, but these new housing targets are highly contentious.

The planning system has long operated in an extremely politicised context in which the powerful interests of the private development industry are opposed by a strongly protectionist environmental lobby. Both sets of combatants have become increasingly sophisticated in their engagement with the media. Both sides score occasional wins as the take on the 'conflict' surrounding housing targets switches from the folly of decisions to support the building of 'soul-less boxes' or 'concreting' over the countryside to the failure to ensure an adequate supply of homes for first-time buyers and low-income and disadvantaged groups. The planning system, it seems, never wins, largely because, as currently framed, it has been set unattainable objectives.

The goals of the planning system have actually been recast in recent years. The concern is now with spatial planning which the government believes 'goes beyond traditional land use planning to bring together and integrate policies for the development and use of land with other policies and programmes which influence the nature of places and how they can function' (ODPM, 2005a). Spatial planning it is argued involves 'critical thinking about space and place as the basis for action and intervention' (RTPI, 2007). The planning system is now responsible for place making and has been charged with supporting 'sustainable development' and helping to create 'sustainable communities'. But framing planning objectives in these holistic terms creates significant challenges. It is well established, for example, that concepts like sustainable development are too vague to be operationalised (Campbell, 1996). This vagueness and holism introduces intractable tensions between competing policy objectives, especially when these can be seen to independently argue for the primacy of economic development or environmental protection or social equity at different times and when there is a failure to acknowledge the difficulties associated with managing tradeoffs.

The broad scope of the objectives set for 'planning' has made it a relatively easy target for critics. Mainstream economists, in particular, have been engaged in a sustained attack on the outcomes of development control and other land-use planning policies (e.g. Evans, 1988, 2003; Dawkins and Nelson, 2002). It is hoped that, in this book, we will develop a more nuanced and broader-based discussion about the effectiveness of the planning system. One major difference in our analysis is that we see planning as the broad range of spatial policies discussed above, rather than as a narrow set of regulatory functions. Another is that we acknowledge that there are long-standing tensions between the broader visions for planning and the rather more technocratic aspects of practice. The planning practitioners operating within this complex policy environment have little unambiguous guidance on how best to resolve inherent tensions. The argument developed here is that the planning policy environment and the operation of the housing market are both complex and, by extension, it is important to recognise that the solution to contemporary challenges in planning for housing will be complex too. There are no easy fixes. Politicians need to make difficult decisions, planning professionals need to embrace new competencies, and housing economists need to offer greater conceptual clarity and better analytical tools. Significantly, however, it is our contention that the planning system will never be able to effectively plan for the housing market in its current form.

The analytical approach

This book is centrally concerned with building an understanding of the workings of *housing markets*. The analytical focus will be on the *local* spatial scale and will be based on a distinctive *economic* disciplinary perspective. It is hoped that the adoption of an explicit economic perspective might be seen in a positive light. It is not our intention to add another voice to those that have used mainstream economic theory as a basis to attack the planning system. Rather it is hoped that we offer a constructive assessment of the strengths and weaknesses of planning policy and practice. The need for a effective planning system should be taken as a given.

We also hope that, in writing this book, the more esoteric concerns of applied economic analysis (undertaken by these authors and others) are presented in a relatively accessible non-technical manner. We remain aware, that as recently as the mid-1990s, there was a feeling that economists' contributions to housing policy debates were of limited interest to

Aims and objectives

The aim of this book is to argue that effective planning decisions must be underpinned by a detailed understanding of the economic structure and operation of the housing system. There are four key objectives. These are to:

- introduce the main policy challenges that contextualise planning for housing in a market system (with particular reference to the UK);
- explore the ways in which, in extensive international literature, economists theorise urban (local) housing markets and consider the extent to which a framework that emphasises segmentation can help enhance our understanding of the workings of the owner-occupied sector;
- undertake a critical evaluation of the current system of planning for housing based on an examination of the way in which planning decisions are made locally and the aggregate impacts of these decisions and the policies that frame them;
- consider how the system of planning for housing might (or ought to) operate to better steer housing markets.

The structure of the book

The pursuit of these objectives has helped to structure the book. The next part of the book (Chapter 2) sets the context for what follows by introducing the main housing and planning policy challenges in the UK today. The chapter provides an overview of house price trends at the regional and national levels during the last thirty years or so. These trends are explained in large part by macroeconomic forces. The discussion, however, also introduces housing affordability problems, the emergence of housing supply constraints, the nature and extent of tenure change, and growing concerns with sustainable urban forms. These issues are all revisited in subsequent chapters.

The second part of the book (comprising Chapters 3 to 5) is concerned with the structure and operation of the housing market. It offers a highly selective discussion of the way in which economists theorise and analyse the workings of the local systems. Chapter 3 considers market definitions and discusses different mainstream economic approaches to conceptualising the spatial structure of local housing markets. This analytical framework provides a starting point from which to begin to explore the implications of planning policies for the spatial distribution of house prices and housing densities. The final part of the chapter explores the theoretical and practical issues in defining housing market areas for use in policy making.

Chapter 4 considers the internal structure of local housing markets. It argues that markets are highly segmented and ought to be conceptualised as a set of interrelated submarkets. This chapter provides a brief account of institutional economic approaches to theorising market structures and explains how some of the key insights, particularly the notion of the housing submarket, are now combined with mainstream models. The chapter also reviews empirical evidence of submarket existence and discusses the problems associated with identification and delineation of submarket boundaries. It concludes by suggesting that the analysis of migration data offers a relatively powerful practical solution to submarket delineation.

Chapter 5 explores the dynamics of segmented housing markets. It begins by exploring the microeconomics of household locations decisions and then explores the movement (migration) of households through dwellings and relates this understanding of market processes to neighbourhood change (including disinvestment, decay and revitalisation). The analysis explicitly recognises that market dynamics are bound up with tenure patterns and with government policies toward tenure (including notably the right to buy). The influence of planning systems on the dynamics of this structure is not limited to the determination of the quantity and location of new homes. The analysis shows that the planning system has the power to reconfigure the internal structure of the market and redefine the spatial distribution of house prices.

The final part of the book (Chapters 6 to 8) focuses on planning for the housing market. Chapter 6 begins by charting the relationship between the development of planning policy and urban economic development. It provides an overview of the structure of the planning system and then focuses on the operation of the current system of planning for housing and, in particular, recent steps to increase its sensitivity to market information. The chapter offers a critique of the 'housing numbers' games that have become embedded within the system and of the rather weak role performed by strategic housing market assessments. It is argued that the system suffers from the failure to adequately theorise the market and from the relatively unambitious nature of most market assessments.

Chapter 7 draws back from these operational issues and adopts a broader perspective on the relationship between planning policies and housing markets. It locates the analysis of planning impacts in the context of policies designed to provide affordable homes, to deliver a social mix via planning agreements and to achieve sustainable development. This chapter considers the economic rationale for planning and uses this as a base against which to evaluate these policies. The central question concerns whether these policies conflict with basic economic realities. The conclusions point to some inherent tensions within policy objectives.

Chapter 8 draws together the key themes and considers the way forward. It starts by asking: what can be achieved by planning for housing markets? There are two areas for action supported by the analysis of policy challenges and market outcomes.

First, it is argued that the current objectives for spatial planning are ultimately unattainable and, as such, are actually unhelpful. Policy makers need to be clearer about their priorities. The planning system cannot address the needs of all stakeholders at all times but there is too much ambiguity and too many inherent contradictions surrounding the implementation of policy at present. The analysis in Chapter 7 suggests some logical (in economic terms) solutions, especially if policy makers and politicians are serious about their desire to work with markets. It would, for example, be sensible to think again about the desire to attain social mix through planning agreements. This policy will ultimately be defeated by market processes and, in reality, merely serves as an unnecessary distraction and unhelpful complication for those charged with implementing policy and securing planning outcomes at the local level. This does not mean that planners and planning policy should not be concerned with social justice. Rather the argument is that more equitable outcomes can be achieved with a clearer and less ambiguous set of policy priorities.

Second, the chapter considers the practicalities of improving the effectiveness of planning intervention in housing markets. This discussion highlights the need for a clearer conceptualisation of the structure and operation of local markets and the need for this to be reflected in the analytical framework used to examine market evidence. This, of course, has implications for education and training. Simplistic economic analysis will not be helpful but a more complex understanding will not emerge overnight. Investment in training will need to be accompanied by investment in local and national data management infrastructures. At present, the poor quality of market information is also a major constraint on the development of housing market analysis. Overall, it is clear that despite the rhetoric about responding to 'markets', there is little evidence that an understanding of market dynamics is central to planning policy or practice. This need not be the case.

2

The Housing Problem

The operation of the housing market is the focus of much public discussion in the UK, with house price trends a national obsession. In 2000 average house prices were four times average earnings in England but this had increased to more than seven times by 2006 (NHPAU, 2007). This upward trend was partially driven by macroeconomic forces, particularly low interest rates, and the peak of the cycle reached at the end of 2007 was hastened at least by the 'credit crunch'. The subsequent downturn in the housing market provides a 'correction' to the market trend but in itself is unlikely to lead to a new long-term lower plateau for house prices. Beneath the veneer of the long-term increases in real house prices there are a range of housing market issues including the nature of supply constraints, affordability, the changing housing system in terms of tenure, and a growing concern about the sustainability of cities. This chapter seeks to set the context for the book by reviewing the fundamental forces at work and the outcomes in terms of spatial house price inflation trends over the last forty years.

We draw on a number of data sources, namely the government's index of house prices that is only disaggregated to regions, plus two other house price series published by the Halifax (HBOS) and Nationwide Building Society. The chapter begins by summarising the context to the housing market in terms of demographics and tenure. It then examines national and regional price trends and cycles, looking in particular at the role of first-time purchasers and new supply. This review leads to an in-depth analysis of affordability that draws out both the growing size of the problem in the UK and its changing spatial pattern. The statistical analysis ends with the fourth quarter of 2007 representing the turning point of the cycle and a logical benchmark.

Housing market trends

The story of the housing market is a combination of short-term cycles set against a long-term increase in real prices. The average new house price in 1961 was £2770 and the 1960s saw consistent house price inflation with prices doubling (although a formal government house price statistical series does not begin until 1969) (CLG, 2008b). The 1970s saw a period of instability with a house price boom through 1972 and 1973 followed by substantial fall in real prices before a further boom in the latter part of the decade. The cycle repeated with the next boom in the latter half of the 1980s. The subsequent downturn saw house prices fall in absolute terms, not just in real terms, for the first four years of the 1990s as Figure 2.1 illustrates. It is not until 1997 that house prices begin to rise again above 5% per annum and annual house price inflation then persists above this level for the next ten years until its peak in the fourth quarter of 2007.

A key influence on these trends is inevitably the macroeconomy in the form of economic growth, real incomes and interest rates. The general

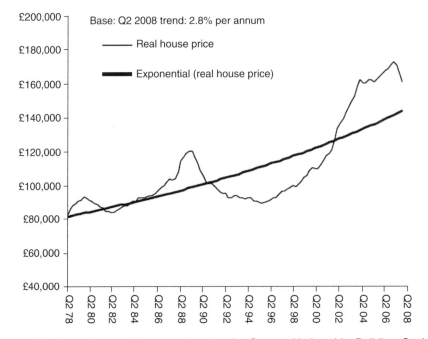

Figure 2.1   Long-term real house price trends. *Source*: Nationwide Building Society (2008).

Table 2.2   Average annual mortgage interest rates 1993–2007.

Year	Mortgage rate (%)
1993	5.63
1994	6.48
1995	7.16
1996	6.77
1997	5.84
1998	6.12
1999	5.98
2000	5.19
2001	5.48
2002	4.58
2003	4.18
2004	5.04
2005	5.23
2006	5.11
2007	5.75

Source: Council of Mortgage Lenders.

availability of mortgage funds for house purchase has also at times been important. The downturns in house prices at the beginning and end of the 1980s were linked both to a rise in interest rates and the onset of a recession. The upswings in house prices of the early 1970s, the 1980s and from the late 1990s were similarly linked to upturns in the economy with rising real incomes and falling interest rates (see Table 2.2). These house price booms are also associated with the easing of mortgage constraints making funds to buy more available as demonstrated by increasing loan-to-value, loan-to-income ratios and mortgage lengths. A mortgage famine also contributed significantly to the housing market slump of the mid-1970s and this has now been repeated in 2007/08 with the tightening of credit following the international sub-prime finance crisis. The write off of bad debts reduced the asset base of many banks which has led to a reduction in available mortgage finance. The effect has been exaggerated by banks moving from lending policies that collectively underpriced risk with very generous credit rationing rules to the reverse, where overpricing of risk has substantially lowered the mortgage terms available. Some homeowners (including landlords in particular) have found difficulties when renegotiating short-term loans and have been forced to sell, thereby adding an additional deflating influence on the housing market.

These economic and financial market factors can be seen in the house price boom that began in the middle of 1996 and gathered pace in 2002. The initial boom coincided with the fall in the bank base rates from 1997 onward and then accelerated with the fall to 4% in the latter half of 2001 (reduced again to 3.75% in February 2003). Over this period average earnings continued to rise at well above the rate of inflation (although the gap began to narrow from the last quarter of 2002, and personal direct and indirect taxes began to rise). At the same time unemployment fell to levels not achieved for over a quarter of a century.

The discussion highlights many common features of these cycles. However, a key difference of the latest house price boom has been the weak response of the house building industry. In previous house price booms the increase in house prices has led, after a lag, to an increase in the number of houses built speculatively for sale. Table 2.3 shows that private sector new house completions fall away in the early 1990s following the recession, but as annual house price inflation begins to rise in the late 1990s there is no substantive rise in new house building completions until 2004/05. In 2003 fewer houses were constructed in the previous six years than during any other equivalent period since the mid-1920s (Ball, 2003).

Table 2.3   New dwellings as percentage of total mortgages.

Year	New dwellings as % of properties mortgaged
1986	10.0
1987	10.2
1988	10.0
1989	10.7
1990	11.7
1991	11.6
1992	11.5
1993	10.5
1994	11.0
1995	12.1
1996	10.2
1997	10.1
1998	10.8
1999	11.3
2000	10.8
2001	8.3
2002	6.7
2003	6.3
2004	5.9
2005	5.2
2006	5.3

Source: CLG (2008a).

These absolute figures arguably understate the required rise in contribution of new building as the number of households expands and the size of the housing market grows. Further perspective is given by Table 2.3 which examines the number of new houses being built relative to the housing mortgage market over time. While the picture might be expected to be complicated by households who downsize, who buy with cash and/or by sitting social tenants buying under the RTB, the trends are remarkably clear. In the 1980s and 1990s the contribution of new building to the housing market never fell below 10% but by the mid-2000s its role had halved. The reasons for these trends are discussed in a later section.

The changing tenure structure noted above is also a reflection of the pattern of new building. New private house building completions in the UK outnumber new social housing units (built by registered social landlords and local authorities) by a ratio of at least 3 : 1 in each year since 1990/91 and by 6 : 1 in the last ten years. However, in recent years many of these properties have been bought by landlords to let out and 2006 saw the first ever fall in the level of owner occupation in England, a trend which continued into 2007 (CLG, 2008b). It is instructive to explain this new phenomenon by considering the changing position of first-time purchasers (FTPs) in the market.

First-time purchasers

FTPs are a varied group and include low-income households and also two-income professional households in their twenties or thirties, although average earnings are lower on average than homebuyers as a whole. The consequence is that these households buy across a wide range of the housing market (Dawson *et al.*, 1982). This is reflected in the trends shown in Figure 2.2 with prices paid by FTPs rising broadly in line with the whole of the market in the UK. There are differences between FTPs and the rest of the market. FTPs normally buy with a high loan-to-price ratio because they have relatively little wealth to support their purchase. This means they are more constrained than other house buyers in boom periods so the prices they can pay falls relative to other purchasers. The difference is shown by the average price paid by FTPs, consistently around 71–72% of all purchasers, rising to 73% in 1995 and 1996 when the housing market reached the bottom of a housing market cycle. The ratio therefore traditionally peaks when the housing market is suffering downturns as the average price paid by FTPs tends to follow a flatter cycle than the market average price.

The prices paid by FTPs tend to be less volatile probably because their ability to pay is linked purely to interest rates and earnings (and bank lending criteria)

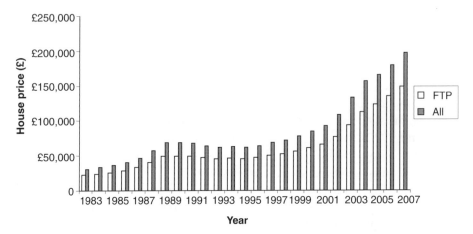

Figure 2.2   Average house prices paid by first-time purchasers (FTP) compared with all purchasers with a mortgage. *Source*: Halifax Bank of Scotland.

and so their housing opportunities expand and contract with the real level of house prices. The ratio of average house price paid by FTPs to all purchasers has been viewed as a (inverse) gauge of these opportunities. However, since 2005 this relationship has broken down and, as house price inflation continued to rise in double figures, the price paid by FTPs climbs in relative terms.

Until the mid-1990s FTPs historically comprised approximately half of all mortgages as Table 2.4 indicates, although housing booms usually lead to a squeeze on FTPs, restricting their access to the market. In contrast during downturns in the housing market cycle such as in the mid-1990s FTPs tend to bolster the market and increase their share of the market. The latest house price upturn has again seen a fall away in the proportion of the market accounted for by FTPs, but unlike in previous cycles their market share has dropped below 40% for the first time, and in 2003 and 2004 was around a quarter. It has subsequently risen but as Table 2.4 shows, because the numbers of house transactions have fallen, the absolute level of FTPs has been at all time low over the last four years. This may explain the rising relative price of houses purchased by FTPs as marginal purchasers are increasingly priced out of the market (see later).

The regional view of these processes is shown in Table 2.5. The proportion of FTPs within the market varies across regions with London having the highest percentage, accounting for more than three out of five house purchases during much of the 1980s and the first half of the 1990s. The lowest share of FTPs are in the East, South East and South West of England where the proportion of the market taken up by these purchasers was just

Table 2.4 First-time purchasers and mortgages for house purchase.

Year	Percentage of mortgages to first-time buyers	Numbers of loans for house purchase ('000s)
1986	50.3	1,248
1987	48.2	1,108
1988	47.3	1,256
1989	52.4	886
1990	53.0	783
1991	47.0	722
1992	50.3	873
1993	53.8	951
1994	54.0	959
1995	51.8	799
1996	47.7	957
1997	44.6	1,104
1998	48.3	1,088
1999	46.8	1,254
2000	43.8	1,123
2001	39.5	1,314
2002	31.9	1,397
2003	26.1	1,252
2004	24.9	1,245
2005	33.6	1,015
2006	36.6	1,126
2007*	35.0^	791

^Estimated; *first nine months.

over 40% in the mid-1980s rising to around half before falling to the order of 30%. Despite these differences the trends are broadly consistent with the national picture outlined previously. The proportion of FTPs falls, for all but four regions, through 1987/88 and rises in all regions through 1989/90. This period represents the peak share for FTPs across all regions and the proportion has been on a downward trend since. There is then a minor dip before a small rise in 1994 (1995 in the North West) and a deep trough in 2003/04 before some recovery. Northern Ireland shows some variation from this pattern as the decline in market share begins later in 2002, is more dramatic and has yet to show an upturn.

These consistent trends across regions and the UK as a whole suggest a commonality of forces influencing the position of FTPs in the market. In every region it appears that the purchasing power of FTPs in the housing market is on the wane although there are absolute differences between regions. This occurs against a backdrop of regional variations in price levels and cycles outlined in the next section.

Table 2.5 Regional variations in the first-time purchaser's share of the market 1986–2006 (%).

Year	North East	North West	Y+H	EM	WM	East	London	South East	South West	Wales	Scotland	N. Ireland
1986	53.7	46.9	50.4	50.3	51.6	44.2	59.4	41.4	42.9	53.7	59.6	63.9
1987	47.0	45.6	48.4	49.0	47.6	43.7	58.4	42.5	40.7	50.4	56.1	64.0
1988	45.6	46.3	47.0	45.5	48.4	42.4	60.0	40.5	40.1	51.1	53.1	62.9
1989	46.4	47.1	49.2	50.7	53.4	49.6	64.0	47.7	49.1	57.4	56.2	63.9
1990	46.8	49.4	46.0	54.1	55.0	51.2	66.1	48.6	54.4	59.1	48.3	65.4
1991	40.2	46.7	45.4	47.0	48.3	45.7	56.4	42.4	45.2	55.1	43.1	54.2
1992	45.8	48.6	49.7	48.1	48.4	49.9	61.8	46.6	49.4	58.8	49.1	52.7
1993	54.2	56.1	52.3	53.1	53.5	51.8	63.8	48.1	48.6	56.2	56.3	60.0
1994	57.5	56.5	52.0	53.5	55.6	51.5	61.7	47.2	48.8	56.3	57.1	66.4
1995	56.2	56.6	52.0	52.7	51.1	49.6	57.5	44.0	46.3	53.4	53.5	63.7
1996	52.7	52.8	51.9	48.2	47.7	45.5	50.4	41.0	42.5	52.5	49.5	54.1
1997	51.4	47.4	47.4	46.4	45.2	41.6	48.4	37.9	38.6	48.5	50.2	54.5
1998	53.6	50.9	50.2	49.6	48.8	44.3	55.9	39.2	42.2	54.0	52.7	58.0
1999	53.2	49.5	50.4	46.2	47.3	43.3	54.5	38.0	42.2	49.7	50.1	57.3
2000	50.2	45.3	46.3	43.0	43.5	42.4	51.0	35.5	35.5	46.5	48.9	59.1
2001	43.6	40.7	43.2	38.7	38.4	36.5	46.9	33.6	33.6	39.0	41.3	56.4
2002	29.6	34.3	28.9	30.7	28.8	33.4	38.6	29.9	26.1	32.3	34.1	42.2
2003	27.5	27.3	24.3	24.8	25.3	25.3	33.9	23.0	20.5	25.3	27.1	34.3
2004	27.6	26.1	25.6	21.9	23.4	23.4	35.2	22.4	19.3	24.6	22.1	31.0
2005	38.7	36.5	34.4	31.1	35.2	29.7	44.1	29.5	27.5	32.4	32.1	30.3
2006	40.8	41.3	38.7	36.7	38.0	31.5	45.2	29.9	29.6	36.6	42.4	30.5

Key: Y + H, Yorkshire and Humberside; EM, East Midlands; WM, West Midlands.

Source: Halifax Bank of Scotland.

Spatial house price trends

There are long-term regional disparities in house prices, notably often described as a north–south divide. These differences can be seen in the continuing gap in the absolute prices between London and the northern regions over the period 1983–2007 as shown in Table 2.6. The London average house price in 2007 is more than double its equivalent in the North of England and Scotland. This gulf in the regional distribution of house prices also existed in 1983 but the relative differences were not so severe and the South East had the highest average house price at that time. In fact, the regional pecking order has changed during this period. London has surged ahead of the surrounding South East with house prices rising on average by 851% compared with 694%. The average house price in the UK at the end of 2007 was over seven times the price that it was at the beginning of 1983, but at the same time house prices in Scotland are just under six and a half times, Northern Ireland more than nine times and in London eight and a half times. These statistics demonstrate that the regional relationships in house prices are fluid not static.

Figure 2.3 indicates that the gap between the north and south widens at peaks of the house price cycle in 1988 and 2002/03 and similarly narrows in downturns. This changing relationship means that comparisons of regional house price relativities vary dependent on the point in the price cycles.

Table 2.6   Average regional house price changes 1983–2007 (£).

	1983 Q1	2007 Q4	Change (%)
North	24,037	157,532	655.4
Y + H	21,711	162,298	747.5
North West	24,186	172,291	712.4
EM	24,350	168,924	693.7
WM	26,992	179,136	663.7
East	28,558	207,054	725.0
South West	31,800	219,311	689.7
South East	39,070	270,949	693.5
London	38,396	326,835	851.2
Wales	24,275	171,422	706.2
Scotland	27,307	175,950	644.3
N. Ireland	24,253	223,945	923.4
UK	29,615	212,973	719.1

Key: Y + H, Yorkshire and Humberside; EM, East Midlands; WM, West Midlands.

Source: Halifax Bank of Scotland.

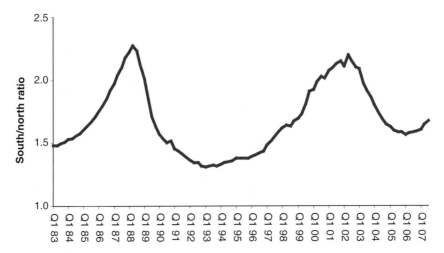

Figure 2.3   The changing north–south house price divide. *Source*: HBOS Halifax Bank of Scotland (2007a).

It is therefore useful to examine the detail of regional house price changes through the different phases as identified in Figure 2.3 between minimum and maximum ranges. A widely held view is that there is a ripple effect rather than a divide between northern and southern regions with Scotland and Northern Ireland having distinct cycles. From this perspective strong increases or decreases in nominal house prices in the south are transmitted first to nearby regions, such as the Midlands and the South West, then to the North of England and lastly to the peripheral regions: Scotland, Wales and Northern Ireland (Drake, 1995). The latest study covering the period 1973–2006 by Holmes and Grimes (2008) concurs, concluding that the speed of adjustment is inversely related to distance from London with Scotland considerably slower to respond than all the other regions (Northern Ireland is excluded). In this way house price 'shocks' that occur in boom and bust conditions cause short-run divergence between house prices in the north and south because the transmission of shocks from the south to northern regions is subject to a time lag.

There is not a consensus between academics on the ripple effect. Ashworth and Parker (1997) argue the case that different UK regions appear to adjust to house price shocks together and the trends in Table 2.7 broadly concur with this view. Average house prices in the North, North West and Yorkshire and Humberside regions move broadly together. The two Midlands regions have similarly closely linked house price trends. The South and South West

Table 2.7 Regional house price index changes at different phases of house price cycles.

	1988 Q3	% Change 83–88	1994 Q1	% Change 88–94	2002 Q4	% Change 94–02	2006 Q1	% Change 02–06	94–06	88–02
North	167.7	67.7	208.5	24.3	306.5	47.0	559.8	82.6	168.5	82.8
Y+H	155.4	55.4	230.8	48.5	339.8	47.2	583.4	71.7	152.7	118.7
North West	167.9	67.9	219.8	30.9	326.9	48.7	553.0	69.2	151.8	94.7
EM	210.7	110.7	210.9	0.1	426.6	102.3	588.1	37.9	178.9	102.5
WM	213.3	113.3	219.6	3.0	417.9	90.3	586.2	40.3	166.9	96.0
East	276.0	176.0	198.0	−28.3	420.5	112.4	557.8	32.7	181.7	52.4
South West	243.7	143.7	189.4	−22.3	457.0	141.3	562.4	23.1	196.3	87.5
South East	248.8	148.8	189.6	−23.8	464.3	144.9	546.7	32.7	188.3	86.6
London	257.2	157.2	195.5	−24.0	537.3	174.8	649.5	17.7	232.2	108.9
Wales	174.4	74.4	203.3	16.6	337.3	65.9	578.4	71.5	184.5	93.4
Scotland	141.8	41.8	199.2	40.5	248.2	24.6	392.4	58.1	97.0	75.0
N. Ireland	128.1	28.1	158.1	23.4	317.2	100.6	586.4	84.9	270.9	147.6
UK	197.4	97.4	204.6	3.6	392.2	91.7	560.4	42.9	173.9	98.7

Key: Y+H, Yorkshire and Humberside; EM, East Midlands; WM, West Midlands.

Source: Halifax Bank of Scotland.

are also likewise paired in Table 2.7 and the East region has gradually joined this group. The remaining regions – Northern Ireland, Scotland and Wales – each seem to have unique house price trends.

Another explanation is promoted by Meen (1999) who argues that interregional migration flows in the UK are too weak to create such price movements. The labour market literature also focuses on the weak migration links between regions and argues that the housing market is causing an impediment to labour market adjustment. There are a number of dimensions to this issue. At its most basic the gulf in house prices between the north and south means that it is difficult, for example, for Scots to move to London because they will not be able to afford a home of an equivalent standard even with a large salary increase. Bover *et al.* (1989) also suggest that labour in the South East of England is dissuaded from migrating to other UK regions because some households will believe the consequence to be missing out on several years of high South East house price growth. This will erode their ability to subsequently purchase housing in that region should they ever wish to return. But regional migration is not just stifled by house price differences; Hughes and McCormick (1981) and Minford *et al.* (1988) emphasise the restrictive role of public sector housing. With such housing administered on a local basis, and allocated primarily administratively, households wishing to move across boundaries within the sector have historically had to organise a house swap, a slow cumbersome and difficult process. The most flexible tenure is private-rented housing but as noted earlier the UK has a low proportion of this stock.

Meen's (1999) preferred explanation (supported by Holmans, 1995) for variable regional house price cycles lies in a combination of changes to relative regional incomes and the relative housing market supply elasticities, the differential responses of the house building industry to house price increases across regions. In other words, on the one hand regions experience different rates of economic growth, and hence household incomes, and on the other there are regional differences in land availability and this influences the ability of the house building to react to house price rises. It is these variations between regions that Meen argues are the main drivers of change, and he shows further how a regional price ripple could be created through such structural changes in regional housing markets. Ashworth and Parker (1997) also suggest that differential house price trends are caused by changes to the fundamental underlying variables such as regional incomes or differences in the structure of regional markets.

In conclusion, there is strong evidence of differential regional house price trends but despite considerable discussion there is no consensus that explains the dynamics of change. There is a belief that the reasons go beyond individual regional economies to encompass the tenure structure of the housing market and the operation of the labour market. Authors on both sides of the housing and labour markets literature note both the interaction between the two and the potential central role of migration as an equilibrating force. Unfortunately, empirical analyses in each camp often suffer from too short a time perspective and conclusions are coloured especially by the experience of the 1980s. Although migration features as a key potential influence in the differing explanations of the regional house price ripple effect, such views are qualified by the constraints on it, and hence the low scale of interregional migration. Nevertheless one explanation of the housing market ripple effect presumes household migration creating a spatial arbitrage process across local housing markets. The alternative perspective is that spatial house price trends are derived from localised regional housing markets. Neither approach presents any substantial empirical evidence to substantiate these dynamics.

Regional house price trends can be decomposed to the local town level although the level of information is far more limited, not only on prices but also on the underlying influences such as incomes. A study by HBOS Halifax Bank of Scotland (2003) looks at how much average house prices had risen in selected towns between 1988 and 2002. It finds the widest variation in interurban price changes were in Scotland over this period. The town with the slowest price growth in Scotland over these fifteen years was Irvine where the average price rose only by 46% compared with 179% for the highest increase that occurred in Edinburgh. The price change differential is therefore almost 4:1 between the highest and lowest 'performing' locations in Scotland. This compares with the equivalent figures in Yorkshire and Humberside of 3:1, around to 2:1 in the South East, Greater London and the North, and 1.5:1 in the South West (HBOS Halifax Bank of Scotland, 2003). These statistics emphasise the particular diversity of local housing markets in Scotland reflecting distinctive local economies and the scale of interurban distances in that region. But they also equally demonstrate the local nature of housing markets despite the panoply of national macroeconomic forces.

Affordability

The ratio of average house prices to average earnings has traditionally been seen as an indicator not only of the state of the market but also of affordability, rising when the market is buoyant and falling during down-turns. Halifax Bank of Scotland publishes a series for this ratio from 1983. In the 1980s as the house price boom takes off the ratio of average house price to average earnings rises from what was seen as its long-term equilibrium value of 3.5 in 1983 to over 4 in 1988 and reaching a peak of 5 in March 1989. It then gradually falls away until the end of 1995 when it stabilises around 3.1 or just over. It then stays at this level for over three years until the spring of 1999 before it starts to gently rise again and reaches 3.5 in November 2001. There is then a strong upward surge passing the 4 barrier in the autumn of 2002, 4.5 the following summer, and 5 in February 2004. There has been subsequently a more gentle upward trend creating a series of new record highs in the ratio, culminating in the ratio reaching its peak figure of 5.95 in the third quarter of 2007. The ratio of house prices to earnings was therefore above 5 for more than four years from 2004 even though it had only once before broken through this barrier in March 1989 and then only for one month.

The explanation is not simply that the market is excessively overheating although that is part of the reason. A major driver has been the relatively low interest rates since the beginning of the decade as shown in Table 2.2. Lower interest rates mean that households can service larger loans from the same income so the house price-to-earnings ratio has only limited applicability as a measure of affordability. In 1989 the mortgage interest rate was over 13% but the next time the ratio reached 5 the rate was less than 5%. Even though mortgage borrowing rates began to rise again after reaching a 50 year low in 2003, by 2007 they remained historically low and this is a major reason why the ratio was at an all time high. Nevertheless, while interest rates rose from 2003 to 2007 the house price earnings ratio also continued to rise implying the relationship is not straightforward and clearly other factors are at work. It also suggests that affordability over this latter period has deteriorated.

More perspective can be gained by looking at the experience of FTPs again. As noted earlier many potential first-time purchasers appear to have been priced out of the housing market. Table 2.8 fleshes out the reasons more clearly as it looks at a better measure of affordability: mortgage repayments relative to disposable income as estimated by Nationwide Building Society (2007). On this basis, at the end of 2007 the UK housing market as a whole is at its most unaffordable for FTPs since records began and worse than at the peak of the 1980s housing boom. The consequences are, as noted earlier, young households deferring buying a home – FTPs are increasingly more likely to be in their thirties rather than previously in their twenties and aspirations of the type of house to be purchased are being downgraded.

Table 2.8 Regional affordability indices for first-time purchasers: mortgage repayments relative to disposable income.

	1983 Q1	1988 Q3	1994 Q1	2002 Q4	2006 Q1	2007 Q4
North	75.3	84.6	45.2	55.2	87.5	99.9
Y+H	77.7	95.5	58.0	71.1	107.6	121.9
North West	82.0	84.5	69.6	78.1	125.2	138.7
EM	74.8	115.3	61.8	87.5	125.2	138.7
WM	81.4	120.4	65.4	95.9	131.3	146.7
East	74.0	154.5	51.9	83.0	104.5	123.3
South West	74.9	142.1	50.4	81.7	107.7	126.5
South East	72.3	157.5	46.6	84.0	106.2	126.7
London	65.3	143.1	46.6	77.8	91.5	111.4
Wales	77.7	97.9	59.9	76.8	122.8	139.3
Scotland	75.6	76.4	56.7	58.7	84.3	111.6
N. Ireland	84.3	73.5	50.5	83.3	121.3	217.9
UK	75.5	115.0	52.4	81.6	109.4	136.4
1985=100						

Key: Y+H, Yorkshire and Humberside; EM, East Midlands; WM, West Midlands.

Source: Nationwide Building Society (2007).

Closer inspection of Table 2.8 shows that this conclusion varies with region and that there is a north–south divide. Northern regions, the West and East Midlands plus Northern Ireland and Wales are all suffering the severest ever affordability problems (although North region affordability index is the same as 1985). In the southern regions of the East, London, South East and South West housing 'unaffordability' in 2007, judged by this criterion, is not on the scale of the top of the house price cycle in the 1980s, but the order of just over 20% below. Nevertheless, overall the affordability problem is deeper and wider in 2007 compared with the 1980s when it was much more spatially focused. It is much more clearly now a national issue rather than the regional issue it was in the late 1980s.

Regional perspectives on affordability cannot fully explain the under-lying dynamics of affordability (NHPAU, 2007). At the local level the HBOS Halifax Bank of Scotland (2007a) reports Henley-on-Thames as the UK's least affordable town, with an average property price more than 13 times the average income of first-time buyer households in the area in 2007. Seven out of ten of the least affordable towns on this basis are not surprisingly in the South East but Ilkley in Yorkshire was the second least affordable town with average home values almost twelve times that of the average local first-time buyer household income (HBOS Halifax Bank of Scotland, 2007b).

This research provides a useful indication of the problem but is limited as it is based on successful FTPs and includes all houses.

More in-depth and systematic studies on affordability examining local differences have been undertaken by Bramley *et al.* (2006) for Scotland and Wilcox (2006) for Britain. Unlike the studies of affordability above they are not based on (the distribution of) the incomes of the population as a whole. Bramley *et al.* (2006) estimate affordability in a series of steps. First, income distributions for under 35 year olds are estimated in each local authority area. Second, the lower quartile point in the local housing market is calculated as a feasible threshold of access. Finally the percentage of these households able to buy a house at this threshold is estimated on the basis that they could borrow 3.5 times their income with an allowance for family wealth providing help with the deposit. A growing number of FTPs look to friends and relatives with financial help with the deposit (NHPAU, 2007). A recent national survey by the Alliance and Leicester (2007) found that parents are paying on average £21,314 to help their children get on the property ladder.

The Bramley research finds that around 47% of new households in Scotland in 2005 could not afford to buy a home, a figure that is 7 percentage points below the equivalent estimate in 2003. In other words, affordability fell significantly over these two years, and has fallen further by the end of 2007 as Table 2.8 indicates. A breakdown of the degree of house price affordability between local authority areas finds that the cities of Glasgow (26%) and Edinburgh (31%) have the lowest levels of affordability for young adults under 35 years of age while most of the other areas with below average affordability are their surrounding suburban districts. It is useful to bear in mind when viewing these statistics that Scotland, judged by Table 2.8, is one of the more affordable regions of the UK.

The approach taken by Wilcox (2006) is similar in that it too focuses on the earnings of young people seeking to buy a home but it targets smaller housing rather than the lowest price housing. The study also first estimates traditional average house price to average earnings ratios for each local authority area for these groups purchasing these house types. Specifically, the ratio is constructed based on a mean price for an equal mix of two and three bedroom houses and estimates of the average incomes of working households aged 20 to 39 years. The results of these calculations reveal a somewhat different picture from Table 2.8, with all but three of the twenty local authorities with the highest ratio, i.e. the most unaffordable housing, in London, the South East and South West. Perhaps surprisingly nine of these twenty are in the South West. The three authority areas outside the core regions are Ryedale and Richmondshire in Yorkshire and North Norfolk in the East region.

The second stage of the analysis by Wilcox (2006) mirrors the Bramley research by estimating the proportion of working households in each area unable to buy a local lower quartile house price of two or three bedroom housing. The analysis assumes a maximum mortgage of 3.75 times income for single earner households (adjustments are made for two earners) and an 18% deposit. Less than half of all younger working households can afford to buy in this low price range in London, the South East and South West, with the South West the least affordable. These figures are lower than Bramley's but is a function of the differences in research method and illustrates the difficulties in providing absolute measures of unaffordability.

A similar but broader study has also been published by NPHAU (2007), although it has the added advantage of comparing the spatial pattern of change for 1998, 2002 and 2006 on a consistent basis. The analysis constructs maps of England that show the ratio of the lowest quartile of house prices to lowest quartile of earnings for each local authority. In 1998 virtually all areas in England have a ratio of less than 4 with a few locations having a multiple between 6 and 8. By 2006 much of England has a ratio over 6 with many experiencing a ratio over 8. The three maps chart the striking growth of unaffordability over these eight years, spreading out from the South East to encompass most of urban England.

To summarise, measuring affordability is not a straightforward exercise but all the indicators point to the affordability of home ownership having deteriorated substantially over the last decade. The research presented has examined the market trends up to the peak of the housing market at the end of 2007 but prices will need to fall substantially to make inroads into the degree of unaffordability. An overview across the country indicates that it is an issue that pervades every region although it is more significant in certain regions and there is some evidence that suggests that it is more problematic in the largest cities. The personal consequences are seen in delays in the ability to buy and parents providing much of the deposits for FTPs. The implications in the terms of the housing market as a whole has been the growth of long-term private tenants. This is illustrated by the following statistics: in the period 1988 to 2004 the percentage of young people aged 25–29 who are owner–occupiers fell from 64% to 50% while the equivalent percentage of private renters rose from 16% to 31% (Andrew, 2006).

Economics of the house building industry

An important factor in the unaffordability problem, as noted earlier, has been the failure of supply to respond adequately to the growth in demand. It is therefore pertinent to consider the economics of house-building. The industry operates in an essentially cyclical market and builds speculatively. Given these uncertainties and that the activity requires capital expenditure for the purchase of land and the building of houses in advance of sale the industry tends to be very cautious (Leishman *et al.*, 2000). There are about 18,000 house-builders registered with the National House Building Council (NHBC) but the speculative production of new homes in the UK is dominated by a small number of major companies. By 2006, the three largest firms were responsible for producing almost one-third of the total output.

The industry's corporate structure has been highly turbulent with merger and takeover activity a pervasive feature (Adams *et al.*, 2008a). Only five of the top house-builders of the early 1980s retained a top ten position by the end of the decade and only two remained in the top ten by 2001 (Wellings, 2005). Most of those that disappeared during these two decades were the subject of takeovers by competitors. Other companies such as Beazer, which was still a regional operation in the early 1980s, rose rapidly to national prominence to become the third largest UK house-builder by 2000, only to run into financial difficulties and be taken over by its rival, Persimmon, in 2001. Such corporate turbulence remains evident in house-building, with the takeover of David Wilson Homes by Barratt and the merger between Taylor Woodrow and Wimpey in 2007, merely recent examples of a well-embedded practice within the industry.

The dominance of a small number of major developers and the nature of the business activity means that industry does not embody the dynamic features associated with the competitive markets found in textbook economics. Rather it is often characterised as being highly conservative and lacking in entrepreneurialism (Ball, 1999; Barlow, 1999). Sir John Egan, who headed the government's construction task force and its enquiry into the skills needed for the development of sustainable communities commented to the House of Commons Environmental Audit Committee (2005, para 152) that the house-builders

> ...have pared themselves down to a relatively comfortable life but that is not the way you stimulate innovation. These are comfortable people doing a comfortable job.

This degree of 'comfort' is such that the industry has been able to overcome very low levels of customer satisfaction with the design and quality of their core product (Barker, 2004; CABE, 2004). This is partly due to the relative lack of local market competition between the products produced by different firms. As Barker (2004: 106) notes:

> When land is in relatively scarce supply, fewer permissioned sites mean that there will be fewer competing housebuilders in any one area. This can reduce consumer choice. In such situations, competition focuses on land. Once land is secured, competitive pressures are reduced: to a large extent housebuilders can 'sell anything'.

This view is partially disputed by a recent OFT (2008) study that finds only 10% of local authority areas where a single firm was granted permission to build more than 50% of units over the period 1998–2006. The study concludes that this occurs where a single home-builder has control of a single large site or a small number of large sites rather than one firm having control over a large number of sites. It argues that this is the consequence of the planning system limiting the number of sites rather than local market domination.

Developers can find themselves in a position that they can exercise monopolistic power in price setting (Fingleton, 2008) and in particular it has arguably been possible to 'sell anything' in the rising market experienced in the last decade. Yet although profit levels have been high in the first part of this decade (Fraser-Andrews, 2004; Adams *et al.*, 2008a), the aggregate level of new building has changed very little. The reasons for the failure to expand supply are contested. The house-building lobby argues that the industry has tried to respond but it has done so in the face of a degree of regulation unparalleled in other markets. The industry is subject not just to constraints on land use but also on design quality, environmental standards and customer care. The role of land use constraints is subject to the most debate and is considered in more detail in a later section.

What is clear, however, is that there are several important factors that impact on the ability of the industry to significantly expand supply. First, there is a lack of financial imperative. There is no incentive for house-builders to expand volume when this might lead to a reduction in price. As the House of Commons Select Committee on Affordability and Housing Supply (2007: 21) note: 'there is no clear reason why housebuilders would be committed to increasing housing supply to such an extent as to compromise their profit margins'. One major builder made it clear that they will 'not chase volumes...[but] would prefer to protect margins and selling prices' (p. 20).

Second, the industry is not solely dependent on the sale of housing for its success. There are two main reasons that house-builders maintain a significant forward supply of land. The first of these is to mitigate against the risk and uncertainty that flows from the delays incurred in seeking planning permission. The second is as a potential source of rewards. Profitability and viability often depend on finding land at the right price and gaining planning permission. These require highly localised knowledge sets. Shortages in developable land are the most significant constraint on the development process and this has meant that the industry has become inherently 'land focused' rather than 'customer focused'. Land is an essential raw material that needs to be controlled well before construction is due to start. The response to its scarcity and to competition in the land market has been to accumulate a stock of land. Sites are normally held in a land bank for at least two years prior to the planned commencement of on-site production. A company's land bank is often regarded as an important indicator of its strength (Calcutt, 2007). The land bank can be seen as a portfolio of assets with different dates of maturity and profit realisation (Ball, 1983), since it will normally contain both 'short-term land' that is immediately available for development and 'strategic land' that may take many years to come to fruition.

Third, the way in which the industry is structured is also important. The nature of production in the house-building industry is, of course, dispersed and localised. This means that, as we note above, the market is highly segmented. Geographic segmentation of the market allows a degree of decision-making independence at the local level. Freedom from central office control is particularly evident in establishing the feasibility of development. The divisional offices of large house-builders will have built up and have control of stocks of land of varying sizes and differing geographical compositions. Some area offices will have been more successful in securing land than others. For many, current levels of production will be high enough to meet their output and profit targets. Others may have inadequate supply of land. This uneven distribution of developable land, of course, has wider implications for the capacity of the industry as a whole to expand the supply of new housing. There is often a mismatch between the capacity to build and the ownership of developable land within and between firms. It is possible that, even in relatively buoyant market, the attainment of a step change in the aggregate level of new housing construction would require highly efficient market processes to redistribute land (within and between firms) to achieve a match between available building land and the capacity to build. The land market, however, is far from efficient (Adams *et al.*, 2005a).

Fourth, even in the absence of land use planning constraints, the industry arguably lacks the capacity to increase output. There is both a long-term shortage of skills within the industry and a lack of innovation (Payne, 2008). This is reflected in a long-standing failure to embrace new construction methods (Barlow, 1999; Gibb *et al.*, 1997). Barlow and Bhatti (1997) undertook a survey of over 100 firms involved in the UK industry, and found that less than 10% were developing new designs or trying out new technologies. Ball (1999) partly attributes this to conservatism amongst buyers who, it is argued, are wedded to particular house types and are preoccupied by concerns about resale values. It is argued that this, combined with the cyclical nature of the market, encourages firms to adopt low-cost strategies that require minimum sophistication and forecasting ability.

At a general level, developers seek to control their exposure to market risk and uncertainty by managing their relationships with other actors in the development process, primarily landowners, planners and other developers. Developers perform most effectively where these relations are well managed and stable and suffer where they are badly managed or turbulent (Adams *et al.*, 2008b). It would appear that this conservative business model has failed many firms in the 2007/08 credit crunch as house price reductions have fed through to land values. Firms saw their share prices fall dramatically in response. Taylor Wimpey, for instance, was forced to write down the value of its land and building sites and to seek an emergency cash injection from its main shareholders (Macalister and Kollewe, 2008). The likely consequence is a wounded house-building programme that will take some time to recover with output stalled.

Adams *et al.* (2008b) show that large numbers of builders became heavily reliant on land transactions as a source of short-term finance. Others, particularly those who are part of more diverse construction conglomerates or who are less reliant on debt financing, saw the downturn as an opportunity to engage in land acquisitions strategies that will enhance or consolidate their longer term prospects. The differences in responses to the credit crunch have not been driven by the size of the firm or the niche or geographic markets in which they operate. Rather responses have been more closely related to the financial structures and business models adopted by the individual firm. There is a lack of sympathy within the industry for those who have been hardest hit. The flawed business model is emphasised and in crude terms there is a feeling that in some cases 'they've built the wrong product, they had no vision' (a builder, quoted by Adams *et al.*, 2008b: 33).

The failure to produce the right product is not a new criticism. The industry has a history of collectively producing very similar products at any one time rather than identifying and meeting local needs. In the early 1980s builders produced mainly small starter homes but when this segment of the market experienced difficulties the industry shifted to upmarket homes (Goodchild and Karn, 1997). Over the last decade new house building has been predominantly at the top end of the market but has also enthusiastically embraced city centre flats.

Overall there remain significant questions about the extent to which, even in the absence of constraints, the house-building industry has the capacity to deliver a significant expansion in the volume of new building. There has been little change in production levels within the private sector in the last few decades. The industry remains inherently conservative and indifferent to innovation and market research. This is an often underestimated contributor to the weak supply response in the UK housing system.

Low-demand areas

Side by side with the affordability problems reported above are areas of low demand in the provincial cities of the midlands and North of England. From the early 1990s neighbourhoods in many of these cities began to suffer from a high concentration of difficult to sell or rent properties. These areas were experiencing population decline leaving high vacancy rates as properties were abandoned and house prices were at nominal values. The government estimates that there were 880,000 properties affected in 2001 across 120 local authorities. The National Audit Office (2007) reports that 5.6% of the properties in Manchester in 2002 had been empty for over six months compared with a national average of 1.9%. These neighbourhoods comprised either Victorian terraces, the classic two-up/two-down with only car parking on the road and no garden, or flats and houses within large council estates built in the 1950s. In some cases they were further blighted by the existence of former coal mine shafts dissuading banks from financing a purchase (Bramley *et al.*, 2001).

The government's solution to these problems were the establishment of 'pathfinder' projects in these low demand areas. In 2003 the government set itself a ten to fifteen year target to rebuild the markets in these areas (ODPM, 2003). The plans for the areas incorporate a mixture of selective demolition, land reclamation, financial assistance to developers for new building for rent and sale, grants to improve the physical environment and better neighbourhood management. The subsequent reshaping of markets in these areas has included raising the local levels of owner-occupation and reducing the number of low-value properties by demolition, and more indirect measures to improve the local economy and household incomes (National Audit Office, 2007). Chapter 5 discusses these policy issues in more detail.

Wider planning policy context

So far the chapter has analysed the housing market rather narrowly in terms of the internal dynamics of supply and demand and the influence of the macroeconomy. In the last section the analysis begins to consider policy, and the government's response to localised low-demand problems is discussed. Now the chapter turns its attention toward the government's response to the affordability problem. However, unlike in the case of the low-demand areas (although the government has its critics here too) it is not simply a matter of a white knight riding to the salvation of the beleaguered would-be home owner priced out of the market. A key criticism has been that the planning system has retrenched into its statutory duty, emphasising the need to regulate growth (through development control), but neglecting the need to set a positive growth agenda (Gallent and Tewdwr-Jones, 2007).

The story really begins 50 years or more ago with the establishment of green belts around the major cities of the UK. When green belts were originally planned it was not anticipated that they would simply constrain urban growth, but also manage otherwise unchecked growth, although precise logic varied across cities (Lloyd and Peel, 2007). Green belts were also a means to avoid the coalescence of towns and the protection of agricultural land. In addition, they were conceived as public spaces for city dwellers to escape to at weekends from the polluted cities they surrounded (Prior and Raemaekers, 2007). In one sense green belts as defined 50 years ago in a world before the advent of the family car could be described as an anachronism. Few green belts fulfil this role today but they have been given a new lease of life by the popularisation of the 'compact city' concept which has in turn reinvigorated planning (Bramley and Kirk, 2005).

The green belts today do not simply restrain the physical development of cities but in doing so also shape local housing markets as part of planning policies more generally. The relationship between planning and the housing market is a central theme of the book. Chapter 3 considers the impact of green belts on the spatial house price structures of cities, Chapter 6 examines the detail of the mechanics of planning processes, and the housing market impacts are assessed in Chapter 7. The analysis here is concerned with the overall market effect of the planning system including the green belts. A major policy issue referred to earlier is whether sufficient land has been made available for housing. The issue has stimulated a polarised debate between the house-building industry and the planning profession, and centres on the level of land banking and take-up of land by house-builders on the one hand and the amount of planning permission granted on the other.

The answer is complicated by the complexity of the process – land banks comprise sites under construction, with detailed planning permission, outlined planning permission, and land under option without permission. Sometimes land with planning permission cannot be built on because of factors such as delays brought about by incomplete infrastructure. There is no doubt that major builders hold land banks but the issue is to what extent there is hoarding. An OFT (2008) study estimated that only 3% of builders' land banks have detailed planning permission and it gives the builders a clean bill of health on the issue of land hoarding. It concludes that house-builders' build-out rates on sites they own reflect market conditions. Adams and Leishman (2008) suggest a caveat to this conclusion arguing that house-builders have unambitious build-out rates partly because of the nature of the industry and partly because of the way the planning system works.

The evidence on whether there has been sufficient planned land release has been a very contentious subject. Bramley (2007) reports that there was a fall in the stock of land in England with outstanding planning permissions between 1988 and 1997 in all southern and midland regions, and a sustained fall in the flow of planning permissions from 1988 to 2000. He also notes that regional planning targets in the late 1990s in England were less than household projection rates. Market reports suggest that the number of plots available with planning permission declined subsequently (Wellings, 2006). Conversely, critics of the industry have suggested that the land supply problems caused by planning constraints have been overstated. Counter-evidence has been reported that suggests that, recently, planning permissions rose from 200,000 in 2000 in England to more than 300,000 in 2005 before dropping back to 280,000 in 2006. The problem has been that the proportion of permissions converted to starts declined from 75% to 65% (Green, 2008). The interpretation of these statistics is difficult and should ideally be examined at a spatially disaggregated level to take into account local market conditions and time lags. Monk *et al.* (2008) suggest that the system has underestimated the time required for the land development process, especially with regard to brownfield and large sites. Notwithstanding a potential improvement in the flow of planning permissions in the recent past, the statistics suggest that there has been a long-term shortfall.

These trends are reflection of the operation of the planning system in the UK as Evans and Hartwich (2005) explain. First, the public participation in the planning system – they argue – discourages development because people usually prefer development elsewhere, often referred to as NIMBY – not in my back yard. This has been a particular problem for large developments (Bramley, 2007). Second, this influence extends not only to local neighbourhoods but also to the district-wide local five-year development plans drawn up by councils which gained greater control over development in the 1990s. Third, Monk and Whitehead (1999) indicate that planning itself, including the requirement for planning permissions, slows down the development process. Finally there has been increased use of brownfield rather than greenfield land that has also contributed to the complexity of housing development. A fuller discussion of these issues is found in Chapter 7.

From the perspective of this chapter these overall development constraint policies, including the key impact of implementing the compact city concept, restrict aggregate supply in an aggregate urban housing market. Gunn (2007) reviews the theory and evidence and shows that house prices rise as a consequence but the ramifications can be seen in wider terms. A growing number of households and higher house prices contribute to many households being priced out of the immediate local owner-occupied housing market. This effect has a number of dimensions. As already discussed it is seen in young households continuing as private tenants for longer than they would like. Other households, unable to afford the type of housing they require, are prepared to commute longer distances. This in turn has had implications for rural areas as incomers outbid low-paid agricultural workers.

The constraining role of the planning system on development is important when the affordability problem is viewed as a disequilibrium problem, supply not responding fully to demand. While an undersupply of new housing in one year may have limited impact on house prices it is the cumulative force over a long period that has created this imbalance. At the national level house-building has not responded to the growing demand as demonstrated by the rising number of households since the early 1990s, with the direct consequence that real prices and affordability problems have substantially risen. There are potentially a number of reasons for this including the decline in social house building, the conservatism and inefficiencies of the house-building industry, and land and infrastructure constraints, but undoubtedly the planning system must take its share of the blame. Some of the planning blockages and the need to take more note of market forces have been recognised in recent government reports (Barker, 2004, 2006) and new planning advice (CLG, 2006b). The result is that the affordability problem cannot be seen simply as an inevitable short-term issue brought about by the cyclical nature of the housing market but as a long-term phenomenon.

Curiously, as a major cause of the affordability problem the government now ironically extols local government to use the planning system to generate affordable housing (CLG, 2006c). Most affordable housing is provided via planning agreements with developers (Monk *et al.*, 2006). The essential logic is that planning not only raises house prices but also land values: there can be large differentials between agricultural land prices and land with planning permission for housing (Evans, 1991). Planning agreements tax this increase – known as planning gain – so that some of the land values generated by the planning system are returned to the local community. The assumptions and housing market outcomes of this policy are reviewed in Chapter 7.

The government has also tackled the unaffordability problem by offering special schemes aimed at key public service workers such as nurses and teachers (and social tenants) unable to afford to buy on the open market. These schemes offer a range of mortgage products that offer an equity sharing arrangement to buy a home where the home buyer initially buys only a share of the house. The government has struggled in recent years to find the right (and often complex) formula to balance the attractiveness and take-up of these schemes to their target audience while minimising their costs (Jones, 2009a).

Conclusions

Analysis of the housing market reveals a combination of trends driven in particular by rising real incomes, demographic factors and the level of inflation/interest rates and cycles linked to the economy and the slowness of new supply to respond. The last decade reveals a divergence from a typical property market cycle – supply has not responded and more and more FTPs have been priced out of the market. Although the housing market peaked at the end of 2007 prices will need to experience an almost unprecedented fall to bring the relationship between house prices and incomes back into equilibrium. Any exogenous correction brought about by the credit crunch is likely to be short lived because the affordability problem is very different from that in the 1980s when it was a short-term regional and cyclical phenomenon focused on the South East and London. The affordability problem today is national and represents a long-term disequilibrium driven by forces internal to the housing market. There are local differences which are important but they can be seen as extremes of a wider picture.

The state of the housing market is a culmination of long-term trends and the question must be: why has this occurred? Planning constraints is the simple answer but the more interesting question is the underlying reasons for the failure to deliver sufficient housing. Part of the explanation lies in NIMBY-ism but a key issue is the relationship between planning and the market. The inefficiencies of the house-building industry are a factor but to a degree it operates within parameters set by the planning system. Planning is changing ostensibly to be more market oriented, and there is a commitment to build more but to date this does not appear to be a change in delivery. At the same time policies designed to provide affordable housing via planning gain and other schemes are cumbersome, have had only limited success and only scratch the surface of the problem.

3

Spatial Structure of Housing Markets

The analysis so far has examined primarily national and regional housing market trends but also showed considerable variation at the urban level. The focus of the book now shifts to analysing housing markets at this local level. The purpose of this chapter is to first consider a theoretical understanding of how urban housing markets work and then to consider the interaction with the planning system. The initial section outlines an economic model of an urban housing market to develop our understanding of the underlying forces at work and establish key trade offs that households make when deciding where to live in a city. From this base the chapter then considers the theoretical implications of planning policies on the spatial structure of house prices and densities. In the following section the empirical evidence is assessed to explore to what extent the theoretical perspective can be justified. In the final part of the chapter the analysis is extended to view urban housing markets within a wider regional context and to consider how housing market areas can be defined in both a theoretical sense and in a practical way. Finally, the chapter examines the implications of the definition of a housing market area for planning.

A model of an urban housing market

The starting point for the analysis is the development of an economic model with a series of simplifying assumptions. First, the model creates a very simple town by assuming the following.

- The town or city occupies a featureless plain, so any topographical features that might distort key relationships are ignored.

- Employment is concentrated in the city centre, the central business district (CBD).
- Travel costs are the same in every direction and are directly proportional to the distance travelled.
- Households make a fixed number of work trips per week.
- The prices of goods and services and taxes, including property tax rates, are the same wherever you are located in the urban area.

The logic of this approach stems from the seminal work on urban housing markets led by Kain (1961), Wingo (1961), and Alonso (1964), followed by Muth (1969) and Evans (1973).

Given that most people in the model work in the city centre, the cost and time of travel to the CBD is a key determinant of residential location. However, because the city is built on a featureless plain and travel costs are the same in each direction a household is not concerned with whether it is living to the east or west or north or south, simply the distance from the city centre. The model assumes that people wish to minimise their travel when choosing where to live but evidently also have to take into account housing costs or prices. In fact, house prices are determined by transport costs and market forces set within this spatial framework.

The housing market in this model is assumed to have perfect information and that households then make bids for particular locations and through this process a price surface emerges. Because people are indifferent which sector of the city they live in this price surface is the same in each direction but prices will vary with distance or accessibility from the city centre. In deciding the price to bid households take into account the transport cost of any location to the CBD. Households are prepared to bid a higher price for an equivalent house (of the same size, etc.) in more accessible locations with lower travel costs than one on the periphery.

Having set out the assumptions and the underlying dynamics of this model it is instructive to examine the detail of the model developed by Muth (1969). Households' decisions are subject to an income or budget constraint and seek to maximise their satisfaction or utility. In this simplified world households only have three choice variables – housing, travel (distance) to the CBD, and all other goods to spend their income on. To allow the model to be easier to interpret housing is presumed to be of uniform quality.

The model can be expressed in algebraic form and this enables it to be used to establish the conditions for a local market equilibrium. In particular it can be shown that for spatial equilibrium to exist then the following equation holds:

$$-qp_k = T_k \qquad (3.1)$$

where

q = quantity of housing consumed,
p = price of housing per square metre,
T = travel costs from the city centre,
k = distance from the city centre,
p_k and T_k are the rate of change in price and travel costs with distance from the city centre.

The rate of change in house prices with distance from the city centre (p_k) is actually the house price gradient from the city centre. From this equation it can be seen that as both q and T_k, the cost of travelling an additional distance, are both positive the rules of algebra mean that p_k must be negative. In other words, the price of housing per square metre declines with distance from the city centre. As travel costs increase with distance from the CBD the model has become known as the 'access–space' model since households' decisions are focused on trading off journey to work costs for housing expenditures. Housing costs per square metre fall with increased distance from the city centre while travel costs rise.

Muth (1969) goes on to show that for the equilibrium to be stable the house price gradient has to be a negative exponential function. Further perusal of the equation above also reveals that it is a function of travel costs. The lower the travel costs the flatter the house price gradient. Delving further into the detail of the model reveals that low-income households consume a small amount of housing at a high unit cost in inner-city, high-density locations while high-income households at outer locations consume a large amount of housing at a low unit cost per square metre in suburban areas (in Western economies). Under a set of further assumptions Muth (1969) further illustrates that a negative exponential density function can be derived from the city centre.

These conclusions are based on assumptions of a perfect market and represent a long-run equilibrium. Undoubtedly the output of this model provides valuable insights into the spatial structure of urban housing markets. The access–space model can explain the long-term suburbanisation of cities brought about by growing household real incomes and new transport technologies lowering transport costs. Lower travel costs mean that the house price gradient is flatter and people can afford larger houses at a further distance from the city centre. Similarly, as household real incomes rise so does their desire to consume larger housing; this effect swamps the increasing travel costs of living further out and hence commuting distances increase. So, all other things being equal, cities with higher incomes have households who value travel time greater, have larger houses and have a more dispersed urban form.

These conclusions are tempered in the real world by the role of planning through, in particular, the use of green belts, the historic development of local housing markets and the trend toward decentralisation of employment. The nature of the city is changing and its offices and retailing centres have been radically reconfigured in the last two decades (Hall, 2001a; Fernie, 1995; Jones and Orr, 1999). The location of manufacturing in cities has also been radically resculpted by deindustrialisation and decongestion (Robson *et al.*, 2000; Dunse and Jones, 2005). The growth of the motorway network has not only changed supply networks but also the optimum locations of industrial units and distribution warehouses to peripheral urban locations close to motorway junctions.

The decentralisation of employment in a sense challenges the heart of the access–space model. Research in the USA, for example, finds that commuting distances remain constant despite continuing decentralisation because such trips are no longer necessarily only from suburbs to city centre (Richardson and Gordon, 1993). Nevertheless, despite the existence of decentralised urban systems that have been variously described as polycentric development or city regions, the city centre remains the dominant commercial location and the point of greatest accessibility for UK cities. As such it remains the focal point for local housing markets and hence at the peak of the urban house price gradient.

A further apparent challenge to the model is also presented by the growth of city-centre living by affluent professional people especially since the beginning of the 1990s. In fact there have always been enclaves of high earners in inner city locations such as the new town of Edinburgh and in European cities more generally. The expansion of this demand can be traced to demographic and household changes that create the potential for new patterns of housing demand. There has been a significant growth of small, one-person households derived from later marriage, lower rates of marriage and increased divorce and relationship breakdown. This phenomenon can be accommodated within the model by the introduction of locational/house type preferences, as the basic model assumes households do not differentiate between neighbourhoods and house types. While there is some evidence that residential preferences amongst smaller, childless households, may not be that different to other household types (Hooper *et al.*, 1998) it seems likely that the growing numbers of childless households are associated with a desire for city-centre living and its associated culture and lifestyle (Lambert and Boddy, 2002).

The theoretical impact of planning

Planning in the UK is a combination of individual development controls, indicative land-use zoning and strategic planning that includes green belts. The logic of green belts is introduced in Chapter 2. Green belts act as boundary constraint on the market restricting the urban land supply, and hence distorting the outcomes of the simple model. It is not just a matter of creating a discontinuous price gradient where the green belt is located as shown in Figure 3.1. It also extends beyond the analysis in the last chapter where the role of green belts is seen simply in terms of rising house prices and the crowding out of households from urban cores. The outcomes are more complex. Rising house prices lead to rising land prices as developers are able to pay more and competitive pressures ensure they are prepared to. But higher values also mean that land is used more efficiently and new development is built to a higher density (also encouraged by recent planning policies as Chapter 2 notes) so that flats rather than houses are built, for example. It also leads to an intensification of existing housing land, as houses

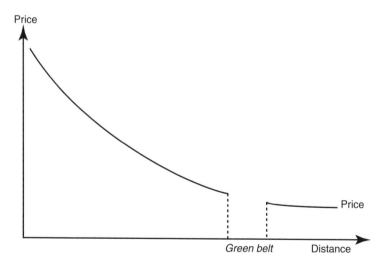

Figure 3.1   Distorted house price gradient caused by the green belt.

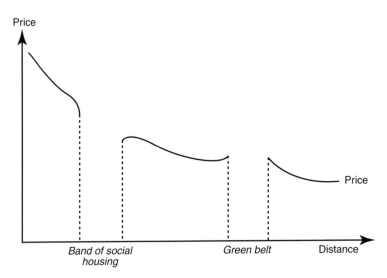

Figure 3.2   Distorted house price gradient due to bands of social housing and the green belt.

are adapted by converting lofts and through building extensions, and a contraction of green space within the urban environment (Evans, 1991).

The impact is not just that demand is constrained by supply pushing up the housing price gradient and residential densities uniformly across the city, although that is part of the story. Demand displaced from its 'natural' spatial equilibrium in the green belt is likely to seek close substitute locations. The lower density of development and scale of land availability in the suburbs also offers greater opportunities to the adaptation of the land-use pattern. There is likely to be a piling up of demand either side of the green belt as shown in Figure 3.2 (ignoring the potential general upward shift in the price gradient from the overall planning constraint). Such an effect may be exaggerated if there are household preferences to live near the green belt.

This last point highlights other simplifications in the model – the lack of locational or house type preferences. Both stem logically from the assumptions of constant housing quality and a uniform plain. While such simplifications assist the power of the model to focus on the access–space trade off, empirical analysis cannot so easily discount such factors. Thus there may be building type preferences, such as the desire of families with young children to occupy housing with gardens. There is a further limitation with regard to the UK in the form of tenure, especially social housing provided outside the market by public agencies. The existence of such housing does not merely distort the model; it challenges all the assumptions of the model because social landlords do not maximise profits, rents are not set entirely on market criteria and households are administratively allocated to housing.

The presence of social housing emerges as discontinuities in the urban housing market space in the same way as the green belt does. In many UK cities, social housing was built in an inner ring around the city centre following the slum clearance programmes of nineteenth-century housing. The impact on the house price gradient of such a phenomenon is shown in Figure 3.2 which also assumes there are negative preferences to living near large social housing estates. The figure also illustrates how introducing just the discontinuities of a green belt and a ring of social housing can substantially distort the negative exponential house price gradient. The real world is less straight forward and the discontinuities are amorphous spaces rather than rings, and a city's house price surface can be viewed as an umbrella with 'holes'.

The analysis presented in the figures has focused on the differential spatial impacts of public policies within cities but it should also be remembered that the overall planning constraint will shift upward the price gradient and densities (the latter actively encouraged in recent years). The consequences for the housing market are that the high-density planning policies referred in Chapter 2 (see Chapter 7 for more detail) are reinforced and magnified by market forces. As noted in the last chapter, households that seek low-density housing, especially families, must move to more decentralised locations.

Empirical evidence on the impact of planning

The analysis to date has focused on theoretical impacts and it now turns to review the empirical evidence. A number of studies have sought to provide evidence of the impact of the planning system on the housing market as well as an assessment of the scale of the impact on a range of market outcomes (Adams and Watkins, 2002). In addition to measuring the price and quantity effects discussed above, the studies also consider the extent to which the planning system might also affect the density and type of new development. Unfortunately, the range of methods used and variations in the focus of the projects make direct comparison of the research findings difficult. There are, however, some worthwhile insights (and interesting debates) generated by this series of academic studies.

Early contributions

The earliest of these studies were essentially descriptive. Using data from a survey of developers, Hall *et al.* (1973) show that the ratio of land prices to house prices (for a constant density unit) had risen steadily over a ten-year period. In the London area, for example, the ratio increased from around 10% in 1960 to between 25% and 38% in 1970. The authors conclude that these increases are more attributable to the effects of national and local planning policy than increases in demand.

Within a more explicit economic framework, Evans (1991) notes that land in agricultural use near the city of Reading might cost around £2,000 per acre compared with between £500,000 and £1 million when planning permission has been granted. Although he acknowledges that the price difference is not so great elsewhere in the country, he maintains that the difference in other regions is also substantial and he attributes the difference primarily to planning constraints. The nature of Evans's work is such that there is no rigorous investigation of the nature, scale or causes of the post-planning outcomes. The analysis side-steps the possible impact of a range of other influences including local land and housing market conditions, social and demographic trends, and institutional factors. The discussion also ignores the extent to which planning regimes may impose different levels of restraint on the operation of the market. Although Evans's assertions about the effects of planning are only supported by fairly selective anecdotal evidence drawn from the South East, the paper provides a robust introduction to the debate about influence of planning on development.

Cheshire and Sheppard studies

A number of subsequent studies seek to re-examine these issues. In one of the earliest empirical studies, using data from 1984, Cheshire and Sheppard (1989) undertook a comparative analysis of two local housing markets. As case study areas they chose Reading, in the South East, a market with strong constraints on new development and Darlington, in the North East, a market with a less restrictive planning regime. They used a standard econometric modelling procedure, known as the hedonic house price function, to isolate the impact of different attributes on house prices. A hedonic price function is a statistical way of linking the price of a house to its characteristics (such as size, type of house, garage) in order to compute comparable constant quality prices for different house types and locations.

The hedonic price function or model can be interpreted as measuring the value of a range of individual physical dwelling components or attributes, as well as neighbourhood and locational characteristics. The statistical technique can therefore estimate the value of an extra bedroom assuming the other features are unchanged. Cheshire and Sheppard also used the model to shed light on the impact of the planning system on house prices. They compared hedonic price functions estimated for Darlington and Reading. Their main conclusion was that the effect of the planning system was passed on mainly through higher densities and not through vast increases in price. The results suggest that plot sizes and the area of the towns would respectively have been 65% and 50% larger in the absence of planning controls because, with lower prices, house purchasers would have been able to buy larger homes. The price effects of the local planning regimes were shown to be between 2% cent and 12% depending on house type.

In a more recent paper, Cheshire and Sheppard (1996) update their analysis using data from 1993. In this research they focus on the distributional consequences of planning, and in particular, ask what the consequences might be for a household in Reading if the planning regime was relaxed to the lower levels of constraint found in Darlington. The research showed that the reduction in housing costs would lead to a rise in household income of approximately £640 per annum at the urban periphery and approximately £775 per annum in the urban core.

Cambridge land economy studies

A team of researchers based at Cambridge also present findings on this issue. This evidence is based on a series of research projects and academic papers. This body of work adopts a more qualitative approach than that used by other economists. The first of these studies examines the extent to which land supply, and the operation of the planning system, affected house prices in Britain during the 1990s. The study sought to identify whether the planning system had merely constrained supply or whether it had led to a reorganisation of that supply. The analysis was based on national and regional trends and a series of local case studies of Wokingham, Reigate, Beverley and Barnsley. The second study examines land supply within a local market. It seeks to explore the differential effects of planning constraints at a local level, and to examine the extent to which land allocations in one area can act as a substitute for land in another area where tighter constraints have been imposed. The research focuses on south Cambridgeshire and the Fenlands.

The price effect arguments introduced by Evans find rather more empirical support from this research. The results show that land prices are much higher at the margins of urban areas compared to agricultural land and that the inflationary impact of planning is also reflected in differentials between areas. The studies, for example, show that, as a result of planning constraints, prices increase by between 35% and 45% in the South East, while the work suggests land prices are 200 times greater than agricultural land in highly constrained areas compared with 60 times greater in less constrained areas (Monk and Whitehead, 1996, 1999). Furthermore, the temporal dimension of this research suggests that the planning system tends to exacerbate price increases at times of economic growth although reducing downward pressures during downturns in the market. Taken together with the failure of the system to help increase output at times of low market activity, the analysis suggests that the planning system adds to the volatile, cyclical nature of British housing markets. In addition, the research points to the negative role of the planning system in narrowing the densities and types of dwellings produced.

Heriot-Watt University studies

In a series of studies Bramley develops a model that explores the relationship between the housing land supply, the planning regime, and the supply and price of new housing. These models uniquely combine secondary data with information from planning documents and from a survey of local authority planning departments. His first study looked at a cross-section of 90 local planning authorities in the South, South West and the Midlands. The estimated equations were used to test a range of policy scenarios including supply responsiveness (see Bramley, 1993a,b). The results suggest that the price and quantity effects are likely to be more modest than those suggested elsewhere. The Joseph Rowntree Foundation interprets these results to suggest that 'large land releases are ineffective and environmentally damaging ways to reduce prices' (Joseph Rowntree Foundation, 1994: 30).

These conclusions are contested by Evans (1996) who highlights the weak statistical relationships between several key variables and questions the validity of rolling forward potentially unstable estimates established using data from a single-time period. These criticisms were addressed in a second study that extends the geographical and temporal coverage of the data-set. The new data, which covers 162 local authority planning systems and two time periods (1988 and 1992), lead to similar conclusions. The simulation model shows that with a one-third increase in land available for housing, prices will fall by 4% while new output will increase by around 9% (Bramley and Watkins, 1996).

A more recent work uses a panel data-set to develop a system of equations, within a long-run equilibrium framework, to estimate the impact of different packages of public policies on a range of outcomes, including the price and quantity of housing in high- and low-demand housing markets (Bramley and Leishman, 2005a,b). The model also allows the authors to simulate the effects of policy changes, such as an increase in the level of building, over a seven-year period from the end of 1997. The results suggest that a combination of supply-side and demand-side (through the local economy and labour market) policies could achieve substantial impacts on the price of housing and quantity of new development. More specifically, they show that policies that allow output to increase by 40% could achieve an 8% decrease in house prices. This latter study seems to imply slightly larger price effects than the earlier work. It also shows that increased new building depresses prices by a proportionately larger amount in low-demand areas.

Summary

While these studies all tend to concur that the effect of planning constraints is more severe in high-demand areas a caveat needs to be attached to their findings. The results vary dependent on the models applied and there is little agreement on the 'best' research method. There is a further problem in that there has never been a period in modern times when there has not been planning, so what would happen in the absence of planning is unknown. There are also differences in planning policies between localities. The reality is that it is not easy to strip away the institutional effects. As Adams *et al.* (2005b) note 'market behaviour becomes adjusted to prices that already incorporate policy imperatives, making outcomes path dependent on inherited patterns of state-market relations'. It does not change the fact that planning has an effect, as the theoretical analysis shows, but it does make accurate measurement almost impossible (hence the debates).

Planning the housing market

The analysis in earlier sections has established the importance of planning in shaping urban housing markets. Strategic planning – if it is to be effective – must not only have an understanding of the impact of its decisions but also of the nature of the spatial housing market systems. Logically the forecasting of future housing demand/requirements should be within a context of a local housing market area (HMA). The identification of a sub-regional system of local HMAs is therefore a necessary framework for strategic planning.

Perhaps surprisingly this view has not been embraced by planning, at least not until recently. Instead UK planning forecasts of population, and hence housing requirements, have been historically based on local authority administrative boundaries. Furthermore, the forecasting was based not on housing market trends or dynamics, but National Health Service data on households moving to a new doctor in a Family Health Service area that lack any reference to tenure (Baker and Wong, 1997). It is doubtful, given the limited relationship with the functioning of the housing system, whether these projections calculated in this way had any real meaning (see Chapter 6 for further discussion).

It is only recently that the use of HMAs has begun to be adopted within the planning process in England. Regional spatial strategies adopted in 2005 noted that housing statistics will have to be compiled for individual districts or appropriate sub-regional HMAs (ODPM, 2005b,c). The government also published a housing market assessment manual developed by DTZ Pieda (2003) that identifies broad approaches to defining a local HMA for the first time. In contrast, Scotland has been the leading the way in the use of HMAs for some time.

HMAs began to be used by planners in Scotland in the 1980s and this proved a major stimulant to research on their definition. From this period Scottish strategic (structure) plans have required planners to estimate housing demand and allocate land within a HMA framework. The first systematic attempt was undertaken by the former Strathclyde Regional Council (1994) when it identified seven HMAs based on migration patterns between district council areas in the west of Scotland. A later study for the successor authority (following reorganisation) refined this approach by deriving HMAs based on migration within the structure plan area essentially between settlements and administrative sub-areas of Glasgow (Glasgow and Clyde Valley Structure Plan Joint Committee, 1999).

A critique of this approach by Maclennan (1992) argues that a definition of an HMA should take into account the spatial market search patterns of households following the search analysis expounded by Smith and Mertz (1980) and Smith and Clark (1982a,b). Maclennan argues that simply looking at migration rather than search patterns creates a definition that is too narrowly defined because migration reflects the existing spatial pattern of the existing housing stock. In other words, such an HMA is defined by supply rather than demand. By looking at search patterns Maclennan argues that it is possible to reveal where there are local market pressure points (i.e. where there is high demand relative to supply). These search patterns apply not just to locations but also relate to house types. Search patterns, it is therefore argued, can identify the nature of area-based or housing-type demand that is being crowded out or simply not provided for by the market.

The planning advice in Scotland on defining an HMA as issued by the Scottish Executive implies some reference to housing search patterns. The definition has had periodic marginal changes and the most recent version gives the following definition:

> A Housing Market Area (HMA) is a geographical area where the demand for housing is relatively self contained, i.e. where a large percentage of the people moving house or settling within the area have sought a dwelling only within that area (Scottish Executive, 2003, para 20).

This definition is in itself insufficient as the whole of the UK would meet this test. The planning advice directs readers to the practicalities set out in a research manual (DTZ Pieda, 2003). This research manual identifies HMAs in a series of stages, as follows.

1 Identification of core centre and settlement hierarchy ranked by size within a structure or strategic plan area. The main centres are taken to be the anchors around which the precise spatial definition or boundary will be drawn.
2 Determine household movement/migration patterns from the principal anchor urban area to surrounding lower-order settlements and if a set proportion of purchasers are from the anchor area (10% is suggested) then they are incorporated into the anchor HMA.
3 If the percentage is less than the (10%) benchmark but 'still not negligible', say 5%, then the research should examine the proportion of households moving from the 'satellite' area into the anchor HMA. If this proportion is substantial (8% is recommended), the community is incorporated in the anchor HMA.
4 If this second test is still inconclusive then the two preceding tests are repeated only for new housing.
5 The final test for inclusion, if the preceding are inconclusive, is to consider the general migration patterns of the satellite area and their interaction with an enlarged anchor area including other areas incorporated by the above steps.
6 Finally, a spatial definition to the HMA is established by drawing a continuous border around the outermost settlements.

This procedure seems designed to provide a relatively simple process although it becomes more complex when a settlement has close links with a number of anchor centres (especially if they have equal rank). In any case, the process is repeated for the unallocated areas to test whether they can be grouped with lower ranked anchor HMAs. The system of HMAs derived in this way is then subject to potential revision because of projected policy initiatives (see later) that may influence the boundaries and finally to consultation and feedback by stakeholders.

The logic behind this procedure is:

> The geographical extent of a housing market area can be defined as the area within which people will search for housing and within which they are willing to move while maintaining their existing economic – e.g. employment – and social relationships … (DTZ Pieda, 2003, para 4).

In other words, households will move within an HMA to meet their individual domestic requirements as income changes or as they pass through the family life cycle without the requirement to shift employment.

The English manual of housing market assessment developed by DTZ Pieda (2004) is less directive but offers two dimensions to a definition: HMAs are areas within which people are prepared to search for housing, and geographical areas which contain both the origin and destination of the great majority who move home. The manual suggests that a 70% containment benchmark would be appropriate for an HMA.

Housing market areas and processes

This brief review of planning approaches to defining HMAs raises a range of theoretical issues. Planning advice has an element of pragmatism and, although the Scottish research finds considerable consensus, there is a lack of an explicit theoretical underpinning, and doubts are expressed that such an approach can reflect constraints rather than choices. For these critics the solution is the application of housing market search analysis. A full assessment, however, requires a fundamental review of the concept of an HMA as a spatial market area. To achieve this task the analysis first returns to the access–space model to consider its view on an HMA. The analysis then examines the internal dynamics of an HMA and, in particular, the relationships and distinctions between spatial arbitrage, migration and search processes. This discussion draws on parallels with the definitions of local labour markets which, as another spatial market, should be based on the same essential principles.

The implicit logic of the access–space model outlined earlier is that the housing market and the city are defined by the travel to work area (TTWA) as people work predominantly in the city centre, and choose where they live by reference to travel and housing costs. A useful starting point is therefore to view a TTWA as an HMA. This was the approach applied by a series of Joseph Rowntree housing finance studies of six UK cities in the late 1980s (see Maclennan *et al.*, 1990). In the access model the urban periphery is the edge of the TTWA as this defines how far people commute to the city centre. A more in-depth view of this process reveals that, actually, the relationship is the other way round. More precisely, the operation of the housing market determines the TTWA so, for example, lower transport costs leads not only to a flatter house price gradient but people living on average further from the city centre. In this way suburbanisation can be explained by the model as noted earlier as a consequence of falling travel costs.

This theoretical analysis is based on an extensive range of assumptions that provide insights into the urban spatial structure of housing markets. The necessary assumptions used to highlight these points also limit its practical usefulness as a planning tool. In particular the spatially diffuse nature of employment and variable landscape topography mean that there is normally no clearly defined edge to a city or built-up urban area and commuting patterns (TTWAs) may encompass several urban areas linked by good transport networks. It also implies that an HMA does not in reality have a 1 : 1 relationship with the physical boundary of an urban area. To achieve further insights into the definition of an HMA the analysis now reviews the internal dynamics or the processes of finding and purchasing (or renting) housing within a local HMA. In other words, the analysis focuses on household movement or migration.

Search

Searching is the first stage in the household migration process within a heterogeneous housing market that offers incomplete information on prevailing prices. The search process may be influenced by 'gatekeepers' such as estate agents and mortgage finance lenders. It can be seen as a series of (potentially) hierarchical stages, for example through the narrowing of spatial focus over time or through initially receiving information on a wide range of available property to visiting a sample. This process informs demand and can shape migration patterns. Ultimately households, in the last step in this process, adjust their consumption of housing by moving house. Migration patterns therefore represent effective or revealed demand.

Search patterns have been argued by some authors, noted earlier, as the most appropriate way to define HMAs but they suffer from a number of problems. First, there are problems of practicality. There are a whole series of questions here. Which level of the hierarchical spatial search process described above should be used, and how could such data be collected on a consistent basis? Not all households search in the same way. How do we account for the variation in search processes of households, for example, some households may only undertake one stage? Should all search areas be weighted equally? In reality households may search several areas but always have a preference. To date, data on search processes have primarily been collected from households who have moved but this excludes those who searched but who were unable to move or did not find a home that met their requirements. The practical data requirements of deriving an HMA solely from search data are severe and probably prohibitively expensive, and this explains why a search-based HMA has yet to be developed.

Second, and the most over-riding point is that even if these problems could be overcome household search areas are unlikely to coincide with a housing market area. In practice each household may have a separate search area based on their existing location. The area could be smaller than a town and similarly it is unlikely that a vendor would actively expect buyers from across a large city (see Chapter 4). Combining individual searches into mac-ro-search patterns does not change the fundamental narrowness of house-hold searches. The boundaries of these search patterns will also vary with different socio-economic-demographic household profiles and house types and prices.

The issue can be taken further by the example of a city and a satellite town, and presume there are significant decentralising moves from the urban core to the satellite. If all the households who move to the satellite search only in that town, and HMAs are defined by search, then this will imply that the satellite is an HMA in its own right. However, these households have implicitly compared and rejected the urban core. This is an extreme example but is useful to illustrate the difficulties of the use of search patterns. The conclusion ignores the underlying relationships between core and periphery that are influencing these search patterns, in particular relative house prices and available house types in the city and the satellite town.

The urban core and satellite are logically simply internal household moves from one location to another within the same HMA. Furthermore, moves between the city and its satellite will create spatial arbitrage: shifts in demand to the satellite could lead to a change in relative spatial prices. A search-based criteria could therefore define a set of HMAs that denies the underlying decision criteria, the interaction between city and satellite housing markets, and hence the existence of spatial arbitrage. This contradiction of the guiding principle of spatial arbitrage arises because search is seen as a process in isolation, not as simply the first step in the migration process; it is not a transaction in the housing market in its own right.

Spatial arbitrage and migration

The analysis that identifies a key part of what creates a local housing market is the process of spatial arbitrage – people comparing prices when making decisions and influencing prices by these decisions. This process is an essential component of a market and is an important building block to identify an HMA from first principles. Further insight can be gleaned from Cournot, quoted by Stigler and Sherwin (1985: 555) who defined a market area as 'a market for a good is the area within which the price of a good tends to uniformity, allowance being made for transportation costs'. This basic economic principle implies that for this to occur buyers can and do consider transactions at any point within the area to be an appropriate substitute and therefore spatial arbitrage occurs.

Local labour markets are defined as the TTWA using this principle (Coombes *et al.*, 1986). This is consistent with Cournot's underlying principle of the requirement of spatial arbitrage to exist: the TTWA is an area within which people commute to work and in which buyers (local firms) and sellers (workers living in area) of labour interact to establish wage rates (prices). Applying the same guiding principle to the definition of an HMA, namely an area within which spatial arbitrage applies, implies the use of migration to define contained areas within which house prices are determined (for the owner-occupied market).

One potential criticism is that household migration is effective demand and therefore represents the outcome of the interaction of supply and demand. It is not a pure measure of the level of demand and is it is also influenced by the spatial pattern of housing supply. This is the main argument against it. It is reflected in the arguments presented earlier in the chapter and is also illustrated by Evans (1990) who argues that planning constraints on supply in the South East of England in the 1980s forced up house prices. Migration patterns in the South East over this period do not measure the excess demand that forced up prices. Those households who were rationed or crowded out of the housing market are not included in the migration statistics (nor usually in search analysis), others who searched and reappraised their options are. The unsuccessful buyers are households who will presumably have searched the housing market before giving up. This example illustrates the issue but further consideration of these processes also draws out the argument in favour of the use of migration. Whatever their reasons for the lack of success there is no reason why (or evidence to show) the spatial search patterns of successful and unsuccessful purchasers should be significantly different. Household migration patterns, while only measuring effective demand, provide the better measure of the spatial extent of a local HMA as they also take account of the essential tenet of spatial arbitrage.

Defining a market area

A spatial market implies self-containment, an area within which the arbitrage process occurs or is focused. If a settlement has an open migration pattern in the sense that it has high proportions of movers into and out of the area, then from this perspective it is clearly not a HMA in its own right but part of a larger HMA. The analysis now develops a set of criteria based on the use of migration patterns to identify such areas. A necessary key to the spatial definition of an HMA is a high degree of closure or spatial containment. The logic of our definition also implies conversely that there is a lack of spatial arbitrage between HMAs which in turn implies no or minimal overlaps between HMAs. Taken together these criteria imply that such an area should, at the very least, be a settlement or contiguous group of settlements with a high degree of housing market self-containment, or that in-migration from the surrounding area is of only minor significance.

One important question remains: is there a threshold size for a local housing market size? This raises a number of subsidiary questions. At one extreme there is the question of whether a small settlement which satisfies the self-containment criterion can have enough transactions to really act as a market in its own right? At the other extreme there is the doubt that a large settlement can be really only one HMA or can it be broken down into a series of segments? This is discussed in Chapter 4 as both of these problems are related to the potential existence of submarkets. Hence in the first case, it is possible that the small settlement might best be characterised as a submarket of a larger neighbour. As these issues are linked to interaction rather than size it is presumed here there is no minimum size.

To summarise, HMAs are defined by the existence of internal spatial arbitrage and the absence of spatial arbitrage/substitutability between each other. The identification of an HMA could incorporate two (potentially sequential) tests comprising migration containment and weak interconnection between areas. A third and subsidiary 'test' is the relationship with TTWAs: the discussion above with regard to the access–space model suggests a close relationship between HMAs and TTWAs in which the former may be equivalent or embedded in the latter.

Practicalities

So far in this section the paper has formulated the concept of a local HMA based on the principle of the existence of spatial arbitrage. This is translated into practical form through the analysis of migration patterns between settlements to identify self-contained areas. In this way a theoretical concept is defined by reference to actual household behaviour. But as 100% self-containment in reality is impossible to achieve the precise level of self-containment which ensures spatial arbitrage remains an unanswered question. To some extent this can only be answered empirically. We can, however, receive some guidance on the scale of HMAs from the previous discussion. The access–space model for a uni-nodal town presumes perfect spatial arbitrage within a totally self-contained HMA that equates to a TTWA. In a multi-nodal city or urban system with dispersed employment there is still likely to be a close relationship between HMAs and TTWAs in which the former may be equivalent or embedded in the latter. In other words, the vast majority of households will move within their existing TTWA. Those who move to another TTWA are likely to do so following a change of job that necessitates a move.

Before proceeding it is useful to draw on the parallels with the definition of a TTWA, and associated problems identified by Coombes *et al.* (1979) and Coombes (1997). TTWAs represent the UK official approximation to local labour market areas (Coombes *et al.*, 1988). The official UK definition of a TTWA draws on the criteria of dominance and containment. The minimum size of a TTWA is a resident workforce of 3,500 and, of the resident economically active population, at least 75% actually work in the area, and, of everyone working in the area, at least 75% actually live in the area (Bond and Coombes, 2007). Based on these criteria a map of TTWAs has been constructed using a computer algorithm which amalgamates Census zones. There are 243 TTWAs based on the 2001 Census that are internally contiguous and the final map contains no overlapping areas and leaves no area unaccounted for.

Case studies of HMAs

There are few independent academic studies that have identified HMAs or discussed these relationships. This section reviews the detail of three studies in different regions: the west of Scotland, the North West and the North East of England. The analysis examines the implications of changing definitions and the relationships between HMAs and TTWAs, and provides insights into the spatial structure of housing markets.

West of Scotland

The first academic study is by Jones (2002) and derives HMAs based on migration patterns within the occupied sector. The spatial focus of the analysis is the area broadly covered by the former Strathclyde Regional Council. It covers a population of approximately 2.5 million people and hundreds of square miles. The area encompasses the Clydeside conurbation and a large number of free-standing towns. Settlements range in size from the city of Glasgow to small villages. To simplify the task deep rural areas are excluded and so the research here does not consider Argyll or the islands, with the exception of one with close links to the mainland. The area can be broadly defined as west central mainland Scotland.

The migration data are derived from the Land Registry/Register of Sasines covering the ten-year period 1984–1993. Each transaction record provides details of the address, type of property, sale price, date of registration, the origin of the buyer and a code which provides information on the nature of the sale (i.e. whether the sale was new build, by a district council, to a property company, a part share and so on). The analysis is based only on 'pure' new and second-hand private house sales ignoring all sales that appear to be non-market sales, including sales to sitting tenants and houses sold for less than £10,000. The approach here is based on the grouping of *settlements* to establish HMAs by examining migration interaction. These settlements range in size from the city of Glasgow to small villages, their attraction as building blocks is their internal coherence.

From the discussion above an HMA can be defined as a contiguous area comprising a settlement or group of settlements with a high degree of housing market self-containment, and where in-migration from outside the immediate HMA is of only minor significance. In the analysis below it is the former principle that is initially applied, but the use of spatial containment, as noted earlier, to define a HMA requires a set of criteria. The theoretical analysis above reveals there is no strict *a priori* theory to guide us on these issues. As household migration is not part of a daily urban system like commuting, it seems logical that the appropriate measure of containment should be lower than the 75% applied to TTWAs. The initial benchmark of a HMA is taken to be 50% of house purchasers moving within the area, but this is later relaxed. More formally, this 50% criterion can be applied to the number of moves starting and finishing within an area's boundaries as a percentage of the total number of moves into that area. HMAs are also assumed to be contiguous areas.

The grouping of settlements is undertaken using an iterative algorithm in which 'open' settlements are married to 'closed' settlements which already meet the containment criterion. Twenty-two HMAs are identified from this algorithm that satisfy the 50% closure criterion. The city of Glasgow is by far the largest with the next largest almost a fifth of its size. Some quite small HMAs are also identified based on towns that have closed housing markets. If we now add the criterion, the lack of interconnection with surrounding areas, the simple containment benchmark is augmented and can be rewritten as:

- at least 50% internal migration, or
- in-migration from an adjacent HMA equivalent to less than 5% of the market.

Based on this criteria one seaside resort area, a residue in the containment algorithm, would qualify as an HMA giving 23 (50%+) HMAs in all.

The basic algorithm is based entirely on a self-containment criterion and there are still significant flows between HMAs especially from Glasgow to adjoining areas. Therefore the HMAs do not meet the original second criterion set out above. Further detailed research shows that this out-migration from Glasgow is to adjoining settlements (rather than to HMAs as a whole). This suggests a little fuzziness at the edges of HMAs, and a different algorithm could include these within Glasgow.

Jones (2002) now applies the two test criteria simultaneously, namely the 50% containment benchmark *and* in-migration from an adjacent HMA equivalent to less than 5% of the market to derive a system of (50*%) HMAs. There are just 11 (50*%) HMAs. The Glasgow HMA now incorporates the surrounding areas within the Clydeside conurbation. Some small HMAs still remain as entities in their own right but HMAs with significant pair-wise migration inter-flows have been combined. This system (of 50*%) also broadly satisfies our third test with respect to TTWAs; there are a number of minor discrepancies at the margins of the enlarged Glasgow HMA.

The benchmarks so far applied are not based on a rule embedded in theory. It is possible to reapply and extend the algorithm to meet a criterion of 60%, but only a few areas meet such a criterion and yet there would still be one strong pair-wise migration inter-flow. A 60*% definition would leave only six HMAs, less than the nine TTWAs identified by the government within the study area. A 40% benchmark would create at least 41 HMAs with many of the suburban satellites of Glasgow meeting this criterion but with significant flows between areas. Overall, the 50*% benchmark, Jones argues, best achieves the original theoretically driven criteria while at the same time best meeting the third test: a close (embedded) relationship with TTWAs.

These results provide useful insights into the open structure of spatial housing markets: 23 HMAs are identified in west central Scotland based on the simple 50%+ criteria but there are still significant migration links between these HMAs defined in this way. This does not satisfy the second test. Extending the 50% containment criterion to include weak inter-connectedness reduces the number of HMAs to 11, and achieves our *a priori* theoretical understanding of HMAs. The region is dominated by the city of Glasgow, and migration patterns appear to ensure an immediate house price spatial arbitration process which can encompass large areas. Yet there are also relatively small communities in rural areas and some free standing towns which have relatively closed HMAs.

North West of England

A delineation a system of HMAs for the North West of England has been undertaken by Brown and Hincks (2008). The region has approximately 6.9 million people and two major cities – Liverpool and Manchester. The research is based primarily on migration data between wards from the 2001 Census but the first stage is to consult estate agents to identify *prima facie* HMAs and thereby to provide 43 core points for the analysis. A 70% containment criterion is used to define an HMA and is applied to both the percentages of in-migrants and out-migrants of an area. The authors use a more sophisticated computer algorithm than Jones (2002), i.e. a hierarchical step-wise aggregation procedure, that groups wards on the basis of migration between and within areas. The first round of this procedure finds that not all 43 potential HMAs stated by estate agents achieved the target 70% containment and so the analysis is repeated and ultimately 25 are identified.

The reduction from 43 to 25 HMAs through strict application of the 70% containment criterion removes a number of small rural HMAs where the market is distorted by second home purchases. After further consultation with estate agents, some small towns are included in larger HMAs. The geography of these 25 HMAs show they are not entirely consistent with local authority boundaries. Similarly, comparison of the 25 HMAs with the 23 official TTWAs in the region reveals great similarities especially in urban areas. The differences in the boundaries occurs in rural areas suggesting to the authors that the self containment criterion should vary by type of area.

North East of England

A study by Coombes *et al.* (2006) seeks to provide a set of policy relevant definitions of HMAs in the North East that can be used for different contexts. In particular it examines how different approaches to this task meet the criteria given in the guidance manual (DTZ Pieda, 2004). Like the North West study the analysis is primarily based on migration statistics from the 2001 Census at ward level. However, the authors point out the limitations of this data set as it includes all tenure groups which means that an area with high levels of social housing will have low mobility compared with areas predominantly of private-rented accommodation. To resolve this problem Coombes *et al.* (2006) include non-movers in their research and rather than using the containment criterion of 70% for movers use its new equivalent of 97% (when non-movers are included).

HMAs are again identified using an iterative procedure that follows the basics of Jones (2002). First, areas are ranked by the set criteria, if the worst does not meet the criteria, then reallocate to maximize the integration of flows, and repeat until the criteria is met for all groups. The results again find that HMA borders split local authority areas. The southern HMAs straddle the regional border with Yorkshire and Humberside. The study then changes the containment criterion to 65% or 96.5% and shows how a rather different map is produced.

Finally, the analysis delineates tenure-specific HMAs by looking at moving groups rather than individuals but this latter task suffers from greater data limitations and produces larger HMAs – the whole country for private renters because of long-distance moves by students. The social housing HMAs (not really markets but allocation systems) are found to be more fragmented than system-wide definitions. The owner-occupied specific HMAs do not differ much with the overall ones but this is not surprising as it is the dominant tenure. The study derives a 60% owner-occupied HMA but ultimately argues that the 65% owner occupied HMA which leads to just

10 HMAs is the most appropriate division for policy although criteria for this choice seems subjective.

Overview of evidence on HMAs

The empirical evidence shows that the national housing market is a system of relatively self-contained spatial HMAs. However, they are not closed systems. The precise containment criterion varies with data set, and varying the criteria produces very different maps of HMAs. The geographies of these HMAs are generally not wholly consistent with local authority boundaries. As spatial markets they have common features with TTWAs. Coombes *et al.* (2006) argue strongly that the research method for the derivation of TTWA can be transferred to HMAs. TTWAs have influenced the accepted 70% containment criterion used in official guidance and by academic authors, but this is quite arbitrary and the parallels between daily commuting patterns and much more infrequent migration need greater justification.

The research does not establish a set of definitive containment criteria. There are strong theoretical arguments why HMAs should be embedded within TTWAs and this provides a useful benchmark for choosing the appropriate criteria in practice. The theoretical arguments based on spatial arbitrage imply that HMAs are tenure specific and there is likely to be significant differences between local owner-occupied and private-rented HMAs. Ideally this distinction should be reflected in the data sets used. To date, private-rented HMAs have not been fully researched and, in particular, the choice of containment criteria needs some more investigation. There are also differences between the characteristics of urban and rural housing markets and it is perhaps necessary to have flexible criteria to deal with this, for example with regard to size and containment.

Implications of HMAs for planning

The evidence that HMAs do not conform to local authorities' administrative boundaries and vary by tenure confirms that traditional approaches to forecasting future housing demand/requirements have been incorrectly specified. The result is that strategic land allocations for housing have been based on inaccuracy and have unintentionally distorted the housing market. Earlier it was argued that the forecasting of future housing demand/requirements should be within a context of a local HMA. This has belatedly been accepted across the UK but the identification of a sub-regional system of local HMAs as a framework for strategic planning is still in its infancy. Official guidance is weak on either specifics or the underlying theory and so the potential for distortion is still very much an issue.

DTZ Pieda (2004) succinctly illustrates part of the potential problem. An HMA that is too narrowly defined may have adverse consequences on both sides of the boundary. This may mean excess supply of housing sites as the land allocation will not take into account demand that may be satisfied across the border in the adjoining HMA. At the same time there may be excess demand in the neighbouring HMA. Similarly if an HMA is too widely defined then land could be allocated to sites beyond the actual market leading to excess demand. The converse of this is that there will be unexpected land available to meet demand in the other HMA. This example has only a partial perspective as the allocation of land by the planning system, notably by the restrictions created by green belts, in itself shapes the housing market and contributes to the definition of an HMA and planners must also take responsibility in this regard.

To date the identification of HMAs has been devolved to regional or sub-regional planning authorities and identification incorporates a degree of local discretion, but there is a strong argument for the identification of a national system of HMAs (following TTWAs). This is reinforced by the research in the North East that finds HMAs encroaching across regional boundaries. A national system would provide a consistent and transparent geography for this task derived from Land Registry or Census data.

HMAs should not be seen as cast in stone. The government updates its national system of TTWAs every ten years because of the changing nature of the transport infrastructure (Bond and Coombes, 2007). Over time TTWAs have become larger and the same forces that are driving this phenomenon are also extending HMAs as the access–space model shows. The dynamics of urban settlement systems could ultimately lead to changes in the pattern of migration flows and hence to the definition of HMAs. There is therefore a requirement to regularly revisit the definitions of local HMAs.

Conclusions

The spatial structure of an urban housing market can be explained in terms of the access–space model in which households trade off increased accessibility close to the city centre against the desire to consume a larger amount of housing at a cheaper price per square metre at peripheral locations. Increasing suburbanisation can be explained within the model by rising incomes leading to people consuming greater housing further from the city core and improved transport technology and infrastructure reducing the cost of commuting.

The basic access–space model provides useful insights but it is based on restrictive assumptions including no planning. In reality the operation of local housing markets and planning cannot be divorced, certainly in the UK. The chapter demonstrates how urban housing markets are shaped by the planning system, particularly through the establishment of green belts. The result can be seen in both increased house prices and densities as well as changes in the intra-urban pattern of these phenomena while the underlying force of the access–space model remains intact.

The second half of the chapter takes a wider view of urban housing markets in a regional context and examines systems of local HMAs. Much of the focus is on the definition of an HMA by reference to the internal dynamics and the degree of self-containment. City-wide housing markets are shown to incorporate suburbia and contiguous towns, but HMAs do not necessarily fit easily with local government administrative boundaries.

Practical schemes for the identification of HMAs emphasise migration patterns but some commentators and official definitions incorporate a role for market search. The use of search analysis is shown to be theoretically unsound as it is not based on market outcomes. Instead it is argued that HMAs are created jointly by internal spatial arbitrage and by the lack of spatial arbitrage/substitutability between them. They are hence estimated from a combination of self-containment and lack of interconnectedness measured by migration patterns (Jones, 2002; Brown and Hincks, 2008).

There is no theoretical basis for the selection of containment criterion and so the decision to date has been arbitrary. The higher the level of containment means the greater the spatial size of the HMA in general. Residential location theory implicitly defines an HMA as the surrounding TTWA and there appears to be a close association between the two. At very high levels of containment the two are broadly matched but while HMAs theoretically should not be larger than a TTWA the case for a 1 : 1 relationship is unproven. The localised nature of housing demand discussed in Chapter 4 inclines the present authors toward smaller rather than larger HMAs and hence a lower containment criterion.

Planning seeks to predict demand and hence allocate land accordingly and this implies the use of a framework of HMAs to ensure that this process is undertaken efficiently. This approach has recently been embraced by government guidance but there remain problems about the specification and delineation of HMAs. This gives rise to problems of incorrect specification that can invalidate research conclusions and produce unexpected planning outcomes. In addition planners must also recognise a degree of circularity in the process because the land allocations that stem from these decisions and policies more generally ultimately contribute to the definition of a local HMA.

4

Understanding Housing Submarkets

The previous chapter started to explore the structure and operation of local housing systems. It set out a conceptual model of how urban housing markets work that was consistent with mainstream economic theory. This highly influential location choice model (often associated with the establishment of New Urban Economics) assumed away product heterogeneity, by adopting the notion that consumers purchase units of 'housing services', and focused on the locational specificity of dwellings. The model builds from the assumption that households (consumers) purchase housing and employment accessibility jointly. It demonstrates that, with application of the standard neo-classical behavioural assumptions (including the rational optimising behaviour of economic agents), it is possible to predict the pattern of residential location choices (often referred to as the Alonso–Muth or access–space model) and the spatial distribution of property values (as revealed by the bid–rent curve) in long-run equilibrium. An important central feature of the different mainstream models has been the assumption that the urban housing system is a unitary market. Although, as we note in the last chapter, these models offer useful insights in to the workings of housing markets and the way they are spatially structured, this chapter explores the case for relaxing this assumption.

The chapter starts by arguing that it is now widely accepted that urban housing systems are highly segmented and, as a result, are best conceptualised as comprising a set of quasi-independent housing submarkets. The chapter is organised in a further five parts. The next section explores the origins of submarkets as an analytical construct. The discussion highlights the fact that submarkets originally were developed in studies that were quite different in methodological content from those discussed above and in the previous chapter. The third section builds on this by exploring the theoretical rationale for submarket existence. This provides the basis (in section four) for a review of competing definitions of submarkets and the challenges these definitions pose for identifying submarkets and modelling them. This is made more difficult by the limited understanding of the temporal dynamics of submarkets. The final section considers the potential significance of the housing submarket as an analytical construct in local housing market studies. It highlights some of the difficulties associated with incorporating the notion of the submarket in to mainstream economic analyses of urban housing markets.

Origins of housing submarket studies

The access–space theoretical model (discussed in Chapter 3) has dominated urban housing economics since the 1960s. Since then several different strands of mainstream economic analysis of housing systems have emerged. Although different variants of the mainstream model tend to emphasise different dimensions of housing as an economic commodity, the various strands of the literature share common behavioural assumptions. The voluminous literature that applies hedonic theory to house prices (see p. 80 for details), for example, is an extension of this mainstream model. Hedonic models continue to recognise that location has an important impact on property values but also accommodates product heterogeneity.

The appeal of the mainstream approach is that it emphasises the construction of models that offer precision and that are generalisable and definitive. There is, of course, a trade-off between the elegance, formal mathematical rigour and tractability on the one hand, and behavioural relevance on the other. Mainstream economists have found it difficult to accommodate all of the peculiar characteristics (heterogeneity, immobility and durability) of housing (as an economic commodity) within a single model (Smith *et al.*, 1988). As we note above, a central feature of these models is that they assume a single unitary housing market. This assumption has not always been so prominent.

Some of the earliest economic analyses of local housing markets emphasised quite different operation features including the segmented and disaggregated nature of markets. The intellectual roots of this alternative approach can be traced to the work of Richard T. Ely in the 1900s. Ely was a highly influential economist who was involved in establishing the

American Economic Society and the *Land Economics* journal. His methodological position is consistent with 'old institutional' economic approaches where an institution is 'a way of thought or action that has some prevalence, which is embedded in the habits of a group or the customs of people' (Hamilton, 1932 cited in Hodgson, 1999: 89). Old institutional analysis is concerned with the way in which norms, habits and culture lead to the socially habituated behaviour of economic agents. Markets are considered to be inherently social and are, in fact, a form of institution. In comparison with mainstream economic approaches, institutional analysis places greater weight on understanding underlying market processes and relations and less on explaining or predicting market outcomes.

In developing his intellectual programme, Ely was heavily influenced by the German Historical School. This school stressed that historical specificity in socio-economic reality precluded the employment of universal covering laws of deductive reasoning. He was particularly concerned with contemporary housing policy debates and his approach and ideas helped shape the work of a number of distinguished 'land economists' located at Columbia and Wisconsin (see McMaster and Watkins, 2006 for further details). In its research approach this 'institutional' school emphasised the importance of description of institutional structure and historical and spatial context. Significantly, this was reflected in highly disaggregated empirical studies that were explicitly concerned with discontinuities in the urban system and the dynamics of neighbourhoods.

The main contribution of these researchers was to derive analytical models of local housing systems that emphasised the co-existence of distinct but interrelated market segments (or housing submarkets) and sought to explore the dynamic nature of submarket linkages and the extent to which 'filtering' takes place. Despite the richness of the empirical work, this approach was not unproblematic and has often been criticised for being under-theorised (see Smith, 1978 for a discussion). Although considerable effort was expended in seeking clear definitions of key concepts, including submarkets, the lack of precision often resulted in difficulties in applying the analytical framework in a consistent manner. These limitations meant that policy-oriented research findings often lacked generalisability and generated contestable results, particularly in the application of filtering models (see Chapter 5).

In the 1960s urban housing economics, like mainstream economics, was subject to a significant paradigm shift that de-emphasised the 'instutionalist' approach. As a result, discussion of housing submarkets and neighbourhood dynamics became less prominent. As noted in the introduction, much of the mainstream approach was derived from New Urban Economics and, in basic form, the model developed assumed that local housing markets are unitary, equilibrating systems. In this framework, variation in house prices across space will reflect the difference in physical or neighbourhood quality. Any significant differences in the price of dwellings of identical specification located in neighbourhoods of similar quality will be merely transitory. In this abstract 'economic' world, and here it is only fair to acknowledge that this is something of a straw-man caricature of vast and complex neoclassical economics literature, where markets are well-behaved, coherent and without transactions costs, price differences between neighbourhoods are removed quickly by the arbitrage process. Developers will build in high-price segments to take advantage of higher than normal profits and/or households will relocate to take advantage of lower prices (without losing out on the quantity or physical and neighbourhood quality associated with their consumption of housing).

Despite their dominance, these models have been criticised for their failure to adequately explain the spatial distribution of prices in local housing markets (see Chapter 3). They have also been the subject of sustained criticism for their preoccupation with technique and mathematical sophistication at the expense of institutional considerations (see, for example, Grigsby, 1978). It is argued that institutional rigidities associated with information inefficiencies, search costs, transactions costs, planning and financial constraints will inhibit the market adjustment process (see Maclennan, 1982). In these circumstances, housing submarkets are likely to exist. This possibility is explored in the remainder of the chapter.

Theoretical basis for housing submarkets

There are two potential explanations for the existence of housing submarkets. One suggests that housing markets tend towards multiple equilibria (Goodman, 1978). This means that each submarket will exhibit its own equilibrium price. This is broadly consistent with the mainstream economic model and it is also the view that implicitly dominates the existing literature on housing submarkets. Although this is rarely discussed, most studies appear to acknowledge the existence of price differentials between market segments and build (hedonic) models of house prices that must be based on the assumption of equilibrium within submarkets. As such they are concerned with multiple equilibria.

The alternative explanation suggests that housing submarkets exist because housing markets tend to disequilibrium (Maclennan *et al.*, 1987). The prevalence of market imperfections such as search and information costs, which are typically assumed away in formal models, render the concept of equilibrium inappropriate as a basis for analysing urban housing systems. The housing market does not 'clear' for a variety of reasons. On the supply side, slow adjustment is caused by durability of the stock. The short-run supply curve is steeply sloping because of high transaction costs. On the demand side, market clearing is inhibited by the financial and psychological costs of moving, the desire to locate near to friends, family and workplace and/or the difficulties and costs associated with collecting and comparing information about competing heterogeneous vacancies.

Irrespective of whether submarkets are the result of multiple equilibria or disequilibrium processes, it is clear that they arise because a number of factors inhibit the mechanisms by which price differences in different parts of the market are arbitraged away. In other words, there are numerous factors that limit the responsiveness of new supply and/or household mobility.

This presence of these frictions suggests that housing markets should be analysed using a framework that accommodates submarket existence. The prevailing model should reflect the fact that, on the demand side of the market, households can be partitioned into distinct 'consumer groups' on the basis of their housing preferences and tastes, stage in the life cycle, life style, size and composition, and socio-economic status. The housing choice of households in the same 'consumer group' is also likely to be constrained by search and information costs that are broadly the same. The housing stock (supply) is similarly segmented. Following standard hedonic theory that asserts that housing is not demanded for itself *per se*, but for the attributes embodied within each housing unit, it is possible to conclude – as Maclennan *et al.* (1987) do – that the housing stock is sub-divided into distinct 'product groups'. Each product group will be composed of relatively homogenous dwellings which represent reasonably close substitutes to the demanders of housing. Of course, the assumption that submarkets comprise homogenous dwelling units is only partly correct. Part of the difficulty in defining submarkets is that dissimilar dwellings can be linked (Grigsby, 1963). Maclennan *et al.* (1987) specify product groups as homogenous, but in reality they need only contain dwellings which are linked by the degree of indifference of consumers.

It is the way in which segmented demand is matched to the differentiated housing stock which is likely give rise to housing submarkets and to cause differential prices to be paid for given attributes in different market segments. Excess demand for particular dwellings (and their close substitutes) will drive prices in that submarket upward. Similarly, excess supply will deflate the relative submarket price. This contrasts with the bid–rent curves derived in the equilibrating system associated with the standard access–space models.

There is considerable evidence of constraints on market adjustment. For example, there appears to be considerable neighbourhood attachment amongst consumers (Munro and Lamont, 1985). Jones *et al.*'s (2005a) analysis of intra-urban migration patterns in Glasgow provides evidence of surprisingly high levels of self-containment within submarkets (see Chapter 5 for further details). Of the six submarket areas analysed, only the city centre, which encompasses a major area of urban renewal activity known as the Merchant City and comprises mainly 'executive' flats in warehouse conversions, has more than 50% of its new buyers from outside the area. This reflects, in part, the nature of the market segment and its attractiveness to buyers who are new to the city and the fact that a resale market has only recently emerged and, thus, the baseline population was low. In contrast, more than 65% of the buyers in the south west of the city originated within that submarket. The level of self-containment observed at submarket level is almost as high as that observed within clusters of local authorities in HMA analysis.

Numerous authors have noted the absence of evidence that optimising consumers seek to benefit from lower prices (Jones *et al.*, 2003, 2005a; Kauko, 2001). This is not least because house purchasers often view housing as jointly having consumption and investment characteristics and, with rising prices, comes an expectation of further future capital gains. It also reflects the fact that, even if we ignore investment motives, this sort of adjustment is prohibited, in part, by transaction and search costs. The pervasiveness of significant market frictions restricts the likelihood of relocation.

The observed price structure of local markets is, in part, shaped by information flows. The infrequent involvement of buyers in the market means that, when compared to purchasers of other goods, they are poorly informed about current market conditions. These information problems can be overcome by an extensive and costly search process (see Maclennan *et al.*, 1987; see also Chapter 3). This may be one of the reasons that many movers often remain within the same submarket. Agents play an important part in disseminating information and shaping search patterns (Palm, 1978). Agents also contribute to the segmentation of the market. The way in which they distribute information about vacancies, including the way in which listings are organised, can shape the spatial extent of housing search. In addition, agents with other professional groups, including valuers and solicitors, help inform the pricing strategies of sellers and the bidding strategies of buyers (Smith *et al.*, 2006). Their advice often reflects knowledge of highly localised trends in market behaviour and acts to reinforce price differentials. The role of agents in making markets, although a subject of considerable general interest to institutional economists, is comparatively under-researched in the housing context (see Evans, 1995 for further discussion).

Spatial differences in house prices are also reinforced by administrative geographies. In a recent paper, Clapp and Wang (2006) make a helpful distinction between 'hard' and 'soft' boundaries (which are similar to the formal and informal boundaries used by Maclennan *et al.* (1998) in their local housing systems analysis). Hard boundaries include the local political and administrative geographies, such as school catchment areas, and can be helpful in identifying the way in which the quality of local public services become capitalised into house prices (see also Cheshire and Sheppard, 2004a). Soft boundaries are those derived from market interactions. These may not be consistent with 'hard' geographies but reflect the influence of information flows and agent activity and other interactions between economic agents. While it is argued that both hard and soft factors are important, Clapp and Wang note that soft boundaries are much more difficult to accommodate within applied studies. They argue, however, that for conceptual reasons it may be important to depart from the use of Census boundaries as proxies for the dimensions of neighbourhoods.

The constraints on new housing supply are even more marked. As we discuss in the next two chapters, it is clear that not only does the planning system restrict the level of new development but planning decisions also have a profound impact on the spatial distribution of new location and on the spatial allocation of different house types. Other public policy initiatives, including regeneration schemes, housing market renewal and the right to buy to name a few, also have a significant impact on changes to the housing stock (see Chapter 5). These policies tend to act completely independently from any market processes.

All of these rigidities work against the spatial arbitrage process that, in theory, would remove the significant variations in prices in different neighbourhoods. The mainstream assumptions about market adjustment are undone by social, cultural and institutional factors. This means that the differences in market performance at the neighbourhood level are of analytical significance. What is less clear is how submarkets should be defined and how they might be identified in practice.

discrimination or desired proximity to friends or workplace'. Some researchers have arguably over-emphasised the significance of structural (property
type) attributes. Allen *et al.* (1995), for example, argue that renters limit
their choices to specific property types, irrespective of location.

More recently, analysts have explicitly acknowledged the importance of
both spatial and structural factors in determining submarket dimensions.
Maclennan and Tu (1996) explain that both structural/house type and
spatial factors, separately or interactively, may generate submarkets. Adair
et al. (1996) also note that submarkets arise from a set of structural and locational attributes. This view is based on the existence of inelastic demand
for, and short-run supply of, housing in given time periods. Differences
emerge when the dimensions of submarkets are identified in these studies. Maclennan an Tu use techniques which jointly identify the important
locational and structural characteristics. The structure proposed by Adair
et al. is 'nested' in that the market is, first, segmented spatially into three
geographic areas, and, second, structurally differentiated submarkets are
identified within each.

Identifying submarkets

There is a fairly extensive international literature that has sought to test
for the existence of housing submarkets in urban areas. As Table 4.1 demonstrates these studies show overwhelming support for the existence of
significant price differentials between neighbourhoods. Only four out of
thirty-four published papers have failed to identify submarkets. The empirical studies that focus on British cities identify between six and ten distinct
submarkets, where each submarket encompasses several contiguous neighbourhoods (Munro, 1986; Maclennan *et al.*, 1987; Hancock and Maclennan,
1989; Adair *et al.*, 1996; Maclennan and Tu, 1996; Watkins, 2001; Pryce,
2004; Pryce and Evans, 2007).

There is some variation in the way in which housing submarkets existence is established. This reflects the fact, as we note above, that there is
little guidance from economic theory as to the appropriate definition or
dimensions of housing submarkets. It is, however, possible to derive a set
of necessary and sufficient conditions for submarket existence. Following
standard microeconomic theory, the extent of the market for an economic
good will encompass all demanders and suppliers involved in the process of
exchange who pay the market price for the good (see Chapter 3). To apply
this principle to an examination of the structure of the housing market, it
is important to consider the processes that shape the interaction of supply

Table 4.1 Testing for breaks in the urban house price surface.

Authors	Study area	Study date	Sample size	No. of test segments	Submarkets?
Straszheim (1975)	San Francisco Bay, CA, USA	1965	28,000	81	Yes
Schnare and Struyk (1976)	Boston, MA, USA	1971	2,195	2/3/2	No
Ball and Kirwan (1977)	Bristol, UK	1970/71	280	8	No
Palm (1978)	San Francisco Bay, CA, USA	1971 and 1978	344	2/7	Yes
Sonstelie and Portney (1980)	San Mateo, CA, USA	1969/70	1,453	25	Yes
Goodman (1981)	New Haven, CT, USA	1967–1969	1,835	5/15	Yes
Dale-Johnson (1982)	Santa Clara, CA, USA	1972	3,021	10	Yes
Gabriel (1984)	Beer Sheva, Israel	1982	89	3	Yes
Bajic (1985)	Toronto, Canada	1978	385	3	Yes
Munro (1986)	Glasgow, UK	1983/84	154	2	Yes
Maclennan et al. (1987); Maclennan (1987)	Glasgow, UK	1976 and 1985/86	863 and 1,257	5	Yes
Michaels and Smith (1990)	Boston, MA, USA	1977–1981 (pooled)	2,182	4	Yes
Rothenberg et al. (1991)	Des Moines, IA, USA	1963 and 1971	1,360	6	Yes
Hancock (1991)	Tayside, UK	1977/78–1986	28,053	6	Yes
Allen et al. (1995)	Clemson, SC, USA	1991	215	3	Yes
Adair et al. (1996)	Belfast, UK	1992	999	7	Yes
Maclennan and Tu (1996)	Glasgow, UK	1984 and 1990	1,257 and 1,342	25	Yes
Goodman and Thibodeau (1998, 2003)	Dallas, TX, USA	1995–1997	28,000	90	Yes
Bourassa et al. (1999a)	Sydney and Melbourne, Australia	1991	2,307 and 2,354	5	Yes
Watkins (1999, 2001)	Glasgow, UK	1991	565	8 and 6	Yes
Fletcher et al. (2000)	Midland Region, UK	1994	18,000	18	Yes
McGreal et al. (2000)	Belfast, UK				Yes
Berry et al. (2003)	Dublin, Ireland	1997–2001 (pooled)	4,312	4	Yes
Bourassa et al. (2003)	Auckland, New Zealand	1996	8,421	18	Yes
Kauko (2004)	Amsterdam, The Netherlands		46,000	Various	No
Bates (2006)	Philadelphia, PA, USA	2000	15,461	6	Yes
Bourassa et al. (2007)	Auckland, New Zealand	1996	4,880	33	Yes
Goodman and Thibodeau (2007)	Dallas, TX, USA	2000–2002	44,000	372	Yes
Pryce and Evans (2007)	Kent, UK	1996–2004	N/A	Various	Yes
Tu et al. (2007)	Singapore	2000	4,192	8	Yes
Keskin (2009)	Istanbul, Turkey	2005	2,175	Various	Yes

and demand to determine market prices. Housing submarkets exist where the interaction between segmented demand – characterised by consumer groups – and segmented supply – characterised by product groups – generate price differences for some hypothetical standardised dwelling.

Thus, following microeconomic theory, a submarket is deemed to exist if the 'law of one price' exists within the submarket; and if a hypothetical, standardised housing unit trades at different prices in different submarkets. The first condition requires that all dwellings within a submarket are relatively close substitutes and are within the same 'submarket'. The second condition is based on the assumption that if differential prices exist then there is good reason to believe that the suppliers and demanders who determine the price are, in fact, operating in different submarkets from other buyers and sellers. In these circumstances it is clear that the market may be partitioned into distinct submarkets which exhibit independent behaviour in terms of current levels of supply and demand, and the determination of prices.

These conditions have given rise to a fairly standard, three-stage test procedure. First, house prices are decomposed into their component parts. This decomposition is largely based on hedonic modelling techniques. The hedonic modelling procedure, associated with Rosen (1974), estimates the implicit price of each property attribute. It allows comparison of prices, even when dwellings have very different specifications because the price of each attribute, or bundles of similar attributes, can be compared. Evans (1995) provides an accessible account of the logic underpinning hedonic property pricing. He explains that the use of hedonic regression analysis assumes that purchasers know the cost of a property or package of characteristics and can list the attributes – or contents of the package – so that we may be able to separate the price of each characteristic. Evans considers this analogous to shopping in a supermarket that does not price individual items and, where people are simply told the total price to be paid for their basket of goods. If each shopper were then asked to list what they bought and how much they paid, then given sufficient variation and that at least as many shoppers have been questioned as there are separate goods, the price of individual items can be found by solving a set of simultaneous equations.

This logic can be extended to explain the analysis of submarkets. If two shoppers spent P_1 and P_2 to purchase Q_1 and Q_2 of the good G_1 and Q_3 and Q_4 of the good G_2 then the equations will be as follows:

$$P_1 = S_1Q_1 + S_2Q_3 \tag{4.1}$$

$$P_2 = S_1Q_2 + S_2Q_4 \tag{4.2}$$

where S_1 and S_2 are the unknown prices of the two goods. As long as the purchases of one shopper are not some multiple of the purchases of the other, then the equations can be solved. As with hedonic modelling, the solution found is the best estimated price that fits the data. So, just as the prices paid for each good will be the same for each shopper, the market price of each property attribute is the same at all points in the market and will be the same for each consumer of property services. This implies that a further test is needed to establish whether prices vary by (sub)market.

Thus, the second stage requires that the price of a standardised (hypothetical) property is compared statistically using a Chow test. This test compares the regression equations calibrated for each (potential) submarket and identifies whether there is parameter equality. In other words, it tests whether the implicit prices for individual attributes (as revealed by the coefficient estimates in the hedonic models) exhibit any statistically significant differences in value. If there are no differences, it is assumed that the prices are equal across the segments compared and that they are part of the same submarket. Third, where there appear to be statistically significant price differences, a weighted standard error test is also computed. The WSE test compares the accuracy of the price estimates generated when submarkets are identified with those derived from a single model covering the entire market (see Schnare and Struyk, 1976; Dale-Johnson, 1982; Gabriel, 1984; Tu *et al.*, 2007). Typically, it is assumed that when the error associated with the submarket level equations is more than 10% less than the error generated by a single market-wide equation then submarkets exist (Munro, 1986; Watkins, 2001). Some variation enters the procedure through the tests used to compare hedonic price estimates. A number of studies do not undertake the WSE test (Fletcher *et al.*, 2000; Adair *et al.*, 1996; Sonstelie and Portney, 1980; Ball and Kirwan, 1977), while Allen *et al.* (1995) and Michaels and Smith (1990) use a Tiao-Goldberger test instead of the Chow test.

The way in which potential submarkets are identified within the statistical testing procedure is also highly variable. Most of the stratification schemes used to identify submarket boundaries are shaped by the broad definition adopted: spatial/geographic, structural/property type or nested/combined. The simplest approach is to aggregate small spatial units such as Census tracts or postcode areas (Straszheim, 1975; Schnare and Struyk, 1976; Ball and Kirwan, 1977) or to subdivide by stock type or quality (Rothenberg *et al.*, 1991; Bajic, 1985). Adair *et al.* (1996) combine the two and identify nine submarkets by subdividing the city into inner city, middle city and outer city, and then differentiating between terraced, semi-detached and detached dwellings within each area.

There have, however, been attempts to avoid researcher bias by developing approaches which allow submarket dimensions to be determined empirically (Goodman, 1978; 1981; Pryce, 2004). For example, Hancock (1991), who describes this as an 'agnostic' approach, started with a single postcode area and then tested the validity of pooling data from other areas on the basis of an F-test on regression equations. Using a computer algorithm, the process was repeated until no further pooling of areas was valid (see also Hancock and Maclennan, 1989). Several other researchers use principal components analysis. Dale-Johnson (1982) and Watkins (1999) apply the technique to housing characteristics to identify substitutable dwellings. Maclennan *et al.* (1987) use the technique to group neighbourhoods with similar dwelling stocks and socio-economic characteristics. Bourassa *et al.* (1999a,b) employ principal components analysis and cluster analysis sequentially. They separately test for submarkets based on clustering the principal components derived from data on both individual dwellings and neighbourhoods. Maclennan and Tu (1996) produce a matrix of submarkets with four city sectors and five product group types. The groupings were also based on principal components analysis of dwelling and neighbourhood characteristics followed by cluster analysis.

The methods employed have become increasingly complex. Tu *et al.* (2007) use the residuals from the hedonic equations to estimate an isotropic semi-variogram from which a residual variance-covariance matrix is constructed. The correlations between residuals are used to assign dwellings to submarkets. Pryce and Evans (2007) also develop a novel empirical approach. They argue that the studies that employ geographic definitions of submarkets are all hampered by the need to use existing administrative boundaries as a starting point. It is suggested that these boundaries are too coarse and that, at times, the units used may in fact include parts of more than one submarket. As a result, they propose a method that builds up from the lowest point in geographic space. The analysis constructs groupings according to similarity in the rate of house price change and contiguity. The approach was piloted using data for Kent for the period from 1996 and 2004 and the results, when mapped, revealed huge variations in constant quality prices, even over relatively small distances. The pattern that emerges does not reveal a clear set of submarkets. As a result, the researchers then employed cluster analysis to group dwellings in to submarkets. This, of course, requires that the number of submarkets generated should be predetermined.

Some researchers have sought to retain independence by consulting independent market experts such as valuers (Bourassa *et al.*, 2003) or estate agents (Palm, 1978). The latter is relatively common and grounded in the view that information flows shape search patterns and estate agents play an important role in the process and understand the outcomes that emerge. Michaels and Smith (1990), for example, invited five agents to classify all 85 key locations in suburban Boston into between five and ten mutually exclusive groups. This produced three useful classifications: one with ten submarkets and the other two with four. They used the responses to produce a composite classification of four submarkets. Despite the intuitive appeal of this approach, there were clearly some practical difficulties in achieving a consensus. Keskin (2009) used a similar approach to identify submarkets in Istanbul. She interviewed ten agents, and although she also had some difficulty reconciling their evidence, a broad consensus emerged from six of the respondents. Empirically this submarket specification was better able to explain the spatial distribution of house prices than other *a priori* geographic specifications.

It is clear from these studies that submarkets are generated by a complex process of supply- and demand-side dynamics, which reflects both spatial and structural influences on housing choice and urban form. This complexity is, perhaps, an important explanation for the failure of housing economists to adopt housing submarkets as a central concept in theories of market structure and for the lack of consistency in the means of defining and identifying submarkets empirically. It has provided the rationale for some recent studies that have sought to compare competing definitions and methods of delineation.

Watkins (2001) undertook an empirical study of the Glasgow housing market that was intended to facilitate a direct comparison of the performance of the three main competing submarket definitions employed in the housing economics literature. He analysed the accuracy of price estimations using different submarket compositions, while controlling for variations in the study area, test procedure and market conditions. Although the spatially defined and structurally defined submarket specifications provide evidence of submarket existence, the results have shown that submarket definitions should be based on structural and spatial characteristics of the housing market. Interestingly, the most effective means of delineating submarket boundaries was based on the segments used by estate agents when listing properties for sale. The agents typically define spatial market segments and then subdivide properties by type.

Goodman and Thibodeau (2007) also sought to compare competing procedures for identifying submarkets. On the basis that the majority of submarket studies employ geographic (spatial) boundaries their research focused on whether submarkets need to consist of geographic areas that are spatially contiguous. The theoretical rationale is that consumers do not necessarily limit their search to one part of the city. Instead it is possible that they might consider similar profile (and priced) neighbourhoods that are dispersed throughout the market area. The study identifies two alternative submarket specifications: one based on contiguity (within the same school district) and the other non-contiguous but based on substitutability of product and locality. The merits of the two specifications are assessed on the basis of the accuracy of the hedonic house price estimates. There are several stages to the test procedure. Initially, like most other analysts, they compare predicted and observed prices and show that, while the aspatial model has a lower WSE, it has slightly fewer predicted prices within 20% of the observed values. These results are inconclusive. As a result, a second test, based on the Davidson and MacKinnon J test and quite different from that used elsewhere, is employed. This test indicates that neither specification dominates the other. The paper concludes that the 'winner' of the competition depends on how performance is measured.

These results, of course, contribute to the ongoing lack of clarity about the practical specification of submarket boundaries. Even though this review summarises an increasingly voluminous literature that provides evidence (from a variety of markets and under a range of different market conditions) that housing submarkets exist, the assumption that markets are unitary remains central in much of the contemporary housing economics literature. Watkins (2001) argues that the failure to more widely embrace housing submarkets as an analytical construct in housing economics can be explained by: the failure to develop a single, coherent definition of a submarket; differences in the way in which submarkets are identified; and differences in the procedures used to test for their existence. Perhaps, significantly, there are also inherent conceptual problems involved in accommodating a concept associated with disequilibrium processes within a theoretical framework that emphasises equilibrium processes.

This is why submarket studies are often accompanied by notes of caution. Maclennan (1987: 40), for example, observed that: 'The findings of <this> paper are time and place specific and they cannot be used to characterise the nature of urban housing systems always and everywhere'. On a more positive note, he does go on to say, 'However, they do illustrate that the cross section econometric analyses of urban housing markets may be flawed, both in relation to model specification and estimation, if they set out with a strong assumption that competitive equilibrium prevails'. The overwhelming conclusion is that, despite the conceptual and operational challenges, submarket existence cannot be ignored. Local housing markets are complex and dysfunctional.

Temporal dynamics of housing submarkets

Several authors have begun to explore the temporal dynamics of housing submarkets. In the context of widespread evidence of submarket existence, these studies provide useful insights into the durability of submarket boundaries. It is clear that for submarkets to be analytically relevant, they need to exhibit a degree of stability, which is not obvious from the existing literature. As we note above, the standard statistical test applied in most studies of submarket existence is cross-sectional. The existence of statistically significant constant quality housing price differences between *a priori* submarkets is taken as corroboration of submarket existence. But this test is static both in nature and by the assumption of equilibrium in hedonic analysis.

This is arguably inherently problematic, particularly as Grigsby (1963: 37–38) argued that relationships between submarkets are likely to be 'in a continual state of flux'. In practical terms, however, the submarket system is difficult to examine empirically, especially as the market is constantly changing. This is exacerbated by the standard methods deployed in testing for submarket existence. The need to repeat this static analysis over time is often defeated by the paucity of available data, although there are some exceptions (see for example Hancock and Maclennan, 1989).

In their theoretical account of submarket change, Maclennan and Tu (1996) distinguish between short-run and long-run dynamic change in local housing markets. They argue that, in the short run, physical attributes and quality are fixed and prices will fluctuate in response to changing market conditions. In the long run, physical structures can also be changed and, as such, submarket composition may also alter. This resonates with Rothenberg *et al.*'s (1991) argument that submarkets are a function of differences in 'hedonic' qualities. As such, it is suggested that submarket composition will change as stock undergoes conversion or depreciation or as new construction flows onto the market. However, such changes are not accommodated in their empirical exploration of the model.

This debate has informed recent work that has sought to explore empirically the dynamics of submarket structure. Jones *et al.* (2003) used co-integration analysis of the relationship between neighbourhood price differences to examine the stability of submarkets in Glasgow over a fourteen-year period. There results showed small changes in the composition and dimensions of submarkets but also that four of the six submarkets remained unchanged over the study period (see Chapter 5 for further details of this work). The overall conclusion was that, even though there had been considerable new supply (and demolition) and household movement throughout the system, the submarket system had remained remarkably stable.

Gallet (2004) undertook a similar temporal analysis of the submarket structure in the Los Angeles region. This study employed time–series convergence tests (which differed slightly from those used by Jones *et al.*) on data covering a nine-year period. Although the results showed some limited convergence in coastal areas, the general conclusion was that LA did not have a coherent region-wide housing market and that there was little evidence of price convergence across the study area.

Similar conclusions can be drawn from studies of submarket dynamics that use quite different empirical methods. Maclennan and Tu (1996), for example, offer reasonably consistent findings from their comparative cross-sectional analysis of the submarket structure in Glasgow in 1984 and 1990. They show that there has been some reconfiguration of submarket dimensions but the majority have remained unchanged. There is evidence that these results are not unique to this market. Rothenberg *et al.* (1991) demonstrate that submarkets are stable across a range of US cities. This is emphasised further in a detailed study of Des Moines, Iowa. Using a very different approach Meen *et al.* (2005b) explore neighbourhood price changes in Manchester and show that, although price inflation in the most deprived neighbourhood between 2000 and 2004 was similar to the city average, the absolute gain was lower. Price differentials were certainly not eroded over time, although this study may have covered too short a time period.

Leishman (2007) revisited the spatial submarkets identified for Glasgow by Watkins (2001) and analysed over time by Jones *et al.* (2003) (see Chapter 5). He uses a multi-level modelling (MLM) approach to explore the stability of the submarket boundaries. The MLM approach involves the estimation of a single market-wide model that also encompasses submarkets and importantly allows the implicit price of attributes to vary for each submarket. It also permits the analysis of prices at the level of the neighbourhoods that make up the geographic submarkets. The results, like those of the time–series study, show that the previously identified submarkets have remained relatively robust. There is, however, some evidence of limited reconfiguration.

Overall, this literature supports the earlier theoretical arguments about the pervasiveness of factors that contribute to the rigidity of the submarket structure and reinforce neighbourhood-level price differentials.

Modelling submarket structures

Much of the housing economics literature continues to be concerned with the application of econometric methods to housing market data. Significantly, however, a growing number of researchers have begun to explore the use of innovative techniques that might explain multiple equilibria, disequilibrium processes and economic segregation. This has included interest in the application of spatial statistics to the analysis of the housing system (see Pace and Lesage, 2004). Much of this technical advancement has been pioneered in the US. There have also been interesting applications of advanced spatial econometric techniques to capture neighbourhood-specific influences on market performance (Pavlov, 2000; Fik *et al.*, 2003). In this context, Clapp and Wang (2006) seek to uncover the underlying structure of urban markets by using classification and regression tree (CART) modelling to group neighbourhoods into homogenous submarkets on the basis of both the 'hard' and 'soft' influences on behaviour that give rise to discontinuities in the house price surface.

In the UK context, Bramley and Leishman (2005c) demonstrate the potential for robust analysis of neighbourhood-level data. In addition, the work by Bramley *et al.* (2008) on untangling the impact of local, regional and national drivers on neighbourhoods is potentially interesting. It is important that local market models can explicitly recognise that price changes at the neighbourhood level reflect changes in the both supply and demand conditions that are specific to the submarket and the trends that operate at the system-wide level (Galster, 1996).

Some of this recent work appears to recognise the value in the conceptual and empirical research of early institutional analyses and emphasises the need to embrace evidence about the role of neighbourhood segmentation and housing submarkets in economic analysis of local market structures. Gibb (2003), for instance, links the concepts of filtering and neighbourhood segmentation to the behavioural assumptions of mainstream economics within a quantitative modelling framework. This represents a relatively rare attempt to develop a UK-based simulation model that seeks to determine the likely effects of policy change on intra-urban housing market dynamics. Elsewhere, Kauko (2004) proposes the general use of neural network techniques in the analysis of neighbourhood-level market dynamics. He argues that this approach falls 'between simple equilibrium frameworks and more complex-behavioural institutional frameworks' (p. 2576). He goes on to suggest that the non-linearity and 'fuzziness' of the approach offer considerable potential in dealing with complex phenomena.

In general, there appears to have been some significant progress made in the analysis of markets. This reflects an attempt to develop techniques that better capture the behavioural and spatial complexity of the market and, more specifically, to accommodate housing submarkets. This has begun to yield improvements in the understanding of market processes and of the role of the neighbourhood in local housing systems.

Conclusions: submarkets as an analytical framework

Historically, mainstream economic analyses of local housing systems tend to assume that the metropolitan area is co-terminous with market boundaries and that there is a single, unitary housing market. In this chapter we contend that local housing systems are too complex to be modelled this way (see also Whitehead, 1999). It is argued that local market analysis must recognise and accommodate the existence of housing submarkets.

This assertion appears to be supported by theory. Institutional rigidities associated with information inefficiencies, search costs, transactions costs, planning and financial constraints will inhibit the market adjustment process. When this happens a unitary market will not exist. Instead significant price differences (even for homes with the same features) will be observed in different parts of the market. These differences reflect unevenness in the spatial expression of housing demand and a mismatch between the available stock and neighbourhood-specific levels of demand. This implies that housing submarkets will exist and should be incorporated within the conceptual framework used to understand the workings of local housing systems.

There has been increasing interest in local market dynamics and considerable progress in accommodating submarkets in housing models. The existing literature highlights numerous analytical problems that require a clear grasp of the submarket structure of local housing systems. Adair *et al.* (1996), for example, explain that failure to accommodate the existence of housing submarkets will introduce bias and error into regression-based property valuations, while Maclennan (1976) highlights similar implications for the robustness of house price indices. Elsewhere, Adair *et al.* (2000) demonstrate the importance of identifying the submarket structure in analysing the likely impact of new urban transportation links to particular groups of households; Bates (2006) illustrates the utility of a submarket-based analysis in revealing the wider market impacts of housing renewal policies; Berry *et al.* (2003) examine the differential impact of spatially targeted tax breaks for owners and investors; and Galster (1996) explores the system-wide ramifications of demand-side and supply-side housing policies.

It is clear, at the general level, that this sort of disaggregated analysis provides a useful platform from which to develop our understanding of the workings of the market. This framework supports the assessment of the effects of policy intervention and facilitates greater understanding of neighbourhood change in local housing systems. The central argument in this book is that land-use planners need to understand the dimensions of, and linkages between, housing submarkets to most effectively make decisions about the quantity and location of land to be allocated for new housing development. The submarket framework provides a basis to monitor and forecast the likely outcomes of housing plans (see also Jones and Watkins, 1999 and Hancock and Maclennan, 1989). It is important that the system of planning for housing is able to recognise that demand is not homogenous. What is built and where matters, and the implications of these decisions can only be understood when located within a clear appreciation of the internal structures of the market. The next chapter explores some of the insights that submarket analysis brings to local housing market dynamics.

On a practical note, it is worth knowing that submarket identification need not unduly add to the burden of market analysts and planning professionals. Despite the fact that a wide array of complex statistical procedures have been deployed in identifying submarkets, some simple techniques have proved to be highly effective. It is interesting to note, for example, that agent-based definitions have tended to perform well empirically in a range of market contexts (see Watkins, 2001; Keskin, 2009). In addition, Jones *et al.* (2003) show that different techniques often generate submarkets of similar dimensions. Their study, which is discussed in more detail in the next chapter, shows that analysis of migration data is both powerful and straightforward. The application of this approach does not require much more than an extension of the analysis currently undertaken to identify housing market areas.

5

Dynamics of the Housing Market

The housing market is subject to constant change as the stock gets older and may need repair, improvement or even demolition; similarly the people who occupy the stock get older and their circumstances alter through a change of job, retirement or household composition. In the preceding chapters the analysis has focused primarily on the spatial structure of housing markets and submarkets rather than these short-term changes. In Chapter 3 the theory of the spatial structure of housing markets examines fundamental change but only from a static and long-term perspective. It uses the access–space model to explain the causes of long-term change, such as suburbanisation, but the model is a long-term equilibrium model and tells us nothing about the process of transition from one such equilibrium to another.

In this chapter the focus is on the underlying dynamics of change and transmission processes at all different spatial levels of the housing market – regional, urban, submarket and neighbourhood. The analysis is concerned with real time and seeks to contribute to explanations of regional house price ripples, the impact of urban growth or decline on local housing markets, and the variation in house price trends between submarkets of a city. It also critically appraises the role of some traditionally accepted processes, such as filtering, trading up and gentrification.

The dynamics of the housing market is also bound up with tenure patterns, differential access to these different tenures and government policies toward them. The focus of this book is the owner-occupied sector but the availability and cost of the private and social sectors influences the dynamics of the housing market. Resales of council houses bought by sitting tenants under the right to buy have had a substantial impact on local housing markets and play different roles depending on the state of these markets

(Jones and Murie, 2006). The recent revival of the private rented sector, through investors attracted by more relaxed regulation and the availability of mortgages, has had an important influence in shaping new supply especially in cities and in constraining demand for starter homes/flats to purchase (Cobbold, 2007). These subjects are not considered in this chapter although the latter is addressed in chapter 7.

The operation of the housing market is set within the national macroeconomic context as Chapter 2 demonstrates, and is also subject to the performance of the local economy through the level of unemployment, wages and in- or out-migration. As the 'credit crunch' shows these national influences can have a severe short-term impact on the ability of households to move home and this inevitably impinges on the dynamics of local housing markets. Furthermore, a macroeconomic environment that provides for stable long-term economic growth offers strong positive support to new housing development and is arguably a prerequisite for the success of housing-led urban renewal initiatives (Jones, 1996a). Given that the attention here is on urban housing markets these issues are not addressed systematically in this chapter but are encompassed in discussions of exogenous factors.

The chapter begins by considering the microeconomics of household decisions in the housing market. It then examines the role of migration in influencing spatial house price trends and in particular time lags between areas. The next two sections look at house price trends with urban growth and within housing market areas, and consider the impact of new building as well as migration. The latter part of the chapter considers the underlying processes of neighbourhood change including (dis)investment and decay, the role of externalities and bandwagon effects, the restructuring of the local population, for example through gentrification, and the issues facing the revitalisation of inner city areas by new house building. The conclusions draw together the themes presented.

Choices and constraints

At the centre of the dynamics of the housing market are the decisions households make about investment in and consumption of housing. These decisions are the outcomes of the choices and constraints that households face. Choices can be conceptualised in two stages – to move or stay, and where to move. But this is a simplification, in fact there may be a prior decision between moving and improving or extending. Subsequent moving choices can be seen in terms of the selection of neighbourhood, house size and type and are influenced by wider considerations than simply the household's demographic characteristics. Attitudes toward housing as an investment vary with lower income groups tending to be less concerned with capital growth and seeing housing more as a consumption good. This, in turn, has an important role in housing choice.

Despite the apparent emphasis in the housing market on choice, constraints are often the dominant force on households (Jones, 1979a). Affordability (i.e. income constraint) has been a crucial factor periodically in the housing market (see Chapter 2). Constraints may be in terms of what properties are available in a particular area, partly brought about by planning decisions. Indeed this gives rise to a further alternative decision – move and improve/extend. Many households follow this approach to adjust their housing consumption.

Financial constraints also apply in terms of the crediting rationing criteria of banks and building societies. These can be in terms of the loan-to-value and loan-to-income ratios a bank will offer a potential mortgagor. Variations in the terms available have been crucial influences on macro-house price trends (as discussed in Chapter 2) but other lending criteria are also important to the dynamics of local housing markets. A number of studies in the 1970s reported on the existence of 'red-lining' (delineating neighbourhoods on a map) whereby financial institutions would not offer loans in inner parts of cities because they were unconvinced of the subsequent marketability of such properties. These areas were dominated by small properties in relatively poor repair in neighbourhoods with high proportions of private rented housing. Jones and Maclennan (1987), in a study of Glasgow find that, while there were no such maps, the criteria used in the 1970s did explain the weak lending in some inner city areas. In other words, restrictive lending criteria did translate into areas of cities that received little or no mortgage finance, although there were variations between institutions.

Over time, the housing markets in these neighbourhoods have been absorbed into the normal lending scope of banks with the decline of the private rented sector in these areas, improvements in the stock and new building in these localities. A further factor has been the relaxation of lending criteria over time as signified by the evolution of 'sub-prime' lending in the 1990s to households with weak credit ratings and histories (Munro *et al.*, 2005).

Nevertheless, there are now new versions of these problems emerging following the sale of council housing under right to buy. In large, former public-sector estates, where only a few properties have been sold under the scheme and resale markets have not been developed, banks are reluctant to lend (Jones and Murie, 2006). Similarly many banks will not offer mortgages on flats above the fifth storey (Jones, 2003a). The sub-prime crisis that has led to the 'credit crunch' that began in 2007 has inevitably had ramifications for the tightening of lending criteria on households and housing.

Moving can involve substantial transactions costs, expenditure and future commitments in terms of perhaps an additional mortgage, and are therefore threshold sensitive. To some extent this varies with tenure as moving within the private rented sector involves fewer legal costs, for example, but even in this instance there may be search costs, deposits required, besides the physical upheaval. Dissatisfaction with a current household's accommodation may build up over time, be anticipated or may be a consequence of a change in circumstances such as a birth, a family member leaving home or redundancy/unemployment (Jones, 1981).

A key dynamic of the owner-occupied housing market is the trading-up process or the housing market (step)ladder. There is essentially a series of (optional) stages in a housing 'career', a person sets up household on leaving (the family) home and then lives in rented accommodation before the purchase of a home at the bottom end of the market. The household then trades up in the market as it passes through the child-bearing and child-rearing stages of the family life cycle until the children leave home and the 'empty nesters' trade down.

In reality the 'trading-up' model is an upgrading process based on a series of assumptions which are far from universal. The model assumes that households invest the capital gain from one sale into the purchase of the next house (and potentially continue to be highly geared). In practice this process is more likely to apply to higher income groups who place emphasis on housing as an investment, although many first-time purchasers who have two professional incomes buy toward the top end of the market (Dawson *et al.*, 1982). Many first-time purchasers, especially from higher income backgrounds, receive financial support from parents (as Chapter 2 notes). Similarly, household incomes are also assumed to rise or at least remain constant, whereas manual workers tend to have variable incomes and certainly the low skilled are susceptible to unemployment. This is important because a high proportion of owner–occupiers can be described as living in poverty (Burrows and Wilcox, 2000). Many households may utilise the capital gains from a house purchase to repay debts and potentially trade down in response to financial difficulties. Others may trade down simply to reinvest in a cheaper, larger property (see gentrification later). Overall, trading up is too simplistic a view of the way the housing market works but it is a useful starting framework to assess diversity of migration behaviour.

These decisions are not simply derived from personal choices and constraints but are also based on the state of the housing market as perceived by the individual household. Household decisions are made with incomplete information about the housing market and can be seen as satisficing (satisfying and sufficing) rather than optimising behaviour; in other words, achieving a set of essential benchmarks in the absence of full knowledge about the housing market. When households move they accept they cannot optimise and instead select a house that (almost) meets a list of criteria they have set (which may have changed through the search process). However, these individual decisions collectively influence the housing market through the competitive process of bidding, the 'magic hand' of the market and the establishment of a pattern of prices. In previous chapters migration has been applied as a measure of spatial arbitrage and as such it represents one potential transmission mechanism within the housing market.

Migration and spatial house price trends

The potential causes of the regional house-price ripple effects are discussed in Chapter 2. To recap: there are a number of unproven hypotheses that seek to explain the changing regional house-price differentials but these explanations centre on two hypotheses – interregional migration or a combination of changes to relative incomes, and the relative housing market supply elasticities. The argument against the former is that interregional migration flows in the UK are too weak to create such price movements (Meen, 1999). This section sheds light on this issue by considering it at a different spatial scale, namely local housing markets at the sub-regional level. It is based on Jones and Leishman (2006) and focuses on the role of migration and interurban house price dynamics.

The urban level is theoretically more appropriate as regions are only just administrative units. In addition, there is a greater scale of migration that exists between local housing markets compared with regions, so the level the significance of ripples should be greater at the local level. The analysis is set within the same framework of local housing market areas identified in Chapter 3 covering the west of Scotland and uses the same dataset. The analysis by Jones and Leishman (2006) addresses the two specific hypotheses.

1 The housing-market ripple effect is caused by household migration creating a spatial arbitrage process across local housing markets.

2 Variations in spatial house-price trends are derived from the interaction of supply and demand within local housing markets. This, in turn, is dependent on local supply constraints, household incomes, demographic trends and so on.

Their research assesses these hypotheses by examining the pattern of leading and lagging local housing market areas (HMAs) and their relationship to migration links. The study period for the research is 1984–1997, and it should be noted that the housing system in the area did not experience the shocks associated with the boom and bust of the eighties and nineties in the UK. Private housing price indices for each of the local HMAs are estimated on a quarterly basis for the fourteen-year period. Tests of the hypotheses for particular housing markets (subsystems) are undertaken by applying the statistical techniques of Granger causality and co-integration.

As chapter 3 discusses, the choice of definition of local HMA is, to a certain extent, a question of judgement as to the degree of closure provided it meets the condition that it is more narrowly defined than a travel to work area (TTWA). As the purpose of the research by Jones and Leishman is to examine migration links the analysis chooses to use a relatively open definition, (50%+) HMAs, that therefore enables greater scope for spatial price interaction. For these 23 HMAs the authors seek to identify dominant inter-migration paths as the basis of leads and lags in house price trends.

The review of migration patterns between HMAs reveals a significant role for the Glasgow HMA, with household migration from it representing a significant proportion of the transactions in most of the other local HMAs studied. Up to 23% of the purchasers in some of the HMAs originate in Glasgow. On the basis of this migration analysis Jones and Leishman test a series of specific hypotheses. First, that Glasgow is the leading HMA in the sub-region and, subject to a lag, changes in house prices are transmitted to other housing markets. There are also clusters of HMAs with strong migration interlinks and therefore potentially common house price dynamics. They examine two such clusters, one which shares strong migration flows from Glasgow and the other with a weak relationship.

The subsequent analysis of local housing price indices finds that price trends in the HMA cluster with strong migratory links with Glasgow are closely associated with, and lag, the Glasgow HMA. The HMA cluster with weak migratory links is broadly independent from Glasgow and no lead-lag price relationship is evident. The study therefore gives strong support to the hypothesis that, through the medium of household migration, price ripples may be transmitted through systems of HMAs. But it also shows that localised spatial markets can also exist where the interaction of internal supply and demand factors are the dominant influence (as well as macroeconomic factors).

The analysis reinforces the argument that there is no such phenomenon as a regional housing market. It also supports the message that the key to understanding regional price ripples is not a regional perspective where interregional migration is weak and housing markets act independently. Instead it is necessary to see the ripple effect as the outcome of a spatial arbitrage process brought about by interactions at the local level through a national system of HMAs. The study similarly reinforces the view that the analysis of the housing market is best conceptualised as a system of interlinked local markets. The extent of common price dynamics and lead-lag relationships is likely to be partly contingent on the extent of local links through household migration. It also suggests that there is a hierarchical structure to local housing market systems, local ripple effects and lead-lag relationships.

New house building, urban form and local housing market dynamics

The lagged response of new house building to rising house prices at the national level is documented in Chapter 2. However, the analysis of the impact of new housing supply on local housing markets is very limited. In theory, excess supply can lead to reduced house prices but the effect is difficult to identify and the lagged response of supply is more likely to create house price inflation. Bramley *et al.* (2007) find that new supply, *ceteris paribus*, does not have a significant influence on house prices in a study of local authority areas as proxies for HMAs in England.

In fact, the issue is more complicated than this macro-urban or aggregate HMA perspective. The influence of new supply on a local housing market, as Chapter 4 indicates, is more appropriately viewed at a disaggregated level in terms of location or neighbourhood/submarket. The role of new supply on housing market dynamics should also not be seen simply in terms of price changes but how it shapes and interacts with the spatial structure of a local housing market and sub-regional spatial structure.

An example is provided by the experience of Aberdeen, a relatively remote city in north east Scotland. The discovery of North Sea oil at the end of the 1960s led to Aberdeen becoming the main centre for the development of that oil. The subsequent transformation of the city's economy offered an opportunity for Jones and Maclennan (1991) to study the relationship between the expansion of demand and a positive housing supply response, together with the impact on spatial market structure and house prices. Their research is based primarily on data on housing market transactions and offers an insight into the wider issues described above.

The analysis presented by Jones and Maclennan, and reviewed below, applies to rapid urban growth. Supply, as noted above, will normally lag demand and in these circumstances the house building industry will not be geared up for expansion either in terms of workforce or land banks available. Furthermore, developers will need to be convinced that the demand boom is sustainable before they respond. The ultimate outcomes in terms of the subsequent spatial structure of the housing market depend at least in part on the existing geography.

Jones and Maclennan suggest that the market response is a dynamic process that can be usefully discerned as a series of stages – pre-shock, transformation, upheaval and consolidation. In the pre-shock stage the housing market is in a state of relative stability, but in the transformation stage the sudden exogenous shock leads to an increase in demand for labour but this is initially in the construction industry where employment is traditionally casual. The upheaval stage is equivalent to a development phase with a degree of uncertainty; house builders are unsure of the potential scale of future demand and the planning system faces the same problem in terms of the amount of land to zone for housing. During this period land and house values will rise given the excess demand and will be fuelled by speculation. In the final consolidation stage the ultimate supply response meets these demand pressures and there is a new 'plateau' with the population now much expanded.

The empirical analysis of Jones and Maclennan finds that the Aberdeen housing market experiences a substantial boom in the early 1970s relative to Scotland as a whole and that the upheaval and transformation stages are compressed into just four years during which the output of the house building industry rose by more than 250%. Despite the increase in supply, by the end of a decade of change, house price-to-earnings ratio had risen by 60%. The picture is more complex than a simple house price boom. The full implications for the housing market are seen by disaggregating between the urban core and its periphery. For example, most of the new housing was built in the surrounding villages and small towns but only 40% of sales in this area are bought by movers into the sub-region and a quarter originate from the city.

In the upheaval and transformation stages there is a rapid rise in the ratio of city prices to periphery prices, followed by a drop when the lagged new supply eventually occurs only for the ratio to rise again two years later (probably the consequence of spatial arbitrage feedback). Jones and Maclennan note a number of consequences for the housing market within the city including a decline in the relative prices of expensive suburbs as new large attractive houses have been built in the periphery. Further, general higher prices in the city leads to a tenure transformation as many rented properties are sold for owner occupation, and (re)development becomes viable leading to higher densities. Many city owner–occupiers benefiting from their capital gain can choose to move upmarket by moving out of the city to the new housing available. In the peripheral areas the former villages, small market towns and service centres designated by the planning system as growth points are transformed from farming to commuter communities. As a consequence the local internal housing markets become much more open to immigrants from outside the sub-region as these centres experience dramatic expansion to their stock and hence a restructuring of house types available.

The example of Aberdeen can be seen as unique in the UK – an expanding city within a predominantly agricultural sub-region. However, it demonstrates the dynamic interaction between urban cores and their surrounding areas and the role planning has in shaping spatial housing market change. In many other parts of the UK, the planning system is working in reverse by restricting development in areas surrounding urban cores even though demand is expanding. The processes in these areas are more protracted than those in Aberdeen but there are equivalent interrelationships. The message is that physical spatial form is dependent not only on the timing and permitted location of development but also on the subsequent housing market dynamics that result.

Intra-urban housing market dynamics

The interaction between migration, house prices and house building can also be seen at the intra-urban scale by centring on the role of housing submarkets. In Chapter 4 the existence of housing submarkets is reviewed and the economic underpinnings examined. To recap: our conceptual framework suggests that there exists a series of interrelated submarkets in which submarket-specific supply and demand schedules interact to determine price. This means that there should be relatively distinct house price trends in different submarkets within a city and the existence of submarkets also suggests that migration within them should be relatively closed. An issue that follows is the stability of these submarkets over time as there is clearly potential for dynamic change. This potential instability stems from supply changes via new house building or transfers from social housing to owner occupation via tenants having the right to buy or a change in household demand leading to new migration flows.

The analysis here summarises the findings of the only study that examines intra-urban house price changes, new house building and migration patterns within a submarket framework. This study, published in a series of papers by Jones *et al.* (2003, 2004, 2005a), is embedded within the Glasgow HMA and is based on six spatial submarkets identified by Watkins (2001) – central, west, east, north west, south and south west. The research can be viewed as both a test of submarkets' existence (as discussed briefly in Chapter 4) but also as a perspective on urban dynamics through the housing submarkets prism.

The picture that emerges from the analysis of new additions to the owner-occupied stock over the study period, 1983–1998, is that two of the submarkets experienced a considerable proportional increase in the stock – more than a third for the city centre and a quarter for the south west. However, the more established areas of the owner-occupied market, the west and south, grew by only 13% and 7% respectively. The east, a down-market area, also experienced only modest growth of 11%. These statistics suggest that the submarket structure could change over time as a result of the new supply.

To examine this issue of stability the authors examine the relative price trends between the six original submarkets by first constructing a price index for each one and then testing to see to what extent the time series are different using the co-integration technique. There are marked differences in price trends in the short and long term with house prices rising in real terms by 46% over the study period in the west at one extreme, compared with only 8% in the south west at the other. The statistical analysis of the price–time series reveals that the submarket structure is relatively stable, but it concludes that the six submarkets collapse to four, with central and west submarkets, and north west and east submarkets combining because their prices move together in the long run.

Comparison of the changes in the housing stock and these house price dynamics suggest that new house building is effectively reinforcing the existing price structures especially for established residential areas; the expansion of the city centre housing market over this period being a policy led exception. This stability occurs for a number of reasons – developers are likely to be risk averse and concentrate on established house types in a given neighbourhood. Planning authorities may wish to appease local residents' fears about new development by permitting only the construction of properties similar in character and design to the existing housing. The planning system and new development therefore reinforce the submarket structure rather than break it down.

The study by Jones *et al.* also examines the migration links or household mobility flows between and within the six submarkets. The existence of submarkets imply relatively closed migration patterns and Table 5.1 indicates in excess of 50% of all house purchasers relocate within the same submarket; the exception is the city centre segment, where only 32% of residents originate in the area. These migration closure rates are shown to be consistent across the whole price spectrum (bands), and therefore imply a broadly strong coherent pattern with the exceptions of the central and north west submarkets. Most of the existing owner occupiers are trading up market within the submarket they currently live. No more than 11% of movers into any one segment move from another submarket. Often these households are trading down and suggest that trading down is an important element within the market and perhaps easier to do by moving away to a new neighbourhood. The city centre submarket 'gains' the most from the surrounding region and interurban/regional moves from elsewhere beyond this hinterland, with 27.5% and 14.5% of house purchasers respectively.

It is possible, as discussed in Chapter 3 that there are there are also potentially submarkets based on house type and price range nested within spatially defined housing submarkets. To accommodate this possibility the analysis breaks down the migration links across submarkets by house type (houses versus flats) and new versus second-hand housing. New houses are considered to be priced at a premium and be especially attractive to in-migrants. Table 5.2 presents these disaggregated migration patterns between submarkets, and demonstrates a consistency between spatial submarkets.

The disaggregated household migration patterns therefore reveal a substantially high level of submarket self-containment for the various types of sales considered, with the exception of the central submarket and new-build sales. The consistency of these results reaffirm the argument that the role of migration is central to a system of submarkets and that there is a degree of segmentation in Glasgow. Within the six submarket frameworks there is some evidence of 'overflow' movement from the west to the central and north west, and from the south to the south west although it is not consistent across house types. The analysis suggests the possibility of nested submarkets based on house type within spatially defined submarkets. It also indicates that there may be wider spatial submarket structures for flats and new-build properties that do not conform with the six submarket

Table 5.1 The migration pattern in the six submarket system in Glasgow.

Destination	Moves into submarket	Origin								
		Central	West	North West	East	South	South West	Greater Glasgow	Surrounding region	Elsewhere
Central	918	32.0	10.8	5.2	2.0	3.8	0.8	27.5	14.5	3.5
West	3259	3.8	57.3	4.6	0.8	3.0	1.1	18.0	9.3	2.2
North West	1709	4.3	9.0	58.6	1.8	2.4	0.9	16.6	5.4	1.0
East	1696	2.8	3.6	4.7	52.0	4.1	1.3	25.0	5.4	1.2
South	4229	1.5	3.5	2.2	1.5	58.5	3.8	21.3	6.5	1.1
SouthWest	2016	1.3	2.9	2.2	0.7	9.5	65.9	13.1	3.2	1.1

Numbers in each cell are a percentage of the respective row total: 'Moves into submarket'.

Source: Jones *et al.* (2004).

Table 5.2 Proportion of house buyers moving within a submarket of the 'six submarket system' broken down by dwelling type, new and second-hand housing within Glasgow.

Submarket	Flats	Houses	New	Second hand
Central	36.9	22.3	18.0	33.5
West	48.0	69.8	55.5	57.3
North West	46.9	68.4	33.6	62.3
East	43.2	64.3	44.0	52.4
South	54.6	65.5	57.4	58.5
South West	59.1	68.9	44.0	66.7

Source: Jones *et al.* (2004).

framework as new house buyers are prepared to move longer distances, suggesting that the spatial definition of the six submarkets could be improved.

Overall, the analysis of new building, price trends and migration patterns by Jones *et al.* demonstrates the segmented nature of local housing markets and the distinctive dynamics of each submarket. Submarkets have very distinctive house price trends and this is reflected in their relatively closed migration structures. It suggests that migration patterns provide a useful practical tool to identify submarkets. Nevertheless the analysis casts some doubts on the precise spatial definitions applied, implying more research is required. The city centre housing market is effectively created over the study period (see Jones and Watkins, 1996) and this has clouded the analysis. Nevertheless, comparison of the results of the price dynamics and the coherence of migration patterns across submarkets implies a system of four spatial submarkets in Glasgow. This system is broadly stable (with a new embryonic central submarket) and reinforced by new development and planning decisions.

Neighbourhood dynamics

Neighbourhood change can be seen in terms of changing relative prices, vacancy rates, the general upkeep of the housing, changes to the housing stock and the socio-economic-demographic profiles of the residents. The drivers of this change can be internal or external to the neighbourhood. Some of these external factors are simply macroeconomic influences such as interest rates and real incomes but also important are local neighbourhood and urban influences. At the urban level the access–space model identifies transport infrastructure as the key framework for the spatial structure of the housing market, and so new/improved roads or changes to the public transport system will have knock-on effects at the neighbourhood level. Internal neighbourhood influences relate to the characteristics of the housing, the owners and the occupiers and are discussed in the following paragraphs. In particular the role of externalities or spill-over effects on neighbourhood change is examined.

The value of a house is partly dependent on its physical characteristics but also its location in terms of accessibility and the neighbourhood in which it is situated. Its value is therefore partly a function of the quality and type of the immediately surrounding houses and also the investment activities and expected future decisions of the owners of these nearby properties, including landlords. In this regard low-income owner–occupiers, as noted above, may be less concerned with their home as an investment and see it more as a consumption good. Similarly, the interests of some private landlords who focus on short-term gains may not be served by investing large sums if they believe rents would not rise accordingly. Spill-over from these types of decisions is likely to be exaggerated in high-density areas where there are predominantly flats and common maintenance/repair agreements are required (Dawson *et al.*, 1982).

The dynamics can be seen by looking at neighbourhood decay although they can also work in the opposite direction. Neighbourhood decay is identified as an area where properties on which outlays for repair maintenance and repair renovation (modernisation) have been less than necessary to maintain their original condition or more likely to ensure they meet modern standards. This effective disinvestment in housing is the cumulative effect of decisions by individual owners that relate to individual circumstances or constraints, such as income and prospective benefits. The incentives to invest can be seen as also deflated in inner city neighbourhoods by the predominance of low incomes, high-density and private-rented accommodation often in multiple occupation, contributing to weak expectations of capital (and rental) growth. Disinvestment and neighbourhood decay can be further accelerated by planning blight, for example in areas identified for redevelopment. The uncertainty engendered discourages current residents from investing or potential incomers from moving in, thus trapping the current population and leading to falling prices.

The issue of blight illustrates the role of market forces. An active market is an essential prerequisite for housing investment and neighbourhood stability (Dawson *et al.*, 1982). It enables individual households to move to adjust their housing circumstances through the family life cycle and demonstrates, via market prices, the benefits of investing and improving your property.

Inner city locations can suffer a number of market constraints, such as thin numbers of transactions. In the past the lack of mortgage finance in inner city areas (as discussed earlier) reduced marketability and deflated prices as loans were difficult to find to purchase properties, and if available were at higher than standard interest rates and shorter pay-back periods. At the same time mortgage finance was freely available on new housing, mainly at the periphery. The consequences were a discouragement of investment potential in inner city areas, thereby contributing to neighbourhood decline. The market outcomes of urban decay can be seen in areas that are experiencing population decline which leave high vacancy rates as properties are abandoned and houses sell only at nominal values.

In a thriving neighbourhood the reverse is true and a household derives a high level of enjoyment from the external, surrounding neighbourhood. A highly sought after area will have high house prices with properties that come to market and sell quickly. Where an area is subject to excess demand, for example where supply or planning constraints hinder or do not permit further new development, then real prices will rise. Increased housing prices can be seen in the medium- to longer-term to increase housing density by making redevelopment more viable. However, where there are planning restrictions on new development it is more likely to be seen in households adding an extension or a loft conversion to their existing homes; a move stimulated by both the lack of suitable large properties to move to and the increase in the investment worth of their homes (Evans, 1991). Curiously, expectations of rapid price appreciation can also lead to properties being kept vacant (rather than rented) (Cobbold, 2007).

The use of housing turnover as an indicator in these dynamics has to be interpreted with care. Very few formal transactions in a neighbourhood may be an indicator of weak demand but it could also indicate a stable elderly population. Similarly, a large number of transactions does not necessarily indicate strong demand. High turnover is naturally associated with areas of predominantly rented properties from private landlords or small houses and flats that are effectively 'starter' homes for households at the beginning of the family life cycle. These homes are typically occupied for periods of five years or less before the households move to larger properties. On the other hand, high turnover could imply that decline in a neighbourhood has accelerated with owner-occupiers selling out to private landlords. It is therefore important to examine the nature of these transactions within the context of the neighbourhood type.

There is the potential for bandwagon effects in these neighbourhood dynamics. A bandwagon is normally defined as households buying more of a commodity the more other households buy. In the urban context the role of spill-over plays a key role in the potential for bandwagon effects on a localised housing market and land use change (Von Boventer, 1978). Expectations about the changes that are likely to occur to a neighbourhood and the responses of households, investors and developers are crucial elements in any bandwagon process. The stimulants for such an effect can come from both the demand and supply sides of the market and include the introduction of new house types or concerns about congestion and pollution but do not necessarily need to be externally induced. Implicit in this concept of a bandwagon effect is the notion of a threshold, or tipping points, beyond which the process takes hold and accelerates. Quercia and Galster (2000) have identified the importance of thresholds as a critical point that triggers substantive change. On the other hand, Galster *et al.* (2007) hypothesise that neighbourhood dynamics may just become unstable beyond a particular threshold.

Empirical evidence on these dynamics is very limited because of the extensive time–series data required. One recent exception is the study by Galster *et al.* (2007) that examines annual price changes and sales rates of Census tracts in the American cities of Cleveland, Ohio and Oakland, California over seven and eleven year periods respectively (but still short for these types of processes). The authors are concerned with how a neighbourhood responds to some transient or exogenous shock, and test a statistical, rather than causal, model that estimates local house price in a given year as a function of its deviation from its stable steady state. Given the data limitations of the study the results can only be treated as tentative but the authors conclude that a self-regulating adjustment process that promotes neighbourhood stability is the norm. For example, the authors suggest that it is in the interests of residents not to place too many properties on the market at any one time (see later).

The overriding conclusion from this analysis is that an active local market is an essential prerequisite for housing investment and neighbourhood stability. A further message is that incremental neighbourhood dynamic change is the norm and while there is the potential for both negative and positive bandwagon effects, these are subject to threshold or tipping points. From an urban policy perspective it would seem that initiatives designed to reverse urban decay require an active property market and a long-term commitment in terms of investment to reach a threshold point at which sustainable positive change can occur. However, the analysis to date has ignored the modification of the socio-economic-demographic composition of households inherent in neighbourhood change. Arguably, it is the flows of households and owners that can fundamentally alter the shape of neighbourhoods and these processes are now considered (Grigsby *et al.*, 1987; Galster, 2001, 2003).

Neighbourhood succession

A useful starting point to examine neighbourhood succession, the replacement of one group of residents by another with different characteristics, is the traditional view of the internal dynamics of an urban housing market given by Hoyt (1939) and others. Hoyt developed what became known as the sector theory of urban structure and growth that is based on steadily rising incomes continually creating a demand for modern peripheral housing which is assumed to be preferred by high-income households. High-class residential areas gradually move outwards along the radii of a city. In this process of succession lower status groups continually move out from the inner city areas into the properties vacated by higher income groups

A related and more comprehensive approach to succession is given by the concept of 'filtering' that recognises that changes in occupancy by different groups also involve a change in housing quality and price. It has been the subject of considerable debate and there is literature on this concept and its differing definitions that has been reviewed by Grigsby (1963) and Jones (1978) among others. Ratcliff (1949) defines the filtering process as the change of occupancy of housing that is occupied by one income group and then becomes available to the next lower income group as a result of a decline in price. These filtering theories share with Hoyt the idea that higher income groups move because they find their present housing 'obsolescent', perhaps as a result of a change in technology or tastes, and that lower income groups move to improve their living conditions too.

The important features of the filtering process are that households move upward in terms of quality, as dwellings move down in terms of relative price, quality and income bands. As such, empirical studies have focused on either the decline in price (Lowry, 1960), vacancy chains (Watson, 1973) or the mobility of individual households (Myers, 1975). Although filtering is defined in terms of housing another important feature of the model is that it could be usefully extended to examine the relationship between neighbourhoods rather than individual dwellings. Fisher and Winnick (1951) explain that, providing areal boundaries are not subject to too much change over time, it is possible to examine the changing market dynamics by monitoring price changes across neighbourhoods relative to other parts of the market. Grigsby (1963) then refined this approach by introducing the concept of the housing 'submarket', and by partitioning the housing stock into sub-markets, he was able to examine how dwellings were linked by patterns of household mobility. Household migration patterns were, in turn, seen to lead to changes in prices and in structure quality.

The filtering process can be illustrated by looking at large town-houses built in the nineteenth century in UK cities. These large houses were owned and occupied by the wealthy businessmen and their families (and servants) at the time they were built. These properties have now often been subdivided into flats and bedsits and let out to students and young people without families. The buildings no longer represent the state-of-the-art modern housing that they were when they were built and can be in need of repair. They are now occupied by relatively lower income groups relative to their original occupants. Clearly, a filtering process has occurred but the example illustrates that the process has extended beyond simply changes in occupancy, quality and price to encompass tenure change and the quantity of housing consumed per household.

These models emphasise the role of income, via income groups and changing income, as the primary force for neighbourhood succession and are consistent with the long-term forces toward suburbanisation identified in Chapter 3. Implicit in this process is that lower income groups, perhaps immigrants, start their housing career in inner city locations. There are also parallels with the trading-up thesis described above but as discussed earlier there is a diversity to household migration patterns and so these models are inevitably a simplification. The Aberdeen study discussed above also shows how in-migrants are not necessarily on low incomes and do not always move into a central location.

The inherent processes do not embrace the influence of bandwagon effects, thresholds or tipping points outlined above. Yet there is undoubtedly a dimension to the process that incorporates these elements along the lines of Schelling's theory of neighbourhood racial tipping (Schelling, 1971, 1972). As black residents move into a predominantly white neighbourhood he argues that once a certain threshold percentage of black households is achieved then it will eventually become all black. In fact, this racial transformation process can also be envisaged as a filtering type process with price and potentially quality adjustments and possibly the increasing incomes of black households as an important driver.

The most striking counterweight to the filtering concept is the phenomenon of gentrification. The study of gentrification has been almost entirely the domain of geographers and sociologists and there is a range of definitions. In this analysis the narrow interpretation of gentrification is taken to be that defined by Smith and Williams (1986: 1) as: 'the rehabilitation of working class and derelict housing and the consequent transformation of an area into a middle class neighbourhood'.

It was described more colourfully by Glass (1964), who first coined the term, as:

> One by one, many of the working class quarters of London have been invaded by the middle-classes—upper and lower. Shabby, modest mews and cottages—two rooms up and two down—have been taken over, when their leases have expired, and have become elegant, expensive residences... Once this process of 'gentrification' starts in a district it goes on rapidly until all or most of the original working-class occupiers are displaced and the whole social character of the district is changed.

Gentrification has been identified in cities on both sides of the Atlantic and involves the upgrading of buildings, increased rents and capital values, housing tenure changes and the displacement of the original working-class inhabitants from inner city neighbourhoods.

These neighbourhoods usually comprise attractive, even historic, architecture, housing once occupied by high-income earners. As a result of the suburban movement of these households the housing had filtered down to low income groups. Some decades later the middle classes start to buy, renovate and restore them for their own use – and in the process ultimately push up property values with landlords selling up thereby driving out former, typically lower-income, working-class tenants. These neighbourhoods therefore exhibit a cyclical history of investment, disinvestment and reinvestment (Smith, 1996).

The rise of gentrification from the 1960s can be seen in demand terms as emanating from the expanding service sector employment in the city centre, as noted in Chapter 3 (Hamnett, 1991). The initial middle class improvers see themselves as pioneers – Smith (1996) likens the initial process of gentrification to pushing the frontier of the American West against the indigenous Indians. The attraction to these households was cheap, large houses with character, and initially in London the process of gentrification was supported by improvement grants from the state. Smith (1996) identifies what he calls the 'rent gap', the difference between the unimproved value and the improved (best) value, as the principal driver of gentrification, although as discussed this is a changing function of the state of the process itself. In many inner city areas these market conditions do not exist and the improved value of a house is less than the original cost plus the improvement expenditure, even with a grant. This is often called the 'valuation gap' and is invariably a major constraint on the viability of urban renewal (Balchin and Rhoden, 2002; Goodchild, 1997). The final value is very much a function of the income capacity of those prepared to pay and so the existence of demand is a necessary if not sufficient condition for gentrification and also for neighbourhood renewal more generally (NAO, 2007).

Once the neighbourhood transformation is complete its continuation requires the establishment of an active market as set out earlier. In the case of gentrification this requires pioneers to be replaced by households who view the neighbourhood as (a distinctive fashionable submarket of) part of the wider local housing market. 'Gentrifier' households who wish to adjust their housing consumption with movement through the family life cycle need to be able to sell their homes. A study by Bridge (2002) in Bristol examines whether gentrifiers subsequently climb distinct spatial/cultural housing ladders or simply move through a 'phase'. The research is based on only a small number of households but is suggestive that 'a diverse but distinctive range of housing trajectories' comes out of the 'gentrified neighbourhood' (Bridge, 2002: 23). The study suggests that often households are forced to trade their distinctive housing and social environment for more traditional locations that meet their child-rearing needs, including access to good schools, etc.

The importance of family life cycle as a key factor in spatial housing market dynamics and neighbourhood succession is identified by Jones *et al.* (2009). Their study is based on a survey of owner–occupiers in Edinburgh and Glasgow in central, outer and in-between neighbourhoods. Younger and non-pensioner, single households are more prevalent in the central city areas. The central study areas also have the smallest average household size, with the suburban areas having the largest average number of people in the household. The suburban areas also have the largest proportion of households that consist of a couple with one or more children. As households grow older and expand, different factors become important in making a residential location and housing choice so that the age structure of a city is an important influence. While family life cycle may not be as overt an influence as incomes (and race) on neighbourhood succession there is no doubt that it overlays the process of any change and a fundamental factor in the spatial patchwork that composes a local housing market.

Neighbourhood revitalisation

Gentrification has spawned an extensive and continuing debate about the scale of the positive and negative benefits (Atkinson, 2002). This debate has been turned into a planning debate as national urban policy has endorsed gentrification in its widest sense as a solution to inner city problems. Since the middle of the 1970s in the UK, private development has been encouraged in inner city areas through a combination of land and financial subsidies either by building new houses on land owned by a local authority or by renovating/improving council housing for sale (Cameron, 1992). In a parallel trend there has also been the promotion of (edge of) city centre living through the redevelopment of land formerly used for commercial purposes and the conversion of warehouses and offices (see Jones and Patrick (1992) for an early example of this process). The current policy is highlighted by the government-sponsored Urban Task Force (1999: 1) report that sought 'to bring people back to our cities, towns, and urban neighbourhoods' to create an urban renaissance. The insertion of a middle-class population into the inner cities has become a central plank of public policy, often referred to as tenure diversification, amidst some controversy about its efficacy in terms of the benefits to the existing community (Cameron, 2002). Strangely there has been little focus on the mechanics and housing market dynamics crucial to the success of these policies.

In 2002 the UK government established a new market renewal programme in a series of nine 'pathfinder' projects aimed at neighbourhoods of acute low demand across provincial cities that also exemplifies this 'gentrification' theme. Individual projects have their own plans for their ten-year programmes but in general they seek to alter the stock to attract people back to these areas. Policies to achieve this goal include selective demolition of surplus and obsolete properties, financial assistance for new building, renovation and environmental grants, and neighbourhood management during the transition process. These neighbourhoods were characterised by a failing housing market with a large numbers of properties difficult to sell and rent and a significant goal of this initiative is that the policy explicitly seeks to regenerate the local markets as a means to regenerate the neighbourhoods. This is the first time a regeneration initiative in the UK has recognised this goal as a prerequisite for success and it is reflected in the targets that include closing the gap between neighbourhood house prices and vacancy rates and regional averages by one-third by 2010. However, such a target is a relatively crude benchmark that takes little cognisance of the underlying dynamics of urban renewal and the overbearing influence of macroeconomic trends on the housing market.

The dynamics of this process is discussed in Jones and Brown (2002) who examine the establishment of markets for new housing estates for sale in traditional inner city areas and public sector communities in British provincial cities. Their analysis builds on that of Jones and Watkins (1996) that argues that the crucial question that such initiatives face is whether they establish 'sustainable markets'. They coin this term because to be successful, new housing developments that introduce a new product to a neighbourhood, ultimately have to demonstrate that they meet a long-term need in the market. The importance of this success is demonstrated by Murray (1996, quoted in Jones and Brown, 2002: 268):

> Those most at risk are those communities who have been sold 'The Vision' and particularly the many owner occupiers who have invested in it. For them the acid test will come when they need or wish to trade up in the housing market, or decide to leave it. If the process of renewal is stalled their vision may become an anchor manifest in negative equity and debt.

The quote does not spell out how this is achieved but a prerequisite is the establishment of a resale market supported by mortgage finance from banks. The formal conditions for a sustainable market can be spelled out as follows.

1 Market values rise to a point at which they are equal to or above the long-run price that makes development viable.
2 There has been a period of sustained resale activity which will demonstrate the credibility of the product as an investment. The latter condition implies a critical mass with regard to market activity.

This fundamental issue has been neglected by policy evaluations as it cannot be achieved very quickly and can take over a decade (Jones and Watkins, 1996).

The research by Jones and Brown (2002) examines the long-term experience (up to fifteen years after being built) of a range of developments for sale that introduce a new type of housing to a neighbourhood. The research is based on a mixture of qualitative and quantitative sources. They find a variety of outcomes; some had prospered while others were in decline with properties difficult to sell and many owned by landlords. Normally house prices initially rose in these developments because they were competitively priced (some supported by public subsidies) creating excess demand, but that this was not usually sustained. The internal markets show considerable fragility and there are often periods of stationary, or even falling, prices. Thin markets mean there is often no consistent price trend from one year to the next making valuation difficult. Part of the reason is that demand for these estates is localised, or very narrowly defined.

A key internal dynamic of some of the estates are the relatively low and variable incomes of the owners who are prone to unemployment, thereby creating an investment risk associated with purchase of houses on these estates. Repossessions can be an important internal influence undermining house prices in the short term and potentially damning the entire estate in the long term. Externalities from immediately surrounding areas such as vacant land, dereliction and crime can also have serious consequences for resale and growth. In some cases these factors came together to be terminal. These findings are consistent with Jones and Watkins (1996) who find that an embryonic housing market in a city centre was more unstable than that of an established residential neighbourhood.

Resale markets were developed in most of the estates considered but very few of the estates stimulated new development in the neighbourhood, as house prices in general did not reach levels sufficient to make development viable without subsidy. The failure to meet this latter benchmark leads the authors to conclude that sustainable markets in general were not achieved. The wider lessons from this analysis generally reaffirm the earlier discussion; neighbourhood revitalisation is a slow, incremental process in which the path to success is not straightforward and there are both internal and external threats that can create negative bandwagon/threshold effects. It also suggests that to achieve fundamental neighbourhood change by the introduction of new types of housing for sale requires critical mass to ensure an active property market. New development by its very nature does not have the inherent stability of an established neighbourhood and so a long-term policy commitment is needed in terms of supporting infrastructure investment to reach a sustainable market. The monitoring of this process toward a sustainable market should ideally be undertaken within a framework that identifies steps in this progress, as for example proposed by Jones and Watkins (1996).

Conclusions

A local housing market can be seen as a system of processes that is a complex entanglement of dynamic market relationships and externalities. This chapter has explored aspects of this web at different spatial scales and has noted consistently the importance of migration flows as explaining the dynamics of spatial house-price trends. The results of the analysis are also broadly consistent with the static views of the housing market presented in the previous chapters.

Household movement as the main market adjustment process is found to be a driver of the spatial arbitrage process between housing market areas. The degree of these migration interlinks between local housing markets determines leading and lagging house-price relationships. The evidence from the west of Scotland supports the notion of a hierarchical structure to local housing market systems with local ripple effects. Internal closure is also important as urban submarkets which have very distinctive house-price trends are seen also to have relatively closed migration patterns.

The planning system, through its development control function, is a crucial influence in the structuring of local market dynamics. The analysis of the Aberdeen sub-region during a period of urban growth demonstrates a dynamic interaction between the housing 'markets' of the urban core and its surrounding area that is shaped by the timing and location of new development. The system of spatial housing submarkets identified in Glasgow is supported or reinforced by development and planning decisions and this contributes to its stability.

The analysis of neighbourhood dynamics highlights the significance of an active property market to ensure or as a sign of the continuing prosperity of a locality. Change tends to be incremental but there is the potential for negative and positive bandwagon effects that are subject to threshold or tipping points. The major source of substantive neighbourhood change is the succession of one group of households by another, most overtly seen through changes in racial groups or gentrification. More normally this can be seen as the spatial restructuring of different income groups within a city leading to adjustments in the price, tenure and quality of housing within a neighbourhood.

Urban policy has recognised that to transform neighbourhood decay, revitalisation requires an input of new house types and households but it has only recently begun to appreciate that this strategy also requires the regeneration of the local markets too. The review of the experience of a number of new inner city housing developments built in the 1980s finds it is a slow incremental process in which the path to success can be unstable and that there are both internal and external threats that can stimulate negative bandwagon/threshold effects. Many of these estates did not have sufficient critical mass to ensure an active property market. The conclusion must be that not only is a long-term policy commitment needed to reach a sustainable market but also that monitoring tools still need to be developed that understand the nature of the process.

6

Planning for the Housing Market

The structure and operation of urban housing markets and the nature and direction of market change is influenced by a wide range of public policies. Previous chapters of this book have explored some of the specific ways in which housing, urban regeneration and planning policies influence market processes and outcomes. Although this chapter is also concerned with the policy environment, here the focus is on the way in which planning professionals analyse markets and how this analysis is used in making decisions about allocating land for housing.

Recent comments by Kate Barker, in her influential inquiry into housing supply, have raised the profile of debates about the use (or lack of use) of market data in housing planning (Barker, 2004). Barker's observations pick up a well-established theme. Commentators have regularly criticised the lack of market content and economic knowledge in housing plans (see, for example, Cullingworth, 1997; Monk, 1999; School of Planning and Housing, 2001; Evans, 2003; O'Sullivan, 2003). Questions have been raised about the ability of the system to deliver dwellings in the right numbers and of the required size and type and in the appropriate locations. In a review of the content of local plans in Scotland and England, Blackaby (2000) highlights the failure to adequately assess the state of the owner-occupied sector. He also notes that there is little evidence of any attempt to understand the relationship between supply and demand and little appreciation of the neighbourhood interactions within local markets. Jones and Watkins (1999) are similarly critical of the failure of plans to systematically take account of the spatial economic structure of local markets. In the absence of this type of relatively sophisticated market analysis, Maclennan *et al.* (1994) suggest that housing plans lack content, method and credibility. These critical commentaries provide the context and motivation for this chapter.

The chapter is organised into four main sections. It begins by charting the challenges confronting the planning system. This provides the context for a review of the evolution of planning and housing policy. This review highlights the fact that, although the planning system remains recognisably the same as when it was introduced, there have been important changes in the underlying processes (Vigar *et al.*, 2000). More specifically this changing policy environment has had important ramifications for the way in which local housing markets are analysed and how this information is used to determine the release of land for housing and the scale and rate at which new housing is provided. This discussion provides the backdrop for an account of the current process of planning for housing. This commentary reflects critically on the role of household projections, affordability targets and detailed background assessments of housing market conditions and trends, including, in particular, Strategic Housing Market Assessments. The conclusions that emerge in the final section are that, although the housing planning process has become increasingly market sensitive, it still lacks sufficient sophistication to capture the complex dynamics of local housing systems. The guidance on Strategic Housing Market Assessments is not bold enough in setting the standards required from a detailed examination of local markets.

Spatial change, planning and housing

Urban development and spatial economic change

The growth and decline of British cities is intertwined with the history of the planning system. The high densities and poor housing conditions in the cities in the late nineteenth century were a major catalyst for the first planning ideas such as the garden city movement that saw planned decentralisation to model communities as a solution (Hall, 1989). Decentralisation of the urban population began in the nineteenth century with the introduction of tramways in the 1870s (Jones, 1979b) and the early part of the twentieth century saw the beginnings of urban sprawl. This was encouraged by suburban railways and the motor bus as cities spread out from their confined Victorian cores. The intellectual reaction against this spurred the incorporation of the Town Planning Institute in 1914 and the formation of the Council for the Preservation of Rural England in 1925, and a series of interwar planning acts designed to (but unable to until the 1935 Act) control ribbon development.

Around 1940 the population of most British urban core cities reached its peak. Cities had spread out from their centres and had grown by annexing land. The inner parts of industrial towns remained largely unchanged from the mid-nineteenth century. There was a planning consensus that the solution to the congestion and housing problems of these urban cores lay in planned decentralisation. For example Abercrombie's Greater London Plan of 1944 foresaw the planned decentralisation of over a million people from an overcrowded city, and the creation of new planned communities (with only 250,000 via spontaneous migration). The 1946 New Towns Act, included eight new towns to serve London spill-over as Abercrombie had planned, and with the 1952 Act provided the mechanism for the planned spill-over from all the major cities. In many ways this scheme followed faithfully the visions and blueprints of the original planners – new towns as garden cities. These new towns were physical 'solutions' provided by the state in which virtually all the original housing was provided by a public agency, a new town corporation. New towns continued to be established through the 1950s and 1960s with a central element of this strategy the creation of green belts surrounding the cities and containing their growth (see Chapter 3 for a further discussion). This was made possible by the 1947 Town and Country Planning Act with its strong powers of control on development.

The final component of the planning strategy was the rebuilding of the cities. Once the immediate housing shortage following the Second World War had been alleviated, slum clearance began in earnest in the 1960s and reached its peak in the 1970s. This was a unique and significant upheaval to the cities which involved a major displacement of communities. Unfortunately, the rebuilding of the cities primarily in the form of mass-produced council housing did not meet the aspirations of the residents. The end of this era was effectively signalled with the 1974 Housing Act which switched the emphasis of housing renewal from slum clearance to (subsidising) improvement of the housing stock.

Throughout this reshaping of the cities, underlying decentralisation pressures continued to influence urban form. After 1961 the populations of conurbations began to decline. Growth in the suburban rings did not keep pace with population loss at the centre. Although part of this was planned, decentralisation accelerated through the 1970s and 1980s. The principal underlying force behind this long-term trend was falling intra-urban transport costs. This initially led to a movement to the suburbs and, with the continuing growth of car ownership, commuters are travelling further and further to work. The population of at least some of the urban rings began to stagnate in the 1980s as decentralisation continued beyond their boundaries.

A further major factor on these urban trends has been the relocation of industry. The continuing decline in the nation's manufacturing base has led to virtually all major urban centres suffering a net loss of manufacturing jobs. The statistics reflect the cumulative effects of the deindustrialisation process which began in the 1950s. Its effect has been especially severe on the core cities with their historic concentration of traditional heavy industries. The pattern of change to a degree also reflects the decentralisation pressures, stimulated by new production techniques, containerisation and an improvement in interurban road networks. As a consequence Parr and Jones (1983) argue that the urban system has moved into an urban dispersal stage. The decline of the traditional core cities and manufacturing centres has been balanced by the rise of small free-standing centres.

The decentralisation of employment and the increased flexibility provided by the car has led to larger travel to work areas (TTWAs) and housing market areas. In 1977 the White Paper, 'Policy for the Inner Cities', recognised for the first time the economic decline of the core cities. It was the beginning of policies designed to revive the cities, policies which were reinforced by strict adherence to the surrounding green belt. At the same time it spelled the end to new towns as resources were channelled into the inner city.

The flight of manufacturing industry from cities left much derelict and vacant space in its wake. These brownfield sites have provided the opportunity for new house building, especially for sale. Local authorities have actively promoted these sites to speculative house builders as a means of redressing local tenure 'imbalance' and as the only 'viable' use for the land. Such initiatives have included the conversion of derelict, redundant buildings such as warehouses, and central government has supported them through grants to developers where necessary (Jones, 1996b). This policy has been so successful that recent estimates suggest that 74% of new housing is on reused urban land (Dixon *et al.*, 2006). Yet there remain clouds over its continuance at least in some areas: some commentators have argued that there are emerging shortages in some areas and the easy sites (the cheapest) may have been developed first, leaving highly contaminated ones remaining (Breheny and Hall, 1996). These views seem unduly pessimistic for large parts of the country given also the current level of obsolete commercial and industrial property.

The development of the urban system and housing problems has therefore provided major impetus to the formulation of planning structures and ideas. In the discussion above, the focus has been on the policies but urban change also stimulated the creation of strategic planning with the establishment of structure plans machinery in 1968. The analysis above further suggests that planning, in terms of both policies and structures, cannot ignore fundamental spatial economic forces. In particular, urban dispersal will continue.

As Jones and Watkins (1999) argue, the emphasis of planning toward inner cities cannot be all encompassing, the shifting of the optimum location of manufacturing and industry has to be embraced, for example inward investment invariably requires greenfield sites. Similarly, the use of the car continues to support the decentralisation of population. There may also be physical and financial limits to the redevelopment of cities via the recycling of brownfield sites for housing, although recent proposals to tax greenfield sites acknowledges this to some extent.

The changing housing tenure structure

The operation of the housing market has been influenced by a broad range of public policies. Here we consider the general direction of public policy and the key changes with respect to planning for new housing and the workings of the housing system.

In 1945 home ownership represented 26% of all households in Great Britain; private rented was the predominant tenure accounting for 62%, while public-sector tenants were very much a minority, housing only 12% of the total (Malpass and Murie, 1994). The subsequent three decades saw the growth of both public-sector housing and owner occupation. By 1979 public-sector tenants represented 32% of the total and owner occupation had risen to 55% of all households. The growth of home ownership was then given a further stimulus by the introduction of the right of council tenants to buy their homes in 1980. The demise of public-sector housing had begun: few council houses have been built for general needs since that date and the right to buy policy has led to large quantities of dwellings being sold. Now we have around 70% of households (although this varies by region) in owner occupation (see Chapter 2 for more details).

Part of the reason home ownership is so attractive relates to the lack of attractive alternatives. Social housing rents have been driven up since 1980. This has redrawn the financial balance between owning and renting. The housing opportunities in social renting are also limited with many housing estates suffering severe social and economic problems, and in many cases including areas of difficult to let housing (Power, 1999). The solution to these 'surplus' estates has become partial or wholesale demolition with the cleared land then offered to private house builders. The number of new social houses since 1980 has been reduced to a trickle as a consequence of central government's reduction of capital allocations for social housing.

The housing tenure pattern that evolved contrasts with the perceived wisdom at the time of the 1947 Town and Country Planning Act, the foundation of the current planning system. It was thought that the era of the private, speculative builder had gone and that most new building would be undertaken by the public sector within an orderly planning framework. The passive nature of the planning controls in the Act were to be balanced by the positive physical development to be undertaken by public agencies. Indeed between 1946 and 1950 the public sector, local authorities and new town development corporations, built four out of five of all new homes (Hall, 1989).

The Conservative governments of the 1950s placed a greater reliance on the private sector, with house building split equally between the public and private sectors during this period. This position was endorsed by Labour when it returned to power in 1964, and remained largely unchanged through to the end of the 1970s. The public sector contributed 47% of new building in the decade to 1980. In the 1980s and 1990s the demise of new council house building, only partly replaced by housing association building programmes, meant that the majority of new homes were built by the private sector for sale. The Labour government since 1997 has presided over only a modest increase in the building of social housing and the speculative house builder has continued in its dominant position as the principal provider of housing. The vast majority of social housing has been built by housing associations who have also been the extensive recipients of stock transfers from local councils (Mullins and Malpass, 2002). The role of a local authority has changed from direct provider of subsidised housing to that of strategic (housing) planning and enabling.

The functions of private sector house builders and the local authorities are now very different compared to that anticipated when the planning system was conceived over sixty years ago. The planning system has to directly address the demands of private builders and consumers. Further, with growing affluence and car ownership, house buyers are travelling longer distances to work and insisting on better quality environments. The nature of work has also changed. The increasing reliance on successive short-term employment contracts means people putting greater reliance on cars, not moving when changing jobs, and travelling increasingly long distances to work. This will continue to reinforce decentralisation pressures as central regional locations accessible to major road networks will become even more attractive.

The evolution of planning for housing markets

The planning system, established in the 1947 Town and Country Planning Act, introduced a set of instruments and institutional arrangements to act as a framework for the management of land use change. The system was intended to work in parallel with housing (and other) policies. As we note above, the planning system was intended to deal in large part with the redistribution of household and business locations (Cullingworth, 1999). Specific policies developed around attempts to restrain urban growth and to channel development into new and expanded towns and, as we note elsewhere, the Green Belt circular of 1955 proved to be a highly significant influence on the operation of the housing system. The overall system was comprehensive and gave all local authorities the responsibility for the production of strategies for the use of land and development control. The main attributes of the system were its flexibility and discretionary nature. Although there were several changes over the next thirty years or so, including the introduction of structure and local plans in the late 1960s, it is argued that the system has remained broadly recognisable and has exhibited a relatively high degree of continuity, even though the context in which it operates has not (Cullingworth, 1997; Brindley *et al.*, 1996).

As we note above, the late 1970s saw a major ideological shift transform the policy agenda. Housing policy under the Thatcher administration sought to promote home ownership and speed up the transformation of the tenure structure. The detailed reforms introduced emphasised the need for greater efficiency in the use of public resources, for increased use of private finance and for enhanced choice in terms of tenure and housing management (Maclennan and Pryce, 1998). In terms of planning policy the focus of the New Right was broadly anti-interventionist. Numerous reforms were introduced in the 1980s and 1990s to assert the primacy of the market over the state. Circulars in the early part of this period, for example, emphasised that there should be a general presumption towards development (DoE, 1980a) and introduced the requirement of a five-year land supply for house building (DoE, 1980b).

Arguably, however, the main influences on housing supply were not introduced until the Town and Country Planning Act of 1990 and the related 1991 Act. The 1990 Act included, in planning agreements, the basis on which local authorities could, in granting planning permission, agree with developers the funding or direct provision of community amenities (see Chapter 7 for a more detailed discussion). More generally this legislation provided the basis for a 'plan-led' system.

The two-tier structure of the planning system set up in England and Wales by the 1968 Town and Country Planning Act remained intact despite the policy reforms outlined above (Moore, 1995). Under this system, structure plans were prepared on a county basis setting out general lines of development and the policies to be applied, while local plans covered the administrative area of district councils who had a duty to produce a plan in conformity with the structure plan. Only major conurbations had unitary plans covering the constituent councils. The local plans were more detailed than structure plans, and were concerned explicitly with land use – allocating sites for particular purposes and forming the basis on which the (re)development of an area should proceed. A key function of these plans was to ensure sufficient provision of land for new development and a critical input was the assessment of local housing land requirements. The approach to this task tended to be 'top down' in nature with the results fed into the statutory development plan system and with local authorities obliged to take account of the findings in structure/unitary development plans.

A key stage in England and Wales was the preparation of a regional planning guidance (RPG) statement by the Secretary of State, after consultations with local bodies to take into account policy considerations such as environmental constraints, the state of the current housing stock, previous over- or under-supply and land availability. The output from this process was a local housing requirement for local authorities set in terms of an average annual housing provision but, significantly as we will discuss later, with no indication of size, density, house type or tenure. These housing requirements fed into the structure plans. In Scotland the preparation of structure plans was broadly the same: the Secretary of State published local population projections which provided guidance to local authorities, but there was no RPG and plans were still subject to formal acceptance by the Secretary of State. The lack of RPG possibly reflects the lower demand pressure on land: Scotland's population has been broadly stationary in recent times, although there has been an increase in the number of households. A further difference in Scotland is the use of local plans at the sub-district level.

Thus, in general, the structure plan process in England and Wales via the 'imposition' of an RPG constraint involved a top-down approach in which population forecasts are translated into land allocations for each district council. In Scotland, on the other hand, the same task was approached from the 'bottom up' with no formal attempt to ensure the achievement of an overall control figure.

Much of this housing and planning policy agenda and institutional landscape remained in place under the Labour government elected in 1997.

Ironically, given recent events, the early statements by the then housing minister, Hilary Armstrong, were critical of the boom–bust market inherited from the Conservatives. The policy agenda emphasised the need to tackle the dysfunctional features of a system characterised by high levels of home ownership and an inefficient and perfunctory private rented sector (Armstrong, 1999). It is not clear, of course, that this brought about any substantive change. By the late 1990s, commentators suggested that there was no longer a distinctive, meaningful housing policy (Bramley, 1997; Malpass, 1999). They argued that few households were directly affected by active housing policies and, with the push for 'joined-up' thinking, the nature and direction of the system was being shaped by sustainable development, planning and urban regeneration initiatives implemented out-with local authority housing departments. The urban and rural White Papers launched in November 2000 stressed the fact that housing issues were being tackled in a wide range of policy arenas and highlighted the need for greater policy integration, particularly given the prominence of the urban renaissance and sustainable development agendas (DETR, 2000c; DETR/MAFF, 2000).

These documents were shaped in part by ongoing conflicts over controversial planning decisions to permit major new housing development on greenfield land (Burton, 2001) and, as a result, contained plans for the reform of institutions, legislation and policy guidance related to planning for housing. The central thrust of these reforms was to replace the plan-led 'predict and provide' system with a 'plan, monitor and manage' approach that ostensibly encouraged planning to steer the market rather than follow it (Prescott, 2000). The Revised Planning Policy Guidance (PPG3) for housing was a key document in securing this shift (ODPM, 2000). The reform agenda in the rest of the UK has been less substantive (see Prior, 2005): in Wales, the focus was on integrating diverse policy guidance (Welsh Assembly Government, 2002); in Scotland, the changes to the development planning framework mentioned in the previous section were moved forward (Scottish Executive Development Department, 2004); and, in Northern Ireland, plan-making and the development control system have been streamlined (DoENI, 2002).

Bramley (2007) argues that, it was at this point in the early 2000s, that unresponsive housing supply was 'rediscovered' as a major housing policy challenge. This topic had been neglected for three decades until acute housing affordability problems brought the problem back in to focus. The issue initially re-emerged on the policy agenda in the context of the Sustainable Communities Plan (ODPM, 2003) and then more fully in an independent review, commissioned jointly by the Treasury and the Office of the Deputy

Prime Minister (which was the department responsible for planning and housing policy at the time), and undertaken by the economist Kate Barker.

The Barker review produced a total of thirty-six recommendations (see Barker 2004 for full details). Although there were concerns about the quality of new homes and skills shortages within the house building industry, the majority of the proposals emphasised the need to change the policy environment within which the development industry operates. The planning system is the target for most suggestions. In general, Barker highlights the need for a more flexible and responsive framework for planning decisions, although importantly she notes that this should not come at the expense of the quality of decision making. Several of the recommendations focus on the need for greater use of market indicators as a basis of providing land for future development. Two specific suggestions are of particular interest in this book. First, as we discuss below, Barker suggests that the traditional approach of allocating land on the basis of household projections (and related needs estimates) might be improved by setting targets for planning that are based on affordability measurements. Second, she suggests that local authorities might designate a 'buffer' of additional land which could be released in response to 'triggers' that highlight local market pressures (see Chapter 8 for a full discussion).

Current practice in planning for housing

In overall terms, the current planning system has bold objectives for the management of the housing market. PPS1 states that 'good planning ensures that we get the right development, in the right place at the right time' (CLG, 2006a: para 12). The changes that have been introduced over the last two decades, including in particular those associated with planning agreements, have had the cumulative effect of imposing responsibility for meeting a wide range of goals on the planning system. These include the delivery of affordable homes, establishing sustainable communities and securing local economic development (this is discussed more fully in Chapter 7).

The broad process of land allocation and release currently used in England was updated with the introduction of the 2004 Planning and Compulsory Purchase Act (PCPA). There are now two main levels of plan: regional spatial strategies (RSS) and local development frameworks (LDF). Regional planning bodies (RPBs) are responsible for preparing, monitoring and implementing the RSS and, where appropriate, the existing Regional Planning Guidance has become the RSS. RPBs are charged with preparation of draft revisions to the RSS and are instructed to take advice from county councils. As we discuss in more detail below, it is at this strategic level that housing allocations are to be settled. The LDF documents effectively replace local plans, unitary development plans and structure plans and must conform with the relevant RSS.

In general, the PCPA was intended to speed up the system and make it more sensitive to contemporary economic challenges (Prior, 2005). The Act contained some quite major reforms to the plan-making process which were prompted by the relatively poor performance of local authorities in producing plans under the previous 'plan-led' system (Barker, 2008). Significantly, in housing terms, it sought to strengthen the role of national policy by replacing guidance notes with new, more succinct, Planning Policy Statements (PPSs) and led to the publication of PPS3: Housing in 2006 (CLG, 2006a). Current policy, as set out in PPS3, states that the specific outcomes that planning for housing should deliver are: high quality housing; a mix of housing in all areas, particularly in terms of tenure and price; a sufficient quantity of housing that will meet need and demand and will improve choice; housing development in suitable locations with adequate infrastructure and access to jobs and amenities; and a flexible and responsive land supply that also ensures the re-use of previously developed land.

It is argued that the policy – by requiring the identification of a rolling five-year supply of developable land and up to a further fifteen years of potential housing land – should provide market and state actors with greater certainty (NHPAU, 2007). There is also increased emphasis on the need for policy to be evidence based. Subsequent proposals have sought to cement these changes and further improve responsiveness (HM Treasury, 2007). The policy statements, of course, underplay the complex analytical challenges that underpin the attainment of these goals as well as the tension that inevitably occurs between local and national political objectives and the 'evidence' and between the conflicting goals of local, regional and national actors. The approach remains firmly in the top-down tradition.

In Scotland, since devolution, there has also been a move towards more action-oriented Strategic Development Plans (SDPs), with a fifteen-year horizon, to replace structure plans; and National Planning Policy Guidelines (NPPGs) have been replaced by National Planning Policy Statements (NPPSs). But there remain some important differences. SDPs, for example, are no longer statutorily required to cover Scotland fully but instead are only applicable to the four largest cities. This key difference allows the retention of a rather more bottom-up approach than that adopted in England and Wales (Jones, 2003b).

The operation of the planning system

In practice, throughout the UK, the current system of allocating land for new housing involves numerous stages and inputs. At a general level, assessments are made of housing need, and future requirements for new housing are set out. This exercise is, as we note above, partly technocratic. Planners use a range of background data including projections of future numbers of households and assessments of the capacity of regions and sub-regions to provide for this additional requirement. Some of these technical exercises are complex and cumbersome and produce outputs that are contestable. The nature of some of the technical challenges is discussed in more detail below.

Household projections

The role of household and population forecasts in the planning process has long been a source of controversy. Official projections take account of the distribution of the population across age groups, by marital status and gender and consider the propensity of each group to form households. On the basis of data from the decennial Census of Population and regular Labour Force Surveys, assumptions grounded in past behaviour are used to estimate future levels of household formation.

This traditional backward-looking, trend-based methodology has been the subject of sustained criticism and the credibility of the estimates produced is regularly called into question. For instance, in the mid 1960s, it was forecast (before subsequent downward revision) that, by the end of the century, the population would be near 80 m when, in actual fact, it was nearer 59 m (Shaw, 2007; Field and MacGregor, 1987). More recently, Allinson (1999) suggested that the projections published in the mid-1990s, suggesting that 4.4 m households would form by 2016, were likely to represent significant over-estimates of the actual demand for housing. He highlighted the failure of the approach used to incorporate a deceleration in the decline in the size of households. These estimates were subsequently revised downwards (to 3.8 m) in the late 1990s and the rate of actual household formation indeed proved to be considerably lower than the forecasts (Meen and Andrew, 2008). The 2003-based projections imply an increase of approximately 210,000 per annum (between 2003 and 2026) compared with just over 290,000 per annum indicated by the 1996-based projections (covering 1996 and 2021).

The most recent projections suggest that the UK population will increase by about 14% in the next twenty years (ONS, 2007). These figures have also been criticised. Holmans (2007), for example, has provided alternative estimates based on different assumptions about changes in the housing stock, the role of second homes, and levels of vacant and shared dwellings. The alternative approach suggests that household growth might be as much as 30,000 per annum lower than the mid-year population estimates.

At a general level, the projections have been attacked because the top-down approach used is not sufficiently sensitive to local issues (Simpson and MacDonald, 2003). More specifically, the projections have also been challenged on the basis of their inability to take account of issues such as the relationship between household size and house type or quality (Bramley *et al.*, 2004), the failure to disentangle future projections from past outcomes (Bramley and Watkins, 1995), the inadequacy of migration data used between census periods (Baker and Wong, 1997; Champion *et al.*, 1998), the limited role for market data more generally (Hull, 1997), and the failure to undertake the analysis for spatial units that correspond to functional housing markets (Simpson and MacDonald, 2003).

There have, however, been ongoing technical improvements in recent years and, following the House of Commons Environmental Select Committee Inquiry on Housing (HoCESC, 1998), estimates are now subject to sensitivity analysis. The sensitivity analysis partly compensates for the forecasters' inability to take account of the impact of short-term fluctuations in economic conditions. It is clear, for example, that household formation will be suppressed in an economic downturn. Over a longer period, however, these economic fluctuations are thought to be less significant than demographic pressures (Bramley *et al.*, 1997).

These figures continue to be used as inputs determining the adequacy of target numbers of new homes set out in the Regional Spatial Strategies in England. They represent the best 'guess' of the likely impact of net migration, changes in birth rates, longer life expectancy, and changing household sizes but with the new emphasis on market information are afforded less weight than they were before.

Affordability targets

Housing affordability targets have become important in the post-Barker era. These are the key mechanism used in attempts to locate market information at the heart of the evidence base used in planning for housing. An affordability model was commissioned by CLG as a key analytical tool to underpin the response to the Barker Review proposals. This model was instrumental in determining the target of reaching 240,000 new homes per annum that was included in the 2007 Comprehensive Spending Review (HM Government, 2007). A similar model with comparable outputs has recently been commissioned by the Scottish Government (Leishman *et al.*, 2008). In England, it is intended that targets should be set at the regional level and should be included in the RSS. These targets are to be determined using the same methodology as the national figures and are supposed to be consistent with national estimates. The future targets, based on this analysis, are tested by public inquiry and subject to confirmation by the Secretary of State.

The methodology used is based on an affordability model that was established in a major research project and seeks to quantify the relationship between affordability and housing supply at different levels (Meen *et al.*, 2005a). The structure of the model is summarised below in Figure 6.1.

The model works on the basis that prices are determined by the interaction between demand and supply. Housing demand reflects demographic changes (including the effects of migration), earnings (and labour market conditions), interest rates and the relative attractiveness of other tenures

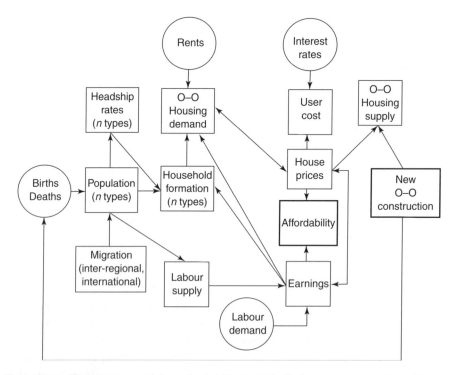

Figure 6.1 The structure of the affordability model. O–O, owner-occupation. *Source*: Meen *et al.* (2005a).

(measured by rents). Supply is generated in the construction sector. By matching estimates of household formation that are sensitive to economic change and the number of new homes, it is possible to model the likely effects on housing affordability. The central affordability indicator is the ratio of lower quartile house prices to lower quartile earnings. This methodology allows the translation of affordability assumptions in to regional targets for new housing supply.

The use of affordability targets of this type can be problematic. There are two main issues. The first relates to the nature of the affordability indicator chosen. There is extensive literature that debates the basis for defining households with affordability problems and the means by which affordability should be measured (Hancock, 1993; Hulchanski, 1995; Chaplin and Freeman, 1999; Stone, 2006). The starting point for affordability analysis requires a normative judgement about the costs of provision of an 'acceptable' standard of housing and the income that needs to be left over for other basic non-housing requirements. There are two broad types of affordability measures used: one is based on the ratio of housing costs to income and the other on the residual income remaining after meeting housing costs. The former allows the researcher to identify the proportion of income that should not be exceeded when paying for a home of adequate size and quality. The latter is tied to an assessment of whether the income left over after paying for a decent home is sufficient to allow a 'reasonable' standard of living. Clearly the standard adopted by the UK government is in the former tradition. Critics suggest that this type of indicator suffers from the fact that, for those on low incomes, an acceptable ratio (where, for example, one-third of income is spent on housing) may obscure the fact that the residual income is well below acceptable poverty thresholds (Grigsby and Rosenburg, 1975).

The second criticism suggests that the proposed approach is unhelpful in that it continues to embed centralised top down analysis at the heart of planning policy for housing. There has historically been dissatisfaction with the tendency to reduce housing planning to a 'number games' (Whitehead, 1997). It is argued that this approach lacks any sensitivity to the local context and, in particular, environmental concerns and existing urban renewal strategies (CPRE, 2006).

More substantively it might be argued that a bottom-up methodology would produce alternative results. There is recognition that the price effects of new supply may be sensitive to variations in the type of new homes constructed (NHPAU, 2007). As prosperity increases, much of the additional demand pressure is driven by the desire for more space and better quality homes. Preliminary analysis shows that a higher proportion of bigger homes might have a larger impact on the rate of house price inflation. In this context, it has also been argued that the micro-location of new development may be a significant determinant of the price effects of additional housing supply (Watkins, 2005, 2008; Adams and Watkins, 2002). Housing is jointly purchased with neighbourhood quality and spatial patterns of demand are shaped by the desire for access to better public services (including school quality) and better social and cultural infrastructure. As we discuss in more detail in Chapter 4, the social and cultural attachment of households creates frictions that inhibit smooth market adjustment and limits the transmission of supply induced price effects. It is almost certain that this will mean that the price effects of new supply are over-stated in top-down models that assume smooth market adjustment and effective transmission mechanisms.

Discussions about household projections and affordability targets are further confused by the fact that they are often intertwined with debates about levels of housing need. There is, of course, a clear distinction between housing need, the absolute requirement for shelter, and housing demand which is a market-based concept and reflects economic conditions, preferences and choice. Housing needs studies, like the official projections, have a strong demographic emphasis but typically, as in the high profile work of Holmans, these bring together information on population flows with information on stock and vacancy rates (see Holmans, 2001). National-level studies of this type have long been used to test the forecasts of housing demand based on projections and it is recognised that these still have a role. The key issue is that, although affordability is a key driver of housing need, there are also normative considerations. The affordability model does not take account of the size and quality of homes that *ought to* be available to households.

In fact, CLG has recently commissioned a housing needs model to be used in conjunction with the affordability model. It is envisaged that this model will produce different outputs that can used with the affordability targets to inform policy advice and planning policy decisions. For similar reasons, local authorities have also tended to rely heavily on local housing needs studies (Fordham *et al.*, 1998). Typically, local housing need studies rely on questionnaire surveys which ask standardised questions about household characteristics, their housing and their mobility intentions over the next five years. Nevertheless, these often lack rigour, are difficult to standardise and quickly become out of date (Blackaby, 2000). For these reasons, the current planning guidance stresses the importance of locating this evidence in its wider market context.

Overall, the use of affordability targets has become the central feature of proposals to locate market information at the heart of the planning system. The detailed approach, however, is not without problems. As we note above, the way in which affordability is measured is not ideal and, as we discuss below, the signals sent by housing needs studies (irrespective of their weaknesses) provide an accessible basis with which to challenge the authority of the estimates. There are also questions about the desirability of the spatial scale at which affordability targets are currently set. As we discuss in Chapter 3, there is little evidence that regional scales bear any relation to meaningful, functional housing market areas, even if they do represent the best level for practical model building for data availability reasons. In fact, the evidence presented in Chapter 2 highlights the fact that the extent of affordability problems varies greatly both between and within regions. The focus on the region in this analysis would appear to be at odds with the attempts to develop increasingly spatially sensitive policies that have followed the 2004 Act. There is tension between the evidence available and ongoing attempts to address sub-regional diversity by moving away from traditional sub-regional boundaries (Bianconi *et al.*, 2006). Thus, although the intentions are laudable, there remain questions about the best way to embed market information, particularly at the sub-regional scale, within the planning evidence base. This is an issue to which we return to in Chapter 8.

Background statements

In the past, top-down assessments of housing demand, based largely on household projections, were modified on the basis of local policy considerations and evidence about the supply side of the system including the state of the current stock, previous levels of supply, and the availability of land (see Adams and Watkins, 2002). Housing Needs and Land Availability Studies (subsequently Urban Capacity Studies) were important background documents in this process.

In the current system in England and Wales, three background statements are now of central importance in determining land release for housing at the local level. These are the designation of sub-regional housing market areas (HMAs), the strategic housing market assessment (SHMA) and the strategic housing land availability assessment (SHLAA). HMAs should be set out in the regional spatial strategy to provide the spatial framework for SHMAs and SHLAAs (see Figure 6.2). Local planning authorities (LPAs) (in line with PPS3) are then required to develop SHMAs that inform decisions about the supply of housing and contribute to tackling housing needs and affordability

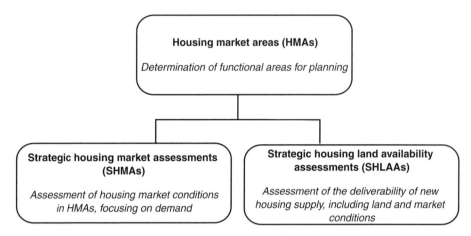

Figure 6.2   Supporting statements for PPS3. *Source*: Ferrari (2008: 8).

problems, while SHLAAs are used to provide a background analysis of land availability. These are required to ensure that the lack of available land does not act as a constraint on the supply of new housing (see CLG, 2007a). The changes to the required evidence base for housing planning has ensured a degree of convergence with the approach used in Scotland where an analytical framework based on HMAs has long informed best practice (Maclennan *et al.*, 1998) and where local housing market context studies, similar in nature to SHMAs, became a statutory requirement in the Housing (Scotland) Act 2001.

Although this general approach is broadly appropriate, as we will discuss later, these supporting statements are not without their problems. SHMAs, which are concerned primarily with the detailed workings of local housing systems often lack conceptual and methodological rigour. Locating local housing needs studies within their broader market context is an important improvement but this is operationally problematic. The SHLAAs occupy the role previously served by land availability and urban capacity studies. They provide a detailed analysis of supply side of the local market and seek to ensure the identification of a continuous flow of land for new housing but there are practical challenges here too.

Strategic housing market assessments

It is intended that each SHMA prepared by local planning authorities should: estimate housing need and demand in terms of affordable and market housing;

determine the distribution of need and demand across the plan area; consider future demographic trends; and identify the requirements of specific groups (see CLG, 2007b). The practice guidance sets out a framework that should ensure 'a good understanding of how housing markets operate' and that the assessments undertaken should be 'robust and credible' (CLG, 2007b: 8). There are several stages to the assessment process. First, a housing market partnership, involving a range of state and market stakeholders, needs to be established. Second, an analysis of the current market is undertaken. This is usually subcontracted to a consultant. Third, the market analysis is examined in the context of estimates of future household numbers and housing need. The next stage takes account of the requirements of particular household types including the elderly and households with special needs.

There is a loose economic (supply and demand) framework that shapes the assessment of current market conditions and the preferred approach emphasises the use of secondary data. Changes on the demand side of the market are explored by consulting a series of proxy measures including the estimated distribution of household income and the employment structure. Supply-side analysis requires consideration of the current profile of and recent changes in the housing stock. Rental levels, overcrowding and under-occupation, vacancies and turnover are also considered. The evidence should be brought together to provide an understanding of how economic, demographic and stock characteristics relate to each other. This involves a mapping exercise and an examination of temporal trends in key variables.

There are, however, serious shortcomings in the quality of the assessments currently produced for local planning authorities (see Nevin Leather Associates *et al.*, 2008 for an illustrative review). Some consultants argue that the reliance on secondary data and existing studies means that the outputs of SHMAs do not actually meet the requirements of the policy guidance (Fordham Research, 2007). These problems are partly a consequence of the fact that the CLG Practice Guidance is under-specified. The guidance fails to provide clear suggestions on how best to conceptualise the workings of the market or how to reconcile data collected from surveys, existing secondary data and qualitative sources. The overall impression is that the guidance asks for too little. Indeed, '[it] focuses upon what to do as a *minimum* to produce a robust and credible assessment and explains how local authorities can develop their approach *where expertise and resources allow*' [emphasis added] (CLG, 2007: 8).

This is particularly disappointing when set in the context of the advancements that have been made in the academic literature. The rich empirical work undertaken by William Grigsby (1963) and others, for example, has long offered a template for the analysis of housing markets within a submarket framework. This approach highlights the need for a fine-grained treatment of spatial segmentation and highlights the substitutability between sub-regional locations. Grigsby also emphasises the need to consider market change through time. The relevance of this sort of analytical framework to planning for housing has been championed by several authors (Maclennan, 1986; Jones and Watkins, 1999). A central assertion has been that the analysis of house prices provides useful evidence of the spatial pattern of any mismatch between supply and demand and that this should inform decisions about the allocation of land for new house building. There have been some ambitious attempts to operationalise the submarket framework (Hancock and Maclennan, 1989). The results of our empirical research, based in Glasgow, offer both conceptual and practical lessons in applied market analysis (see Chapters 4 and 5). This work demonstrates that it is possible to harness secondary datasets to identify market areas, define internal submarkets and explore price change and mobility within this system over time. The objectives, for the increasingly similar approaches to market analysis used throughout the UK, remain very modest when compared with the possibilities highlighted in this research and in Chapters 3, 4 and 5 of this book. And, when framed in this way, it is not clear that the secondary data sources are up to the task.

Strategic housing land availability assessments

SHLAAs are employed: to identify specific deliverable sites that are ready for development in the first five years of a plan; to identify additional potentially developable sites for years six to ten; and, if possible, in years eleven to sixteen (although it may be acceptable to identify broad locations for future growth for this period) (see CLG, 2007a). The sites identified should not include windfall sites that might become available in the first ten years of the plan. The key differences between this guidance note and its predecessor (DETR, 2000b) is that the focus is now on a longer time period and there is an emphasis on the need for the assessments to provide a 'conveyor belt' of land by continually topping up the stock of identified sites. The SHLAA is intended to identify sustainability and physical constraints that make sites unsuitable for development and to identify action that might help bring them forward.

As noted above, the SHLAAs now occupy the role previously performed by land availability and urban capacity studies. In principle, these assessments are intended to provide a detailed analysis of the land market and of the supply of land for housing development. In the past, the effectiveness of land availability studies was undermined by differences in key actors' definitions of 'available' and 'developable' land. Like other aspects of the housing planning system, these studies have historically been criticised for their failure to take account of market conditions (Adams and Watkins, 2002). Arguably the greatest achievement of these exercises has not been in establishing a supply of land but rather in assisting to secure a better dialogue between planners and house builders (Cullingworth, 1997).

The need for interaction between stakeholders is deeply embedded in the new approach. As with the guidance on SHMAs, the published best practice strongly promotes engagement in Housing Market Partnerships of a wide range of actors, including house builders, social landlords, property agents, and community and regeneration agencies. In the SHLAA context, it is argued that builders, in particular, will provide expertise on the deliverability and developability of sites and the extent to which economic viability might change with market conditions. Even though this assumption ignores the flawed economic assessments that are regularly made by house builders (see Maclennan, 1986; Adams *et al.*, 2008b), there is little doubt that these partnerships will provide a useful forum within which market actors can prepare the ground for steering development proposals through the planning system.

Reconciling the evidence: broader political and policy concerns

The technical limitations that emerge at various stages of the process are not the only problems with the current system. The exercise inevitably also involves political choice and debate. Regional bodies take decisions on the requirements to be made and the distribution of these requirements within the region. These decisions are informed by the work on projections, other policy priorities including those set out in Regional Economic Strategies and also by public examination of the requirements. This process is often extremely controversial. There are many cases where local political choices may lead to significant changes in the requirements set out in Regional Spatial Strategies (Crook *et al.*, 2005).

Local planning authorities then prepare their Local Development Documents. In doing so they must ensure that they meet the housing requirements of the entire community. This encompasses the need to ensure choice in terms of the mix of type, size and location of new homes and meeting the specific requirements of those who need affordable homes and those with special needs. These will also include local targets for, and strategies to promote, the reuse of previously developed land. They are also required to take both national and regional policy guidance into account. Hence they consider regional policy with respect to housing. They must take a wide range of national policy into account including affordable housing, the 'urban renaissance' and sustainable development agendas (see Chapter 7 for further discussion of the difficulties this introduces).

The debates and discussions can be made more rather than less complex by the background evidence. Studies undertaken at local and regional levels will often be framed by different objectives (Ferrari, 2008). Regional level analysis is generally concerned with drawing comparisons between areas, which can be done using a relatively simple and consistent model. This, however, is unlikely to explore locally specific issues. As a result, different studies (often conducted at different spatial scales) will yield different results. Although SHMAs are supposed to aggregate and integrate local findings, this can be complicated by variations in the survey methodology employed or the time period in which the studies were undertaken. There is scope for SHMAs to contradict local studies to which considerable weight has been implicitly assigned. Local authorities tend to prefer their locally commissioned surveys. Ferrari (2008) shows, for instance, that in Yorkshire, the regional comparison study suggested that the city of Wakefield has one of the highest affordability problems in the region, even though Wakefield's local studies showed that its housing was among the most affordable in the country. These very different findings reflected partly definitional incompatibilities between the two types of study but also reflected the fact that the model used at regional level was more sensitive to very low incomes in the area.

Despite this complexity, characteristically, after balancing the evidence accumulated in the background statements and accommodating political priorities, LPAs will allocate a number of sites for new residential development, typically larger sites which can take a number of years to build out. These sites will often be those that developers and landowners have been discussing with the LPA over many years (Crook *et al.*, 2005). With allocated sites there is usually evidence of market interest. Plans can, and often do, give detailed indications of what is required on each and every site, including affordable housing requirements and other planning obligations to be negotiated. In addition, local planning authorities will also indicate their expectations as to the number of 'windfall sites'. These are typically smaller sites for which permission will be sought by landowners and developers but whose exact numbers, capacities and locations cannot be predicted in advance. Plans should, however, set out policies showing how local planning authorities will respond to such applications.

The performance of housing planning is, of course, subject to ongoing monitoring and review. Local planning authorities are required to collate information on change in key housing indicators as part of their Annual Monitoring Reports. These indicators include percentage of new dwellings completed, the number of affordable homes completed and the percentage of new dwellings on previously developed land (see Wong *et al.*, 2008 for a review). This exercise is very limited and suffers from the lack of an adequate framework within which to meaningfully analyse and interpret the data (Wong and Watkins, 2009).

Overall, although notionally the new planning system is intended to steer the market, it is not clear that technical framework developed is capable of serving this purpose. The quality of housing market analysis continues to suffer from the failure to establish a clear analytical framework. The use of secondary data, collected for other purposes, ensures that analysis remains wedded to inappropriate and highly aggregated spatial scales. The lack of robustness of much of the evidence base means that (often appropriate) planned actions will inevitably be unable to resist pressure applied from those with (often short-term) political priorities. Despite the best intentions of recent reforms, housing plans will continue to lack credibility as a result of the gap between the reality of plan-making and the intentions of the policy guidance. The vagueness and incoherence of policy objectives will, of course, serve to exacerbate the problem.

Conclusions

The current planning system, together with elements of urban regeneration and housing policy, provides the state with the levers with which to influence the rate and location of new housing development. These levers are intended to be deployed with reference to the prevailing market conditions and the over-arching policy concerns of the government. The number and location of new homes delivered must also be sustainable. New housing must help meet the needs of those unable to afford access to market housing and contribute to intra-urban and regional economic development. It is not clear, however, that the policy framework can deliver on these goals.

The evolution of the planning system has, of course, been intertwined with the development of towns and cities in the last sixty years. The system's guiding principles were framed by the challenges associated with the decentralisation of households and businesses and the need to reverse the decline in the social and physical environment. The extent and nature of the social, economic and physical problems that have accompanied urban change have inevitably evolved. In the housing context, there has also been a significant change in the consensus about the possible solutions to urban problems. The function of a local authority has changed from direct provider of subsidised housing to that of strategic (housing) planning and enabling and the housing system has become dominated by the owner-occupied sector. New development is now almost exclusively provided by speculative builders. A major challenge for the planning system lies in the need to directly address the demands of private builders and consumers.

This has proved problematic in recent times and the system has come under sustained attack from critics, especially for its failure to respond to market pressures. Despite continued calls for radical reform, the picture that emerges is one of gradual but continuous reform. As a result, the system of planning for housing has remained broadly recognisable over time but there have been substantive changes *inter alia* in the way in which relations between state and market are framed (Thornley, 1996); in the role of the planning system in relation to the interactions between traditional sectoral policy interests (Adams and Watkins, 2002); and in the ways in which planning tools and competencies are used (Vigar *et al.*, 2000).

More recently, Kate Barker's proposals on housing supply, and those in the second Barker Review of Land Use Panning, have contributed to the speed and direction of the most recent reform agenda (Barker 2004, 2006). This is reflected in the detailed methods and processes involved in decisions about the release of land for housing. The 'post-Barker' changes have, in particular, emphasised the need to consult market information in making planning decisions and, as a result, affordability targets have become central to the new housing numbers game. However, although the proposals were substantially accepted by the government, the package of measures has actually been implemented on a relatively limited scale and, with the market downturn that started in 2007, much of the impetus appears to have gone from this agenda. As we discuss more fully in Chapter 8, proposals to use market signals to trigger the release of land from a 'buffer', largely because of operational difficulties, were watered down to the extent that these additional market information proposals were relegated to an Information Note (CLG, 2007c).

The revised planning system is thus notionally intended to steer rather than follow the market. It is not clear, however, that there is either the strategic vision or technical apparatus in place to achieve a substantive change in performance. Disappointingly, the system still fails to provide an appropriate framework for a more bottom-up understanding of the workings of local housing systems. The current system of allocating land for housing is only partly dependent on the evidence generated from analyses of the spatial structure of sub-regional markets and studies of the dynamics of local housing systems. Even then, the guidance on how to undertake this background analysis and the quality of the evidence produced is problematic.

The problems faced in practice are similar to those that have been exercising academic researchers concerned with understanding the workings of local housing markets. There continues to be a lack of conceptual clarity and inadequate data to support the production of better market evidence. At a general level, practice continues to be inhibited by the limits of analytical skills and techniques and by the inability to deal with the complex spatiality that characterises the housing market. The next chapter looks more fundamentally at the relationship between planning and the market.

7

Planning Policies and the Market

The changing role of planning in the housing market is part of a wider evolution of planning. 'Land use planning' has over time has given way to 'spatial planning' as the dominant culture representing a shift in emphasis toward a more integrative approach linking land use to related diverse strategies. This 'modernisation' agenda may appear merely semantic but it seeks to shift the emphasis away from narrow, passive concerns of regulation and control of land use, towards a more positive, proactive approach to planning. In 2005 the government in the first of a new set of Planning Policy Statements states that:

> The new system of regional spatial strategies and local development documents should take a spatial planning approach. Spatial planning goes beyond traditional land use planning to bring together and integrate policies for the development and use of land with other policies and programmes which influence the nature of places and how they can function. That will include policies which can impact on land use, for example by influencing the demands on or needs for development, but which are not capable of being delivered solely or mainly through the granting of planning permission and which may be implemented by other means (ODPM, 2005d: 12–13).

The aim is to link land use planning with economic and social policy elements to coordinate urban and rural regeneration strategies, regional economic and housing strategies, community development and local transport plans.

Within this new policy environment a number of housing themes have dominated planning policy and can be summarised as the provision of affordable housing and achieving social mix via planning agreements and sustainable development. These policies have not been developed in a vacuum and are closely linked to housing policy. This chapter explores these policies in the context of a planning ethos that has notionally become more market oriented in the post-Barker world. Central to this critique is an assessment of the impact of planning on the housing market and hence on meeting the needs of society in an efficient way. A key question is to what extent these policies are deliverable or conflict with basic economic realities of the housing market. The chapter therefore builds on some of the detailed issues presented in Chapter 6 by examining the fundamentals of the role of planning and the property market.

The chapter first considers the relationships between planning policies and market forces and explains the economic logic for planning. This discussion also identifies the importance of trade offs between conflicting planning goals. To support the analysis there is a brief reminder of the housing policy context. The next section examines the use of planning agreements to provide affordable housing and dissects both the practical mechanics and the theory supporting the policy. The following discussion on the use of social mix obligations in planning agreements questions its priority given the role of the market in sifting households by income. The analysis of sustainable development centres on whether actual market outcomes achieve the policy goals and whether long-term planning goals can override short-term market forces. Common issues from these evaluations linking economic underpinnings, market outcomes and policy trade offs are summarised in the conclusion.

Planning policies and the market

There is a fundamental and longstanding question about the relationship between planning and the market that has raised much heated debate over the years especially during the Thatcher years. The Conservative government at that time sought to reduce the role of planning in favour of market forces and introduced a range of market-led urban regeneration initiatives (Jones, 1996b). It fuelled an existing ideological debate about the relationship between planning and the market (Brindley *et al.*, 1989; Hague, 2002; Thornley, 1991). In the 1990s concerns about environmental issues and NIMBY-ism led to a backlash and a return to more restrictive policies. However, the relationship between planning and the market is not just about a simple choice between the two but is also about what planning is trying to achieve and to what extent planning can counter the market.

At one extreme there is a belief that the market should be subservient to the plan. In survey work undertaken for the Department of the Environment by the University of Cambridge, one planning practitioner commented 'we would not see the point of looking at price data...Planning should lead, not prices. Land prices should reflect planning, not the other way round' (Jarvis and Russell, 1999: 3; also quoted in Evans, 2003: 198). The alternative model that the planner works with the market to facilitate economic processes while ensuring they are environmentally benign is a more widely accepted view of the planning profession (Davoudi, 2001). Nevertheless, the precise relationship remains a grey area. Planning increasingly wishes to see itself as having a proactive role as demonstrated by the New Vision for Planning (RTPI, 2001) which focuses on delivering urban sustainability. It sees a more central role for planning to negotiate with private sector interests amongst others to create a long-term commitment to sustainable development. Chapter 8 provides a critical appraisal of the development of this agenda but the Vision has set the tone for planning policies over the last decade. In many ways as a manifesto it emphasises the establishment of a strategic plan to which the market is subservient.

In the post-Barker world (see Chapter 6) planning has ostensibly set out to become market responsive and the Planning Policy Statement 3 (PPS3) for England and Wales has been revised to make a step-change in the expansion of housing supply (CLG, 2006b). Similarly, the Scottish Government has amended its equivalent document, Planning for Homes, explicitly to increase the flow of new housing. Market responsiveness in these documents is taken to mean the use of market information when determining HMAs, and consultation with developers and house builders about demand and land supply. There is also much advice on physical outcomes such as design standards and housing mix, but on *market outcomes* the advice is limited to ensuring the appropriate amount and type of 'affordable' housing that is *not provided by the market* (see later for definition). The language remains rooted in physical and deterministic planning and is entirely focused on development with no reference to market structures, potential trade-offs between different goals or the impacts of policies on the rest of a local housing market. This new market-oriented planning seems to accept the importance of market forces but national planning advice appears to implicitly believe that there are narrow boundaries to this approach and its impact.

To explore these issues it is useful to step back from these recent policy arguments by going back to basics and looking at the economic arguments for why planning should intervene in the operation of property markets. The basic theoretical argument lies in the potential for 'market failure' in the property market given that it is very imperfect with incomplete information, no formal marketplace and complex heterogeneous goods that have different legal interests. The economic logic of planning is to intervene in the urban system to resolve this 'market failure'. There are a number of dimensions to this market failure:

- externalities where costs of one firm are imposed on others without payment,
- failure to supply 'public goods',
- market misjudgements, for example excess supply,
- 'unacceptable' market outcomes (Harrison, 1977).

Many of these are uncontentious and planning in its broadest sense has become an accepted part of modern life. Externalities that create costs for nearby users are addressed through development control. Public (green) space in cities is a public good that would not be provided by the market and is promoted and protected by the planning system. Market misjudgements creating an oversupply are frowned upon as a waste of land and often become eyesores. Society accepts and requires minimum standards for various aspects of the built environment that are linked to safety and public health, so that people are not permitted to live in unsanitary conditions.

The consensus about planning belies some wider conflicting policy issues that are relevant to the planning of the housing market. This is highlighted by the following two examples. The countryside can be seen as a public good to be enjoyed by everyone. In particular, planning can be used to prevent the countryside (in the form of the green belts around cities) being 'privatised' by house building. Alternatively what happens if the market does not produce a sufficient supply of new homes for the community? As a housing shortage is an unacceptable market outcome, the planning system is expected to address this failure – but can it achieve this goal while protecting the countryside? This is exactly the dilemma set by the Treasury for the Department of Communities and Local Government in the following public sector agreement target:

Achieve a better balance between housing availability and the demand for housing, including improving affordability, in all English regions while protecting valuable countryside around our towns, cities and in the green-belt and the sustainability of towns and cities (NAO, 2006).

This is, of course, a very real problem for, as Chapter 2 argues, planning policy's emphasis on the conservation of green belt has contributed to market failure (i.e. a housing shortage). How this dilemma is attempted to be resolved is considered later.

In fact, as the preceding chapters demonstrate the impact of planning in terms of the scale, location and type of new supply has a potential impact on the whole of a sub-regional housing system. This is most obvious when restriction of supply within a city diverts demand to beyond the green belt, bringing with it house price inflation with consequences for people living in rural areas and surrounding towns. At the same time excess local demand also pushes up house prices in the city, modifying the internal spatial price structure, and leads ultimately to increased densities. The Aberdeen sub-region growth example in Chapter 5 also shows that, even when the planning system is set on expanding supply, the nature of development permitted in the area surrounding the city has feedback impacts on the city housing market. This is shown in a decline in the relative prices of expensive city suburbs as new large attractive houses are built in nearby villages.

There is one area that planning has accepted: it does have market consequences. With a restrictive local planning regime, as Chapter 3 shows, there are substantive differences between the prices of land zoned for housing and agriculture on urban fringes. The granting of planning permission for housing on this agricultural land, therefore, results in an uplift in its value. This increase in land value is principally a socially generated land value and is not derived from the individual efforts of the land owner and so can be justifiably taxed. There is a long history of attempts to tax this gain in land value and it has become to be known as 'planning gain' (Prest, 1981; Adams and Watkins, 2002). The realisation of this planning gain has been through the use of planning agreements.

Planning agreements emerged in the 1980s and were given statutory encouragement at the beginning of the 1990s. Initially, this planning gain was generally limited to securing developers' contributions towards the specific externalities associated with the development. Today, they are used increasingly to make contributions to wider infrastructure and community needs, including affordable housing (Campbell *et al.*, 2000; Crook *et al.*, 2006). These contributions are legally enforced through Section 106 Agreements in England and Wales and Section 75 Agreements in Scotland.

There is some debate as to who actually pays the tax represented by the contributions. A simple view suggests that the developer who pays the contributions to the planning agreement factors this into the price to be offered for the land. The reduction in land price, in effect, means the land owner pays the tax in these circumstances. However, Crook and Whitehead (2002) show that this is unrealistic and in practice it seems likely that costs will be passed on to a combination of landowner, house purchasers (via higher prices) or developer (through lower profits). The application of these agreements involves extensive negotiation at different stages and results inevitably in the slowing of the property development process. A necessary prerequisite for the use of planning agreements is that the planning system impact has already restricted supply, thereby increasing land values, and their application potentially further reduces supply.

Planning and planning agreements both constrain development and adapt and shape the market forces that operate in the housing market. National planning advice and guidance chooses to focus only on shaping the amount, location and type of new housing developed. Although this is to be achieved within a framework that includes a local demand assessment for housing, it also seeks to raise standards and meet wider land-use policies. There is no explicit reference to the underlying economics to justify some of this general advice. As noted above, this begs questions of to what extent the current planning advice diverges from a free-market position and to what extent are these policies contrary to market fundamentals? The review of economic theory shows that this is not an issue of planning *per se* but of the policies pursued. The rest of the chapter assesses arguably the most important planning policies of the last decade, the provision of affordable housing, the encouragement of social mix and sustainable development. To set the scene for this analysis, the housing policy context is first reviewed.

The changing housing policy context

It is useful as a context to recap the historic role of state intervention in the housing market, even though some of these policies have been referred to in earlier chapters. Initial regulation of the housing market took the form of public health laws in the nineteenth century. During the First World War, in 1915, the first controls of the housing market (as opposed to the stock) were introduced in the form of rent control. Over the next seventy years there were various forms of regulation (and deregulation) of private tenancies encompassing rents and security of tenure. The 1988 Housing Act effectively removed or phased out rent regulation and weakened the security of tenure of most private tenants. The most direct intervention into the housing market was the building of social housing. The first social housing was built in the latter half of the nineteenth century as model demonstration projects for the private sector to show how good-quality, working-class housing could be built and still make a profit. It was only after the First World War that the first national council housing programme began and the state was effectively intervening in the market to provide subsidised housing at a price people could afford. At its zenith in 1980 council housing represented a third of the stock in England and Wales and half in Scotland. The right to buy and low levels of new social housing subsequently built has reduced the role of social housing. The mantle of primary provider of new social housing has also switched to housing associations and local authorities have retreated to a strategic and enabling role in the provision of new housing (Goodlad, 2001). The combined effect of these recent trends is the pre-eminence of market forces in the housing market although there are various forms of consumer protection (Jones, 2009b).

The dominance of private provision and the increasing reliance on market mechanisms for general housing supply has, perhaps curiously, enhanced the role of planning in the delivery of new housing and affordable housing, in particular. The planning system, since its inception, has always been an active regulator of the housing market through development control, planning permission and being the gatekeeper of new supply. The use of planning agreements to provide affordable housing placed it as central to the national housing strategy.

Provision of affordable housing

The green paper for England and Wales, 'Homes for the future, more affordable, more sustainable' published in 2007, emphasises the unaffordability problem and notes that, for several years the supply of new houses has not kept up with rising demand (CLG, 2007c). It argues that a new national drive to support more affordable housing is needed immediately and it outlines the government's plans to build 3 m new homes by 2020. Part of this target will be achieved by more social housing but this represents around a fifth of the new homes to be built. At least a further tenth are to come from other forms of affordable housing for rent or sale. Affordable housing in this context is defined as social and intermediate housing. The latter encompasses homes sold at a discount to market value, various forms of shared equity, part buy/part rent of which shared ownership is the most well established, and properties let at below market rent to key workers (but above rents of social housing) (CLG, 2006c).

Chapter 2 highlights the extent to which the planning system acts as a significant barrier to new house building with its lack of speed, efficiency and transparency contributing to the undersupply of new homes. The consequence is an unaffordability of home ownership that is determined by a long-term disequilibrium in the housing market. Perhaps ironically, governments are now strongly encouraging the use of planning agreements and obligations to expand the supply of affordable housing (CLG, 2006c). There are various mechanisms within planning agreements for the delivery of affordable housing that can incorporate the developer providing such housing directly, or indirectly by making land available, possibly for free to a registered social landlord.

In fact, the use of planning agreements to promote affordable housing has been honed and developed over the last two decades, supported by planning guidance that has evolved to lend more credibility. For example, in England and Wales the revision of planning guidance in 2000 strengthened the policy position further by stating that planning permission could be refused if affordable housing was not provided (DETR, 2000a). PPS3 offers comprehensive direction as to how to negotiate for affordable housing contributions (CLG, 2006b). It notes a national indicative size threshold: on sites with 15 or more dwellings, affordable housing should to be provided. PPS3 also recommends that local planning authorities should: set an area-wide target for the amount of affordable housing to be provided; set separate targets for social-rented and intermediate-affordable housing where appropriate; specify the size and type of affordable housing that is likely to be needed; and set out the approach to seeking developer contributions, with a presumption that affordable housing will be provided 'on site'.

Accompanying the publication of PPS3 is an associated policy statement, 'Delivering Affordable Housing'. It further emphasises the importance of the issue and encourages local authorities to strive for greater achievement of planning gain for affordable housing, preferably without the need for a public funding contribution (CLG, 2006c). Together these documents demonstrate how planning agreements have become embedded within the system and are now are central to the provision of affordable housing. In 2004/5, 46% of all affordable housing provided on sites supported by a social housing grant in England and Wales also included a developer contribution.

The position is broadly the same in Scotland and is set out in Scottish Planning Policy 3: Planning for Housing (Scottish Government, 2008a). In Scotland the government has set a 25% threshold as a starting point for negotiating the proportion of housing that is affordable on a given site (Scottish Executive, 2005). Most local threshold targets are much lower (Newhaven, 2008).

In England there is no such guideline but in some areas the starting threshold is much higher, such as in London where the target percentage is 50%, and Cambridge at 40% (Greater London Authority, 2008; Burgess *et al.*, 2007).

There is a considerable political capital invested in the promotion of this policy but there are a range of underlying issues concerning its successful implementation. First, there is the issue of the appropriate contribution by property developers. This is dependent on the level of uplift in land values socially generated by urban growth and the planning system. Given the imperfections and lack of information on the land market and the limited number of transactions, this is impossible to estimate with any accuracy. Instead, planning agreements attempt to set a local benchmark for financial contribution from developers who, it is assumed, will factor these contributions into the price they are prepared to pay for a site. Unfortunately, as discussed earlier, the process is not that simple as the developer usually will argue that this transfer has not been wholly possible. The result is that planners have to negotiate with a developer on the appropriate contribution.

Part of the problem is that the local benchmark contributions are a moveable feast and developers do not know precisely what their contribution is at the outset. The negotiation is also complicated in England by the way the planning obligations are expected to perform two financial roles: as a means for compensation of third parties negatively affected by the development; and a tax on the planning gain. Barker (2004) proposed that these roles be explicitly separated through the creation of a distinct tax called planning gain supplement. This tax would be set nationally and bring at least partial clarity to expected developer contributions. However, after strenuous criticism from both sides of the supply equation this was not taken up by the government. A further ingredient to the negotiation is the use of planning agreements to deliver social housing mix (see later). There are also often a range of parties to the negotiation including registered social landlords and (sub)developers who potentially may not be identified at the outset, especially on large sites.

The negotiation of planning gain is therefore a complex process that requires skills and resources that can be somewhat lacking in local authority planning departments (Cherrett, 1993, Jackson *et al.*, 1994, Joseph Rowntree Foundation, 1994). Local authorities are often negotiating with private developers who have vast experience of doing so, and this asymmetrical process is hindered by cultural differences between the private and public sectors (Pearce and Wenban-Smith, 1998). Very often different departments of a local authority are party to the process and have different priorities (Barker, 2004). Private developers question whether local authorities and others involved in these negotiations have the understanding and outlook to engage and collaborate with developers (Newhaven, 2008). There are also variations between local planning authorities in the way that, and the degree to which, negotiations are undertaken with developers because of differences in organisational culture (Claydon and Smith 1997), and the strength of bargaining positions linked to the local housing market (Farthing and Ashley, 2002).

As a result of some of these concerns the government considered providing guidance in England and Wales on the use of common starting points for negotiating planning agreements to provide more certainty for developers (CLG, 2006d). However, recent research by Burgess *et al.* (2007) finds that such a national benchmark is not possible and there is considerable variation between sites as well as varying priorities across planning authorities. It recommends only a common starting point for each authority to ensure at least local clarity and to address some of the concerns of Barker (2003). Further, the NAO (2007) in its review of the delivery of affordable housing, concludes that local authorities inconsistently interpret national guidance because they lack the necessary negotiation skills and financial tools.

Negotiating planning agreements is also a protracted process. The NAO (2007) finds that the process can take sixty weeks in some local authorities, although others can complete the procedures in three months. From the developer's perspective this increases costs and adds uncertainty to the development start date. Variations in criteria and procedures between authorities and lack of standardisation, even within authorities, also cause confusion to developers, and slows the process more generally. Another major point of contention are the different types and locations for affordable housing put forward by planners and developers (Rowlands *et al.*, 2006).

The general presumption that affordable housing should normally be provided on the same site as the private development also creates an internal conflict between the goals of these planning agreements (Crook *et al.*, 2006). In particular: is the planning agreement designed to provide affordable housing or to achieve social mix? For example, a planning obligation from a site in a central city location where land values are high could produce more affordable housing if it is used to build the affordable housing in a more suburban area where land is cheaper. More affordable housing could be provided for a given financial contribution at the cheaper location but there would be less social mix. The desire for social mix can have a detrimental effect on the quality and quantity of housing built. There are instances where the social mix of the housing offering alone has been insufficient for the planning authority to permit the development. Government advice and the planning profession prioritises social mix over the potential supply of affordable housing.

Planning agreements theoretically should provide affordable housing without government grant. In fact, a comprehensive study finds that only 30% require no subsidy, and the actual amount of grant has increased significantly, certainly in the middle part of the decade (Monk *et al.*, 2005; Joseph Rowntree Foundation, 2007). The system is therefore actually dependent on the amount of public funding. A study of schemes in Yorkshire by Watson (2006) further finds that the housing units provided by agreements were below general space standards of normal grant-aided affordable housing. The nature of this process means that it is quite difficult to assess the financial benefits derived from planning agreements. The NAO (2007) finds that the value of developers' obligations does not exceed 10% of the development value. Unfortunately, planning gain is subsumed within development value and there are no studies of the actual proportions of planning gain achieved. Nevertheless, there are considerable doubts about the efficacy of the system in generating planning gain.

These problems of the use of planning agreements are summarised by Crook and Whitehead (2002), who argue that, in practice, planning agreements are likely to be both inefficient and inequitable because of the costs of negotiation, lack of information about the extent of planning gain available on each site, the extent of uncertainty in determining land prices, varying negotiation skills of planners, and who actually pays. The success of the policy is also dependent on the buoyancy of the private housing market and new house building rates, as the recent recession has shown (Crook *et al.*, 2006).

Much effort by government has gone into overcoming these problems and promoting the use of these agreements and because of this, the amount of affordable housing increased over the first half of the decade (Crook *et al.*, 2006). While this could be put down to the system working better as local planning authorities move up the learning curve, it has been achieved in a benign macroeconomic environment and rising house prices which have led to increased unaffordability. These housing market conditions (with a relatively weak supply response) led to higher land values and more planning gain available to be captured, and hence greater potential for success (Crook *et al.*, 2008). This success was also heavily concentrated in areas of high demand where planning gain was at its highest – namely London and the South East of England with very few affordable housing units provided through this mechanism in northern regions (Monk *et al.*, 2006; CLG, 2008c). Similarly, McMaster *et al.* (2008) show that between 2004 and 2007 very little affordable housing was provided through planning agreements in Scotland. Four out of five affordable housing units given planning consent in Scotland during the period 2005 to 2007 received no developer contribution

(Scottish Government, 2008b). Very little of the housing provided via planning agreements was in deprived areas; most were around high-value areas such as Edinburgh or Inverness.

The use of planning agreements has enabled registered social landlords access to land in areas of high demand, possibly the only way they could (Crook *et al.*, 2006). But there are fundamental theoretical issues about the policy's application. A prerequisite for its use is high socially generated land values causing unaffordability that can be tapped into by using planning agreements to provide affordable housing. The logic so far is fine. But the government is committed to new market-oriented planning to increase supply to meet demand by making more land available and (implicitly) reducing planning constraints. This policy should logically bring down land value, reduce the potential planning gain and as a consequence reduce the scope for affordable housing provided by planning agreements.

The implication is that the only way planning agreements can be applied on a long-term basis is to ensure that unaffordability continues. In other words, there are substantial restrictions on supply. Put more starkly, the provision of affordable housing by this means can only be achieved if there is a housing shortage and unaffordability. The logic means that the use of planning agreements should only at best be a stop-gap policy in medium-demand areas. It already had limited success in relatively low-demand regions. The government appears not to recognise the underlying economics of the system. In advice published in 2006 the government states:

> In traditional high value areas, local planning authorities already have strong experience of negotiating planning obligations…But there is a need for local authorities in other areas to raise their game and to recognise that such obligations will be increasingly viable on new housing developments (CLG, 2006c, para 7).

This seems an exercise in self-deception or an implied acceptance that the prospect of meeting demand is a long way off. At the very least it is based on the flawed assumption that house price inflation will be pervasive across space and through time.

The analysis also suggests that increasing the land supply and the market output of housing by relaxing planning constraints would be a much simpler solution in many areas than the convoluted approach inherent in planning agreements that has an inbuilt dampening mechanism on supply through taxation and cumbersome negotiation. An increased land supply could ultimately reduce land values and hence house prices but it is not a universal panacea. Actual market outcomes of such a policy would be subject to time lags, local market conditions and the response of the house building industry. A market solution along these lines would also be unsuitable in areas where high socially generated land values are derived from the impact of planning constraints *and* from the weight of demand and historic expenditure on public infrastructure. The relaxation of planning constraints in such areas, for example inner London, is likely to have a very modest impact on land values. Overall, the use of planning agreements as a national long-term solution to the provision of affordable housing has a weak theoretical base and suffers practical difficulties; so does the free market solution. Both are also dependent on a benign macroeconomic environment. There is no simple solution but these are strong arguments for tailored policies based on local market assessments and, in the short term at least, direct intervention through the greater provision of social housing in some areas.

Encouraging social mix

Closely entwined with the provision of affordable housing through planning agreements is the policy to ensure neighbourhood social mix, or in the current planning language, 'mixed communities'. The origins of this policy stem from concerns about increasing social inequality and concentrations of privation particularly on large council estates from the 1970s. Policies designed to address this issue by the introduction of new housing for sale in public-sector communities began in the 1980s and were a motivation for many advocates of the right to buy (Jones and Murie, 2006). It has become a long-standing policy with regard to neighbourhood revitalisation (see Chapter 5). The Labour Government, when it came to power in 1997, brought new impetus to these policies. It set up the Social Exclusion Unit and developed the sustainable communities agenda that aims to promote social cohesion and inclusion while strengthening economic prosperity (ODPM, 2004).

The report of the Urban Task Force (1999) has been strongly influential on current sentiments toward social mix. Under the heading, 'Prioritising social well-being', it argues,

> Without a commitment to social integration, out towns and cities will fail...In responding to social problems we must avoid repeating the mistakes of the past. Developing large amounts of social housing in one location does not work...In future, we must develop on the basis of a mix of tenures and income groups (Urban Task Force, 1999: 45)

This argument has been the subject of some debate and the benefits appear to be an act of faith despite the many papers on the subject (Jones and Brown, 2002). Jones and Murie (2006), for example, point out that historically many homogeneous council estates were seen as very successful and they question the norm of social diversity in neighbourhoods. Atkinson and Kintrea (2000) and Allen *et al.* (2005) also show that social mix does not necessarily lead to social interaction. Meen *et al.* (2005b) argue that there is evidence that tenure diversification improves the physical environment of a neighbourhood. The issue of social mix and tenure mix in these analyses is also rather blurred (Rowlands *et al.*, 2006).

Whatever the precise benefits, social mix has become a central tenet of planning policy and is linked closely to the provision of affordable housing through planning agreements as the previous section shows. The government's policy is explained as,

> For too long we have lived with the consequences of rigid monotenure development; and today no one would promote significant scale development that would include nothing but social rented housing. But the scope of planning obligations gives local authorities the ability to require developers to build mixed tenure developments, thereby helping them secure improvements in mix over the whole of the stock (CLG, 2006c: para 12).

The insistence of social mix in planning agreements is the main vehicle to achieve this goal rather than small-scale, social-rented housing developments. There is a consensus that large social housing estates should not be repeated but the delivery of social mix is contentious. Policy has also entered a new phase, from building houses for sale in public-sector communities to building for rent in new developments predominately aimed at owner occupation.

A useful insight into the issue is to consider the outcome that results from a market in the absence of planning. The market naturally sorts households by income and Chapter 3 explains this process. This perspective is reinforced by Cheshire (2007) who argues that concentrations of poverty are principally caused by income inequality. Berube (2005) reports greater levels of income stratification in the US housing market as income differentials have widened in recent decades. The UK has not had a free housing market because of government intervention for almost a century with the development of council housing in particular distorting the spatial pattern of social groups. One historic visualisation of the market forces on a British city was given in the description of Manchester by Engels in 1845:

> Around this commercial quarter there is a belt of built up areas on the average one and a half miles in width, which is occupied entirely by working-class dwellings...Beyond this belt of working-class houses or dwellings lie the districts inhabited by the middle classes and the upper classes. The former are to be found in regularly laid out streets near the working-class districts...The villas of the upper classes are surrounded by gardens (Henderson, 1967: 27–28).

More than a century later, the relative spatial distribution of incomes has changed little demonstrating the limitations of planning and the use of planning agreements by shaping new development can achieve only a very localised impact.

Planning agreements undoubtedly deliver affordable housing within private sector developments despite the reluctance of at least some developers (Monk *et al.*, 2005; Rowlands *et al.*, 2006). But a fuller assessment of their ability to address social mix is dependent on the type and range of affordable housing being built and whether the initial social mix is sustainable in the longer term.

Some commentators have expressed concern that planning agreements have focused too much attention on the delivery of affordable homes in these developments and placed too little emphasis on outcomes in terms of the types of housing and communities being created (Newhaven, 2008). A particular issue of concern is that there is an increasing percentage of affordable housing units being built in the form of shared ownership rather than for renting from a registered social landlord. There are a number of reasons for this including the fact that most can be built without grant and it has been attractive to developers/landlords in the rising market until recently. These shared ownership units tend to be smaller units and are aimed at a very narrow range of households – childless, marginal owner–occupiers (Joseph Rowntree, 2007; CLG 2008). The problem is not restricted to shared ownership as developers often seek to meet the obligations of planning agreements by increasing the number of units on the development, i.e. higher density for both the market and the affordable housing. This in turn means small properties and again few opportunities for accommodation suitable for families with children (Rowlands *et al.*, 2006).

These concerns about the achievement of social mix on new developments are an important indicator of the policy but only on its own terms. There is a much bigger and more important social mix picture when viewed from the urban perspective that the policy ignores. Planning constraint does not simply contribute to unaffordability; there are distributional implications. Higher income households can outbid those on lower incomes so while the middle classes may have to pay more it is low-income households that are the most affected. The precise consequences are myriad and include young first-time purchasers who cannot buy in the area in which they were brought up and have to move elsewhere. Households crowded out of the owner-occupied market are forced to live in temporary rented accommodation and the overall housing shortage means that the people who suffer most are, ultimately, the homeless. It is highly debatable that planning policies are achieving an optimum 'mix over the whole stock'.

In the longer term there are further questions over the specific policies aimed toward social mix. Chapter 5 has already discussed the problems about achieving sustainable markets for new developments for sale in public sector communities. Not all such developments are ultimately successful. The key point is that initial subsidy to purchase in a given area does not necessarily lead to an active resale market and many houses sold initially can ultimately be bought up by private landlords at nominal prices (Jones and Brown, 2002). Similarly, where social housing is included in predominantly private-sector developments, social mix is not cast in stone, and Rowlands *et al.* (2006) find that many of the market housing in their case study estates were bought to let. Just as in any neighbourhood, mixed tenure may prove to be less marketable than single tenure estates on resale. Given the relative freshness of the initiative there is no long-term study of the viability of these initiatives. Atkinson (2006) notes that long-term worries can be allayed by active management in these developments to ensure equitable treatment between households of different tenures covering such items as service agreements, and if residents are aware of the tenure structure on moving in.

The growing proportion of shared owners, one-third of affordable housing units on planning agreement schemes in 2005/6, also raises some wider issues. In the longer term these properties are likely to be become part of the wider housing market (whether to rent or buy) and so represent only a short-term social mix fix. There are also issues about the investment potential of such investments. The Joseph Rowntree Foundation (2007) points out that at least in the recent past shared ownership has not proved as good a financial deal as 100% discounted mortgages. There are more fundamental worries for investors who buy into a new concept that incorporates social mix given some negative views by potential purchasers (Rowlands *et al.*, 2006). This is illustrated by Jones and Brown (2002) who find that the initial purchasers who bought houses on new estates in public communities acquired a poor long-term investment relative to opportunities elsewhere in the housing market.

Sustainable development

The rhetoric of sustainable development has engulfed planning and has become a core principle. The delivery of sustainable development has been accepted by all the constituent governments of the UK (Batty, 2006), and yet the concept lacks tangibility and a comprehensive definition. In a sense it is a political concept that is merely an expression of our preferences (Batty, 2001), and in another it is a way of parcelling together a range of existing policies. The government sees sustainability in terms of quality of life, economic progress and social inclusion as shown by the following statement:

> Sustainable communities meet the diverse needs of existing and future residents, their children and other users, contribute to a high quality of life and provide opportunity and choice. They achieve this in many ways that make effective use of natural resources, enhance the environment, promote social cohesion and inclusion and strengthen economic prosperity (ODPM, 2004).

Sustainability from this perspective overlaps with the social mix agenda but uses the ephemeral concept of community that seems to imply a place, possibly a neighbourhood. The planning profession has emphasised environmental and ecological concerns and both the government and the planning profession have placed a strong emphasis on urban design as part of sustainable development (Urban Task Force, 1999). There is also a belief that a long-term commitment to sustainability should override short-term market forces (Davoudi, 2001).

Urban sustainability policy has also focused on the compact urban form rather than a dispersed urban form or urban sprawl. The arguments have centred on how, rather than whether, the sustainability of urban forms can be achieved by increasing the density of development, ensuring a mix of uses, containing urban 'sprawl' and achieving social and economic diversity and vitality – the key components of the 'compact city' (Jenks *et al.*, 1996). Compact urban forms are also seen as protecting agricultural and amenity land, and leading to the more efficient use of existing, previously developed urban land. As a result of a mixture of uses in close proximity, the arguments in favour suggest that there would be reduced transport energy consumption by increased use of alternative modes of travel such as walking and cycling, as well as public transport. This, in turn, would lead to environmental, social and economic benefits.

These arguments are essentially normative and untested or disputed but such ideas were taken up in a series of UK government strategy documents (see HM Government, 1994), strongly advocated as a basis for policy and implementation by the Urban Task Force (1999) and accepted in the government's green paper response (DETR, 2000c). The government has been exhorting higher and higher residential densities by following a stringent defence of the green belts surrounding the cities and the reuse of brownfield land. There is a target for building 60% of new homes on reused urban land. National Planning Policy Guidance to local planning authorities at one point advised the following prescriptions:

- avoid developments which make inefficient use of land (those of less than 30 dwellings per hectare net);
- encourage housing development which makes more efficient use of land (between 30 and 50 dwellings per hectare net); and
- seek greater intensity of development at places with good public transport accessibility such as city, town, district and local centres or around major nodes along good quality public transport corridors (CLG, 2006b).

The compact city has therefore become the accepted wisdom for the planning regime in many towns and cities (Jenks and Jones, 2009). Similar concepts can also be found in the US in the form of New Urbanism and 'smart growth' initiatives. All tend to advocate urban forms that are high density and mixed use, which are contained to reduce travel distance and dependence on private transport, as well as being socially diverse and economically viable (Boyle and Mohamed, 2007).

These high-density policies have had a significant impact on the nature of housing development, as Table 7.1 demonstrates. The contribution of flats to new house building in England has risen from 20% of the total at the beginning of the 1990s to 45% in the second half of this decade; if social housing completions are added the proportion of flats is almost 50%. This transformation has occurred in a brief period, primarily over the last five years. Whilst the statistics in Table 7.1 are somewhat cyclical, in terms of house sizes built – presumably reflecting developers' views – the cause of the recent trend is clearcut. The move towards flats has induced a major shift in the types of housing built for sale; it reduced the proportions of three- and four-bedroom housing

Table 7.1   Breakdown of private house building in England by type and size.

Year	% Flats	% 1 Bed	% 2 Bed	% 3 Bed	% 4 Bed or more
1991–1992	21	15	31	31	23
1992–1993	19	13	31	33	22
1993–1994	16	11	30	35	24
1994–1995	14	9	29	36	26
1995–1996	15	8	28	36	28
1996–1997	13	6	26	37	31
1997–1998	12	5	24	38	32
1998–1999	14	5	24	37	35
1999–2000	15	5	24	36	35
2000–2001	17	5	24	35	36
2001–2002	22	6	24	31	39
2002–2003	26	6	28	30	36
2003–2004	33	8	32	29	32
2004–2005	40	9	37	29	25
2005–2006	45	9	41	28	22
2006–2007	44	9	40	28	22
2007–2008	45	10	41	27	22

Source: CLG Live Housing Statistics.

units to smaller units, especially two-bedroom properties. In summary, while Hall (2001b) points out that high density does not necessarily mean flats, it is clear that the market outcome is a predominance of new, small flats.

The consequence of compact city policies then are restricted urban housing development due to green belts, and permitted development increasingly taking the form of small flats. There are many critics of these policies who point to market forces acting in the reverse direction. For example, Evans and Hartwich (2005) argue that high densities are not the favoured choice for residents wishing to purchase homes. As Chapter 5 points out, family life cycle is a key dynamic in the housing market with families with children seeking out suburban locations. In Chapter 2 we note the growth in the demand for city living linked to the growing numbers of childless households (Lambert and Boddy, 2002). However, Hall (2001a) points out that small, childless households do not necessarily wish to live in flatted development and, given that some 80% of housing is provided by the market, they are able to exercise this choice.

The focus on the development of flats exacerbates a long-standing housing shortage by meeting only one segment of demand. Over the urban housing market many households are continuing to be priced out of the immediate housing market; they are not be able to afford the type of housing they require. The consequences are increasing commuter distances for many as households are prepared to travel longer distances from another settlement, hopping over the green belt, to find suitable housing. However, in terms of urban sustainability, the result is increased use of transport energy, the reverse of what the policy is designed to achieve.

The production of so many flats, especially in provincial city centres, raises another question – is there the demand? This is not easy to answer. Part of the reason is that many of these flats were bought up by buy-to-let landlords, some of whom deliberately chose to leave their properties empty, at least in the short term (Cobbold, 2007). Published housing market statistical time series suggest that the prices of flats have followed a similar pattern to house price trends as a whole but they do not provide sufficient detail to ascertain the performance of city centre flats. There is anecdotal evidence in newspaper articles that suggests serious problems of over-supply, although this may be as a result of the market decline, particularly affecting this segment. Innes (2007) reports that up to 35% of city centre flats in Liverpool were lying empty in April 2007 even before the recent downturn, but this seems extreme. A brief qualitative review of city centre markets by Cobbold (2007) finds that some markets do have excess supply, or at best, are in balance. He notes that there are limits to the expansion of this segment of the market.

In terms of sustainability this brief review of the relationship between sustainable planning policy and the housing market reveals that policies cannot focus entirely on high-density living or ignore short-term housing market dynamics. The planning system, for example, cannot promote or ignore 'wastelands of surplus developments' in a particular urban submarket in the short term while wider demand aspirations remain unmet. From a long-term perspective, urban sustainability must meet an affordability constraint that there is an adequate supply of housing for the workforce and their families (Jones *et al.*, 2009).

Conclusions

A traditional justification for planning is in terms of addressing market failure, but this also implies shaping market outcomes. The stated goal of governments is to promote supply by a more market-responsive planning system but actual policies so far have been modest in addressing this goal and there is an ambivalence toward the market as demonstrated by the language of national guidance. There also remains a longstanding undercurrent in planning practice that the market should be subservient to the plan. The scale of this view is unknown but it seems the new market approach will take some time to permeate practice. This chapter has examined three important planks of planning policy over the last decade with regard to the provision of housing set against the backdrop of this more market oriented approach. The analysis has essentially examined the economics and the market outcomes of the three interrelated strands of policy – the provision of affordable housing, encouraging social mix and sustainable development.

Affordable housing policy in the UK is a conundrum. The increasing long-term unaffordability in the housing market is chronicled in Chapter 2 and there is a broad consensus that it is the consequence of the lack of housing supply. The government's 'solution' to use planning agreements to tax socially generated land values is a complex bureaucratic mechanism that has a doubtful, or at best incomplete, logic. There is a very respectable long-standing view that the increase in land value from the granting of planning should be taxed, but its use to provide affordable housing leads to some dubious economics. On one hand planning constraint causes unaffordability and high land values and it is then used to provide affordable housing through a tax. The only way this tax can continue is by ensuring there is built-in unaffordability (partly by planning constraint) but this is entirely counter to the policy goal. Of course it is not as simple as this logic suggests because the removal of planning constraints in some areas will not increase supply. Equally, there are some parts of the country where planning constraint is minimal. Overall, the collection of the tax across all regions is difficult to justify except as a short-term measure. This is reflected in the difficulties that its application has experienced even during a period of rising house and land prices.

Mixed communities have become a major aspiration of planning and is also subsumed in the sustainable development agenda. Arguably it has been a key ingredient of the town planning movement from its earliest days but it has now been embraced by national governments. There are doubts about precisely what it achieves but the interest here is limited to the efficacy of the policy tool applied to encourage it. In a 'pure' housing market there is likely to be minimal social mix except at points of contact between different groups. In fact, the current housing market has much more social mix than theory would suggest because of the historical development of towns and cities and the resultant pattern of housing types and the location of social housing.

The current use of planning agreements to encourage social mix by a presumption that affordable housing is provided on large private developments means that the planning system is not just taxing planning gain but also intervening directly in the market. It is, in effect, an unrecognised restraint on housing development. The negotiation of this contribution is also a dampener on the development process, resulting in planners being unsure as to what negotiation priorities they are seeking and slowing the building of open market and affordable housing. It also opens up a trade-off between social mix and affordable housing. In the case of high value locations, affordable housing contributions could be provided elsewhere on lower value sites and actually increase the amount of affordable housing that could be built. On the other hand the social mix requirement may be the only way land may be available in some areas for social housing. But this does not apply everywhere.

Earlier in the chapter the question is posed about the dilemma between the green belt and affordable housing but actually the policy framework adds a third dimension to the trade off: the desire for the achievement of social mix and sustainable communities. The nature of this debate is neither explicit nor well specified. The wider picture of the impact of planning constraint on the social mix of the local housing market tends to be ignored with the focus of planning decisions entirely on individual sites. There is a lack of perspective in terms of the political energy and bureaucracy to deliver the social mix in these sites relative to the impact of the policy, which can only be at the margins of the spatial distribution of social groups. The recent move toward shared ownership also means that any impact could also be short lived.

Traditionally, planning tools have been passive but the use of planning agreements to encourage social mix introduces a proactive tool in line with the new era of spatial planning. However, it is unclear that the planning profession has the understanding of the housing market and the skills necessary to maximise this goal (Crook *et al.*, 2006, 2008). Similar messages arise from the analysis of sustainable development policies. The impact on the housing market of urban sustainable development policies also demonstrates how the planning system, by focusing on physical measures, leads to market outcomes that are unsustainable in the long term and potentially unstable in the short term.

8

Conclusions and the Way Forward

The overriding message of the analysis in this book is that an efficient planning system needs to embrace the housing system as a series of local markets. The aim of this chapter is not just to summarise the book but also to bring together and underline the key conclusions as a way forward for planning the housing market. The first step is to review current housing market problems and look forward beyond the immediate context. The next section assesses the planning policy response to these challenges over the last decade focusing on market outcomes. The chapter then sets out the nature and dynamics of local housing markets that underpin these outcomes. It then builds on this analysis to assess the practical issues in the application of market analysis to support planning decisions. Finally, the chapter proffers a critique of the current direction of planning in the UK and counters with its alternative vision.

Current and future housing market context

After a period of what is probably an unprecedented rise in house prices in the UK, the market has suffered what could euphemistically be called a 'correction'. The spur for this downturn has not come from internal market forces but from an international banking crisis referred to as the credit crunch. This exogenous shock has fed its way into the housing market as banks have restricted lending by offering less generous mortgages in terms of loan-to-value and loan-to-income ratios. Would-be owner–occupiers and potential movers are rationed out of the market by this process leading to falling effective demand. The number of market transactions has reduced substantially and house prices have fallen. With prices falling some potential first-time purchasers have decided to delay entry until prices stabilise at a lower level which in turn exacerbates the downturn. Land prices too have fallen as a consequence and some commentators have argued that this is an opportunity for housing associations to buy the land and an opportunity to revive the building of social housing. At the time of writing there may be yet be further downward pressure associated with the weak economy. The short-term prospects are uncertain and although there are forces dampening house prices it seems unlikely that these pressures will be sufficient to fully address the affordability problem.

The reason is that the (un)affordability problem can be identified as a disequilibrium brought about by a long-term shortage of supply in the housing market rather than a short-term outcome of a market cycle or the outcome of an exogenous shock. The aftermath of the credit crunch will actually make this position worse as new private house building will take sometime to recover; builders have been particularly badly hit by the sudden downturn leaving many properties unsold and new (incomplete) building at a standstill. Looking back beyond the recent past the book shows that while macroeconomic forces have contributed to the rise in real house prices, especially through relatively low interest rates, the severe imbalance between demand and supply is a culmination of a number of housing market processes which are now summarised.

There has been a continuing and expanding number of households, especially comprised of single people, that has fuelled long-term growth in demand. Owner-occupation has become the norm, brought about through rising incomes and accelerated by the sale of council housing via right to buy. The cumulative effect has stimulated the demand for private housing. To some extent this demand has been thwarted by the revival of the private rented sector stimulated by the popularity of buy to let, and landlords have been able to outbid many low-income households. Supply has not responded to the growing demand and increasingly first-time purchasers have been excluded with their numbers at an historic low ebb. The consequence is an affordability problem that is different in nature from that experienced in the price boom of the 1980s when it was a short-term cyclical issue for London and the South East of England. Over the last decade unaffordability has systematically engulfed most of urban Britain. The problem today is a national phenomenon, although there are significant local variations.

The planning system has been unable to ensure the land supply for new house building to produce sufficient housing (Barker 2004, 2006). Part of the explanation lies in the power and success of NIMBY-ism to deter development. The planning system has been a long-standing strong advocate of green belts around cities that have increasingly constrained urban development. These green belts have been in existence for more than fifty years and have been given a new raison d'être with the recent and enthusiastic embracing of the concept of the compact city by the planning system. Overall, the planning system has arguably emphasised its statutory obligations rather than facilitated the development necessary to cater for the expanding demand. A contributor to the weak supply response has also been the capacity of the house building industry and its interaction with the planning system that has led to a cautious approach to output expansion.

The short-term future is likely to see dampened demand partly because of the (weak prospects for the) economy and accumulated consumer debt but certainly because of the constraints on mortgage finance. The world financial crisis may not bring a full-blown mortgage famine for the foreseeable future but the prospects are certainly a period of mortgage restraint as banks become more risk averse while they rebuild their asset bases. It is uncertain how long the market adjustment will continue but this will ultimately be a transitory downturn stage in a continuing housing market cycle, even if the recession is quite prolonged. Potential first-time purchasers are likely to find it difficult to enter the market for sometime but this is only likely to lead to increased pent-up demand.

Household formation rates will be similarly affected. Financial and affordability constraints will mean more young people in their twenties and even their thirties being forced to live at home with parents or with friends. This will also put pressure on social housing and will lead to increased demand for renting in the private sector. The outcomes will also be seen in overcrowding, families in unsuitable and temporary accommodation (NPHAU, 2007). The downward pressure on household formation should be set in the context of continuing rising forecasts of household numbers, projected, for example, to increase by 23% in England between 2004 and 2026. The prime driver of growth in absolute numbers are single person households that are expected to increase by half (CLG, 2008).

As Chapter 6 notes there has been a history of over-prediction and so the actual trends may be less than forecast. Even so, the projections still suggest that without a sea change in the rate of house building, the long-term prospects of increased unaffordability can only worsen again. UK governments have begun to recognise the problem and set about addressing this issue by a series of initiatives that are now critically appraised.

Contemporary policy agenda and the housing challenge

Governments in the UK are committed to expand supply by an increase in 'affordable' housing, including social housing, but primarily the owner-occupied stock, by a more market responsive mode for planning. A major question mark lies over the ability of the system to change, although policy makers and planning professionals have begun to reshape priorities and practices. At the beginning of this decade, there was an attempt to revitalise planning policy and practice with a new manifesto – under the umbrella term of 'spatial planning' – and a new overall goal of sustainable development. This signals partly a move in emphasis from a broadly passive approach to regulation of land use to a positive or proactive stance that seeks to integrate urban (and rural) policies and apply wider mechanisms than simply the granting of planning permission to achieve its goals. It can be seen as a grand design to bring together land use planning with economic and social policy elements and hence to coordinate urban and rural regeneration strategies, regional economic and housing strategies, community development and local transport plans.

In this new era, planning policy toward housing has been focused on the provision of affordable housing and achieving social mix by placing obligations on developers through planning agreements and sustainable development. These policies fit well into this new paradigm and are closely aligned if not a central element of housing policy. What is less clear is whether these policies deliver a more market oriented planning system in the post-Barker world. Chapter 7 poses a key question as to what extent these policies are deliverable or conflict with basic economic realities of the housing market.

The analysis raises severe concerns about the theoretical underpinning and practicalities of the use of planning agreements to tax socially generated land values to expand affordable housing. The taxing of socially generated land values has a long pedigree going back to Henry George in the nineteenth century but its use to provide affordable housing has a logical inconsistency. It is accepted that planning constraints can contribute to high land values and unaffordability so a tax in the form of an obligation on development can be used to provide affordable housing. The difficulty with this argument is that the only way this tax can continue to be used to provide affordability is by ensuring there is continuing unaffordability by planning constraints. In other words, the policy accepts that the current long-term strategy will not succeed in enabling the market to meet demand. Planning agreements certainly slow the supply response in the short term with long delays for the negotiation process and inevitably some development is deterred.

The actual position is less clear, as simply removing planning constraints in some places will not increase supply because the existing high densities are the dominant constraint. There are other areas where planning constraints have a limited effect on land values and have a minimal restraint on development. This variability also means that the collection of the tax across all locations as government policy and planning advice exhorts is difficult to justify. The use of planning agreements for affordable housing is logical on a short-term basis in some locations. There is also a wider practical cloud over the policy as the delivery of affordable housing depends on the rate of private housing development, in other words market conditions. To date, the policy has been promoted actively during a period of rising house and land prices and there has been a very supportive financial backdrop yet there have been still been difficulties of implementation. With the aftermath of the world financial chaos there must be serious doubts about its output for the foreseeable future.

The current application of planning agreements to provide affordable housing is also restricted by the additional requirement of social mix on the site of private developments. The implications are that planning agreements are not simply acting as a tax but also that planning is positively intervening directly to shape the housing market for the first time. The significance of this development appears to have gone unrecognised, certainly unheralded and without any real national debate, but fits easily into the ethos of spatial planning. The justification for the promotion of social mix in this way is a reaction to the monolithic council estates that have proved problematic. Requiring social mix to be provided in neighbourhoods with very high house and land prices is a very expensive solution and more affordable housing could be provided at cheaper locations. Social housing built on small scale developments achieves the same goal without recourse to complex planning agreements. Such developments could be built in areas of predominantly owner occupation without necessarily being located in the areas with the highest land value. This approach would require to be funded entirely from registered social landlords or the public purse without the private funding from planning obligations. However, it is unclear what is the significance of private funding within planning agreements at present, and there are few schemes that are viable with only private funding.

The insistence of social mix, through this mechanism, undoubtedly has reduced and slowed the supply of affordable and market housing, although it can be argued that in some locations it is the only way land is made available for social/affordable housing. It has created a trade off between social mix and affordable housing because affordable housing contributions on high-value sites could be built somewhere else at a lower cost and still achieve social mix. The bigger picture in the wider context of an urban housing market suggests that this policy of social mix is likely to be of only marginal significance. Market forces will still sift households by income and wealth and determine spatial patterns accordingly.

Social mix has become a mantra of the planning profession with many papers extolling the benefits. The arguments in favour of social mix are outlined in Chapter 7 and are largely faith based but it is implicit that low-income groups benefit. The role of planning constraints on housing market supply in actually reducing the real opportunities for low income households has received nowhere near the same attention in the planning literature.

There is one final issue concerning policies designed to achieve social mix. A wider perspective incorporates not just planning obligations for affordable housing on private sector developments but also previous initiatives in the form of new private development in public sector communities and the right to buy. Both of these involve subsidies to promote owner occupation alongside social housing. The evidence referred to in previous chapters shows that initial subsidies to persuade people to buy a home in a public sector community does not necessarily lead to long-standing social mix. Success depends on a resale market being established over time. Similarly, right to buy has gradually but ultimately led to whole estates being privatised defeating any social mix objective (Jones and Murie, 2006) The long-term role of social mix as part of planning obligations is also becoming increasingly precarious. The recent move toward shared ownership as the form of affordable housing means that any impact could also be short lived once these properties are sold in the market. Social mix policies therefore have to accept that any initial configuration will eventually be subject to and modified by market forces.

Sustainable development is at the very heart of the planning agenda and is characterised by the compact city and high density living. There is an argument that environmental concerns are so important that market forces should be subservient to this long-term goal. The problem is that 80% of the housing stock is governed by the market and the evidence suggests that there is a limited demand for living in flats which is the predominant form of new high-density housing. In addition the market outcome of green belt constraints has contributed to longer commuting distances and less rather than more sustainable cities if judged by emissions from travel. The impact on the housing market of (urban) sustainable development policies that are aimed at physical measures leads to market outcomes that are unsustainable in the long term, and potentially unstable in the short term with surpluses of unwanted housing and shortages of the types of housing people do want. The problem is that with the demise of social housing a subservient population no longer has to accept the housing offered (Hall, 2001b). Planners cannot simply require high-density housing and expect people to live in them or argue that people need to be educated about the benefits of high-density living. Moreover, planning practitioners need to learn how to produce more sustainable cities that offer housing in which people want to live.

The analysis has demonstrated, using examples, that while government policies have charged planning with becoming more market responsive when judged by three core strands of policy there has been a failure to engage fully with market forces. Policies fail to identify, or ignore, trade offs and hence the outcomes achieved have been limited. There is a sizable gulf between the over-arching policy and practice. In the latter part of this chapter we develop this critique further and offer a way forward but first it is useful to recap on the chapters that examined the economics of housing markets as a base.

Towards a framework for housing analysis

The book conceives the national housing market as a system of related local housing markets with national/macroeconomic and regional influences. These housing markets are linked through limited migration but at the same time are largely self-contained. The migration pattern also acts as vehicle of spatial arbitrage transmitting (with a lag) any price changes from one market area to another. Regional house price ripples that are often reported and analysed are, in fact, urban price ripples. There are also local demand and supply forces within local housing markets that determine the internal configurations.

An insight into the understanding of how urban housing markets work is given by the access–space model (see Chapter 3) which can also explain the spatial structure of a city. In the model, which is based on simplifying assumptions, households make location choices which trade off increased accessibility close to the city centre against the desire to consume a larger amount of housing at a cheaper price per square metre at peripheral locations. This trade off provides the basic framework within which an urban housing market exists, although this underlying inverse relationship is blurred by the complexities of the real world such as neighbourhood and house type preferences. The long-term suburbanisation of cities can be explained within the model with rising incomes leading to people consuming greater housing further from the city core and improved transport technology and infrastructure reducing the cost of commuting.

The model can be used to explore the impact of planning on an urban housing market through the introduction of a green belt. The modified model shows both an overall increased level of house prices and densities as well as changes in the intra-urban gradients of these phenomena. This practical application of the model therefore shows that while the underlying force of the access–space model remains intact urban housing markets are shaped significantly by the planning system.

The access–space model focuses of the spatial structure of cities and on the journey to work as a key determinant of house patterns within a local market. In doing so it provides an important perspective not only on household location decisions but also on long-term urban change. To achieve these goals the model's assumptions abstract from the heterogeneous nature of housing. An important central feature of the model is the assumption that an urban housing system is a unitary market. Chapter 4 sets out the case that the urban housing system is highly segmented and, as such, is more appropriately conceptualised as a series of quasi-independent housing submarkets. This view is supported by the imperfect nature of the housing market. The source of these imperfections centre on the heterogeneous characteristics of housing, the lack of one central marketplace and the associated information inefficiencies that necessitate search costs, transactions costs, and financial and planning constraints that can inhibit the market adjustment process.

A sign of a segmented housing market is that there are significant price differences, in different parts of the market for homes with the same physical features and locational attributes. The fundamental reasons for this occurrence is that on the demand side of the market, households can be partitioned into distinct 'consumer groups' and on the supply side housing can similarly be classified by a typology of 'product groups'. Household or consumer groups are distinguished on the basis of their housing preferences and tastes, stage in the family life cycle, lifestyle, and socio-economic status. The housing stock is subdivided into distinct product groups which comprise relatively similar house types which represent reasonably close substitutes for households seeking a home.

The differentiation of demand and supply in turn leads to the potential for particular types of households to want distinct house types and this separation on both sides of the market is likely give rise to housing submarkets. From this perspective a local housing market is decomposed into a collection of submarkets and within each market forces determine house prices. It is therefore possible to have excess demand in one submarket pushing up prices while in another submarket in a city excess supply will deflate or at best leave prices stagnant. An important reason for this occurrence is the inelastic nature of demand with respect to particular characteristics of housing, i.e. households only want to live in a particular neighbourhood (type) or house type (these are of course related) or a school catchment area. Differences in housing market conditions across cities can therefore arise that reflect unevenness in the spatial expression of housing demand and a mismatch between the available stock and neighbourhood-specific levels of demand.

Chapter 4 reviews the growing number of empirical studies on this issue and concludes that despite a number of differences in statistical approach and definition the evidence supports the existence of spatial submarkets (with house-type submarkets possibly nested within). This implies that a tiered approach to housing markets based on submarkets should be incorporated within the conceptual framework used by planners to understand the workings of local housing systems. To effectively make decisions about the quantity and location of land to be allocated for new housing development it is necessary to think and act at this very local level. A practical approach to the identification of submarkets is offered by the use of migration patterns.

The potential for disequilibrium in one submarket at the same time as equilibrium in another illustrates continuing dynamic change within the housing market. In fact, the housing market is continuously adapting in response to the changing socio-economic-demographic characteristics of the population, the spatial pattern of land use and as the stock becomes older and is modified and expanded to meet updated living standards. Chapter 5 portrays a local housing market as a system of processes that is a complex entanglement of dynamic market relationships and externalities. Within these intricacies patterns of migration flows stand out consistently to be at the heart of the dynamic relationships whatever the spatial scale.

The influence of the planning system on these dynamics is not confined to the location of new house building. Supply restrictions lead to higher densities through households adding extensions or attics to their homes. New development itself shapes not only the built form but can change the spatial structure of a local housing market which has ramifications for changing internal migration dynamics and relative house prices. It is also has the potential to reinforce existing internal housing market structures. In a case study of Glasgow, planning and new building reinforced the existing submarket structure, and contributed to the process of creating a new submarket based on the city centre. Planning policy and practice therefore has the scope to reinforce and reconfigure local housing market structures.

An active property market with clear evidence of houses being sold easily is an essential prerequisite for neighbourhoods to continue to see investment in their housing stock, and is evidence of neighbourhood stability. Neighbourhood change tends to be incremental but there is the potential for negative and positive bandwagon effects that are subject to threshold or tipping points. An example of such a process could see the neighbourhood change from being predominantly rented to owner-occupied: on a council housing estate as more and more households exercise the right to buy their home, a bandwagon effect takes over as a resale market is established (Jones and Murie, 2006). Changing tenure does not necessarily imply substantive change, at least in the short term. Significant neighbourhood change occurs when there is the succession of one group of households by another most overtly seen through changes in racial groups or via gentrification. However, more often neighbourhood change can be seen as the spatial restructuring of different income groups within a city leading to adjustments in the price, tenure and quality of the local housing stock.

This analysis of the economics of the housing market, whether from a static, long-term or via a short-term dynamic perspective, reveals that the planning system pervades every aspect of the housing market. Planning decisions directly influence development and indirectly migration, density and house prices. However, there are limitations to its influence as macroeconomic forces dominate for example through rising real incomes or mortgage constraints and house building too has its input. Most importantly, planning cannot change fundamental economic or market forces, so, for example, constraints on the land for housing leads to rising prices and in the long term to higher density. Planning policy cannot reverse market pressures but it can achieve a great deal by affecting the viability of new development and the nature and direction of neighbourhood change.

Reshaping the system of planning for housing

Until recently the main role of planning in the housing market has been notionally in the assessment of demand and the allocation of land to satisfy this demand. As Chapter 6 explains, this process has gone through periodic redesign but the essentials, whether it be 'predict and provide' or 'plan, monitor and manage', have remained intact since this process was conceived at the inception of the planning system in 1947. At that time the housing market was very different with virtually all building undertaken by local councils and planning was perceived as part of an emerging centrally planned economy. Now, of course, nearly all new development is in the private sector. Forecasts of demand were primarily based on demographic trends and ignored tenure. This is less problematic today but a real issue when tenure in the housing market was more mixed and even now could be an issue if there is a return to social house building on a large scale.

This system effectively broke down in the 1990s when the planning system was supposed to be 'plan led' but plans did not materialise and house building output did not reach the targets set by conservative projections. As Chapter 6 describes to some extent these projections were inevitably deflated in high-demand areas by the existing housing stock constraints inhibiting household formation. The whole process in any case made no reference to market signals about demand or supply or (except in Scotland) to housing market structures. The procedures were based on local authority areas rather than housing market areas and it was presumed that demand could simply be shifted over relatively long distances to wherever the land allocated to housing was designated. Similarly it was assumed that the sites allocated would be attractive to private house building although from the 1980s on builders were party to discussions about suitability as brownfield sites became increasingly important.

The lack of credibility of these procedures in England has partially been addressed by the introduction of 'Strategic Housing Market Assessments', and the analytical processes and techniques have been subject to substantial reform in the last decade. In the wake of the Barker report policy guidance has evoked the need to consult market information in making planning decisions and affordability targets have become a central element. However, these targets are curiously regional rather than local and proposals to introduce 'automatic' price signals to the land allocation process have stumbled in the face of conceptual and practical problems. While policies and guidance are evolving there is a lack of clear direction and only a partial recognition of both the local nature of housing systems as set out in this book and the limited nature of market signals.

Planning has also embraced the need to address market signals as part of policies to address neighbourhood decay and stability. Over the last thirty years much effort has been expended to revitalise inner city neighbourhoods and public sector communities through an input of new house types and households, but it is only recently that policy has begun to acknowledge that this strategy also requires the regeneration of the local markets too. But again, the monitoring is rather simplistic requiring only a narrowing of the gap between local house prices and the regional average thereby ignoring the detail of the task. Chapter 5 notes that the experience of a number of new inner city housing developments built in the 1980s is that the establishment of resale markets is a long and uncertain process. There are internal and external threats to the process, especially as households in these areas are on low and variable incomes and prone to unemployment. The consequences are that the path can be unstable and that there are strong possibilities of negative bandwagon/threshold effects. Many of these estates did not have sufficient critical mass to ensure an active property market. This evidence also implies that is not sufficient to simply build new housing for sale, and a long-term policy commitment is needed to nurse and manage these areas to achieve a sustainable market. There needs to be an acceptance that this process of neighbourhood revitalisation is fundamentally an economic process and an appropriate tool kit to monitor and shape the process.

The conclusions from this review of the system of planning to meet housing need is that, although planning policy has begun to recognise that it has to be market sensitive to achieve its central goals, practice or indeed central guidance still does not fully engage with the complex dynamics of local housing systems. There are a number of layers to this dysfunction, including the failure to fully apply spatial frameworks that accommodate economic functionality, to recognise the interaction and spill-over effects within the housing market including the role of submarkets, and to manage the evolution of local markets. Taken together with the earlier analysis of the specific planning policies of the last decade, it seems that there is in effect a lack of appreciation that the role of planning in the property market is one of market engineering. The practical issues that arise and how more reference might be made to market signals is explored in the next section.

Local housing market analysis and planning practice

A convenient starting point to consider the application of local market analysis is a critique of the Barker proposals that emphasise that planning should take more account of and make greater use of market information. The supporting analysis and the subsequent practical use of market signals are examined in detail here to highlight a range of important theoretical and practical barriers. As discussed in Chapter 6, Kate Barker's arguments are reflected in the new role given to affordability targets in Regional Strategies but Barker also argues for greater use of market signals at the local level. She notes that 'one of the striking features of the *local* planning process is the lack of any reference to price signals' (Barker, 2004: 40; emphasis added) and also states (p. 6) that:

> prices provide a wealth of information about the nature of demand. For example, price differentials indicate consumer preferences with respect to housing location and housing attributes. This does not imply that preferences should always be satisfied. Prices are not a substitute for planning. However, using them as part of the decision making process can lend itself to better decision making, not just in high demand areas, but also in tackling problems of low demand and housing abandonment.

Barker's more detailed proposals highlight some of the challenges associated with the application of economic analysis. The proposals serve to illustrate that there are no easy, one model fits all answers to housing land allocation challenges.

The specific suggestions contained in Barker's review appear to be strongly influenced by the price signals model proposed by Cheshire and Sheppard (2004b). This model focuses on land prices rather than house prices. It suggests that constraints on land supply have created price differentials. The resultant pattern of prices provides information on the shortage of land in particular localities. It is suggested that it is possible to use price as a 'material consideration'. When prices trigger a certain threshold then generally, although there will be some exceptional circumstances, permission to develop should be granted. It is further argued that by using prices in this way land availability decisions will be distanced from the political process. The model, of course, ignores the fact that land markets are 'thin' and that data on land market transactions are rare and, when available, are often unreliable or out of date (Watkins, 2005). Nevertheless, this analysis led to recommendation nine which proposes a system of buffers and triggers. Barker (2004: 133) states:

> Local Authorities should allocate a further buffer of land to improve their plan's responsiveness to changes in demand. Additional land for development would be brought forward from this buffer when there was evidence of local market disequilibrium...If predefined indicators of housing market disequilibrium were triggered then authorities would not be able to refuse additional applications on the grounds that their targets had been met.

There are, however, numerous conceptual and operational questions that need to be addressed in designing an effective system of local market signals.

Barker (2004: 40), in fact, acknowledges that 'there are a number of practical obstacles to introducing this model'. Key questions include: how should prices be measured? What is the appropriate spatial scale for analysis? How frequently should signals be computed and consulted? The answer to these questions requires an understanding of the complex economic workings of local housing systems.

In Chapter 4, for example, it was argued that the existence and persistence of price differences between submarkets is a function of the peculiar workings of the market. It is useful to delve further into these market dynamics outlined earlier in the chapter. Submarkets exist as a result of the interaction between the highly differentiated housing stock and segmented housing demand. These submarkets are reflective of differences in the quality of neighbourhoods and the types of property available (on the supply side) and the way in which different groups of households (delineated by size, income, tastes and preferences) demand the various 'products' available. In this context, the distribution of house prices reflects differential, submarket-specific conditions. Even in buoyant conditions, house prices are likely to be rising quickly for only certain types of property and/or in only selected locations. This will reflect excess demand for a desirable product/location, a shortage of supply for that product/location or a combination of these influences. Conversely, a neighbouring ('low demand') area might exhibit falling or static prices for its 'product'. In these circumstances an understanding of the submarket structure of the local housing system is an important pre-requisite for the interpretation of market signals. Planning decisions should incorporate an appreciation of the complex inter-links between neighbourhoods and house-type submarkets.

Barker, however, has little to say about the structure and operation of the housing markets. She acknowledges that:

> There is considerable evidence that the shortage of housing exists, but the nature of this shortage is complex. Simply comparing number of households and number of dwellings fails to capture the mismatches between the location of supply and demand or between the type of housing desired and that which is available (Barker, 2003: 5).

But this complexity is not reflected in other assertions. The central premise of the Barker review is that house price inflation is the result of weak supply response and can be brought under control by a higher rate of building. Although this assertion is uncontentious, and supported by (regional and national level) empirical studies, the potential ramifications for prices in different parts of local housing systems are less clear cut.

The argument appears to be based on numerous assumptions about the structure and operation of local markets. These are not clearly articulated but they appear to be developed from the implicit adoption of a textbook model of a frictionless market. This model appears to ignore the importance of the current policy environment in directing supply, the significance of neighbourhood attachment (associated with social and economic structures) and other associated rigidities and imperfections in the housing system.

In practice, there are numerous technical and operational challenges associated with the interpretation and measurement of price signals in a complex, fragmented market. The measurement and interpretation of house price signals is difficult in its own right. The basic problem facing housing market analysts is that price measures need to be 'mix adjusted' to allow like for like (or 'constant quality') comparisons across space and over time. Prices reflect the inherent value of the physical and locational attributes of a property. It is entirely possible that 'average' price movements may be caused by changes in the type of property sold at different points in time or changes in the mix of neighbourhoods represented in the 'average'.

Mix adjustment allows us to compare prices for a standard dwelling in different locations and at different times and to be certain that any price changes detected will actually reflect differences in the market for housing rather than differences in the composition of the sample used to produce the price signal. Computing mix-adjusted prices for different localities and over time periods is, of course, technically demanding and time consuming. And, even when constant quality indices are used, local house price trends show that real prices are highly volatile over time and that monthly and quarterly series are subject to profound seasonal effects (see Leishman and Watkins, 2002). This analysis suggests that caution should be exercised when interpreting and responding to short-term fluctuations in prices.

Furthermore, if the planning system is to allocate sufficient land for housing to provide new dwellings of the required quantity, type and size and in the appropriate location, it is also important to appreciate the complex structure of the housing market. There are several useful lessons to be learned from the series of empirical studies of the Glasgow housing market discussed earlier in the book. These studies use mix-adjustment techniques and all comparisons of price changes and trends are based on 'constant quality' measures and thus reflect changes in market conditions rather than product mix.

The textbook model earlier implies that new supply and household migration will eliminate submarkets. The evidence from Glasgow, however, suggests that that the difficulties associated with reproducing the full set of desired attributes (including public goods) and high levels of neighbourhood immobility would prevent this market adjustment from taking place. It also reveals that very few households move between submarkets within the city. Spatial submarkets were shown to be relatively self-contained in the sense that a majority of the households that move are likely to settle within their original submarket (Jones *et al.*, 2004 and Table 5.1 for details). This effect occurs partly as a result of households' self-imposed limits on search patterns. It seems that house buyers restrict themselves to the parts of the market (neighbourhoods) that they know best and within which they are socially embedded. This is also a reflection of the influence of high search, information and transaction costs.

This analysis provides preliminary evidence that new development in particular submarkets may only have a limited impact on prices in other parts of the market (Jones *et al.*, 2005a). The relationship between price change and stock change is not constant across space. It seems that the location, and probably type, of new supply can also be as important a determinant of price change as the volume of new supply. This has important ramifications for decisions about the scale, type and geography of new development. The largest price effects do not always coincide with the largest increases in housing supply. The level of new supply required to generate a reduction in price will be difficult to predict and will, of course, be highly contingent on demand conditions. The observed relationships need to be examined and interpreted in the light of evidence from both the supply and demand sides of the market. In the absence of this contextual information, price signals can send misleading messages.

This may be why the proposals were ultimately watered down and resulted in a little known Housing Market Information: Advice Note (CLG, 2007c). The note sets out a method of consulting market data that is intended to provide an appreciation of housing market conditions ahead of the production of strategic housing market areas. The note suggests that planning authorities should consult three indicators: the ratio of lower-quartile house prices to lower-quartile earnings; annual growth in median house prices; and fifteenth-percentile house prices. The approach proposed represents a significant dilution of the original proposal. The merits of a 'traffic light' system for land (with or without standardised thresholds) and accompanied by a computer-based decision support tool and for sub-regional and intra-local authority level analysis were debated and abandoned for many of the reasons including the ambiguity of price signals.

The problems that beset the Barker proposals exemplify a more general point. Good, evidence-based, planning decisions require detailed and complex analysis of local housing systems. There is no simple answer and reliance on automated responses to a small number of indicators is likely to create more problems than it will solve. There are three major impediments to improving the practice of planning for housing that must be tackled as a matter of urgency.

First, there is a lack of conceptual clarity in the guidance provided. Disappointingly, given the discussions in Chapters 4 and 5, there has been a failure to establish a framework for the analysis of the dynamics within local markets. There is no real consensus on the appropriate scale for analysis. The local authority level tends to remain the focus of analysis for pragmatic reasons related to the units at which data are collected and the importance of local authority boundaries in the democratic decision-making process. The discussion of the definition of housing market areas in Chapter 3 draws out the limitations of administrative rather than functional boundaries. The use of local authority boundaries has also meant there has been little discussion about how to identify analytically significant neighbourhood or submarket structures. There is also very limited understanding of the interactions between localities. This includes the specific problem of dealing with the role of submarkets at the neighbourhood level within open systems and the interactions and overlaps between housing market areas. The analysis of links between spatial scales has also long been considered an important area of weakness (Maclennan and Bannister, 1995; Adams *et al.*, 2005b). The temporal dynamics of the market too receive only a perfunctory treatment in current practice. Much of the research used at present offers a very limited basis for predicting future outcomes and requirements.

Second, these problems have been exacerbated by the constraints imposed on applied research by the poor quality of available datasets and the fact that often these can only be examined at relatively high levels of aggregation and for administrative rather functional submarket or market boundaries. The response to these difficulties has apparently been to set the requirements for strategic housing market areas at a low level. The guidance fails to recognise that more can be achieved, even with the resources available at present. In the longer term, the development of a more sophisticated analytical framework would require that consideration be given to improving the quality of market data collected by HM Land Registry (HMLR). The HMLR dataset provides details of sales price, location of the property (the postcode), property type (flat, detached, semi-detached, terrace), and data of sale (or, more precisely, data of receipt of the record by HMLR) and has only been available to the research community in electronic form from 2000. In terms of the detail available on the properties transacted, it compares unfavourably with the data collected by government offices in the US and parts of Australia and Europe (see Costello and Watkins, 2002 for a review). Further investment in the IT infrastructure might help ensure that further steps could be taken to enhance the nature and scope of the data collected by HMLR. This is an important prerequisite for providing more robust measures of absolute and relative price levels and price changes. At the very least, a longer time period would allow the development of constant quality indices using repeat sales. Additional data on property attributes would be required to make other mix-adjustment techniques viable.

Third, there is also a shortage of adequate market analysis skills within the planning profession. This is recognised in the strategic housing market area guidance (CLG, 2007b) and will, of course, need to be addressed before any significant increase in the sophistication of the analysis of the housing system can be achieved. Until these shortages in skills and knowledge are addressed, there will remain significant weaknesses in the way in which the workings of housing markets are conceptualised in planning debates. As part of this process such skills need to be developed as part of the normal basic training of planners and this will require a rethink of the priorities placed on the educational components of university planning courses.

Solving these problems will not be the end of the story. It is worth noting that, should we manage to increase the use of market data in shaping planning decisions, new challenges will emerge. Inevitably any technical analysis used in the planning system will come under considerable scrutiny. It is possible that the enhanced role assigned to market information in the planning decision making framework might provide the basis for challenging planning decisions in the future. There are two areas that might be problematic. First, as discussed above, the data used to construct market indicators is never entirely up to date. This, of course, limits the extent to which the information might be thought to accurately capture current market conditions or might help to determine the future trajectory of the market. Second, the use of publicly available data means that analysts will be able to construct variants on these indicators. It is possible that, as is the case in the US, the technical basis of market evidence might be a fruitful source of income for consultants and expert witnesses. In this new environment, it may be possible to produce alternative estimates by using different methods. There is every chance that, in the years to come, market signals will be open to the same contradictory interpretations and controversy as household projections.

This critique has drawn out many of the pitfalls of applying a 'market signals' approach and the potential for errors. It is not a simple panacea to the current planning approach. It needs to be grounded in a full understanding of the behaviour of local housing market dynamics and meaningful statistical tools and data. The conceptual and technical basis for housing market assessment must be robust and the planning system needs to acquire the skills and knowledge to address this task.

The challenge to planning and the way forward

Disappointingly, the focus of planning debate has not been on the challenges of accommodating the market in wider visions of place making or detailed debates about the competencies required in practice. In contrast, the planning profession has enthusiastically forged forward with its spatial planning agenda. The Royal Town Planning Institute (RTPI) sees itself in a period of 'radical evolution' in which it 'has reaffirmed our core values whilst reinterpreting them to meet changing circumstances and new challenges' (RTPI, 2008). The key words the RTPI identifies in its vision published in 2001 are: spatial, sustainable, integrative, inclusive, value-driven and action-oriented (RTPI, 2001). This document comprises of nine pages that set out a manifesto for planning that seeks to reposition it for the future and is subtitled 'Delivering Sustainable Communities: An Agenda for Action'. It seeks to reposition planning and also promotes fundamental shifts in power.

The vision highlights the impact of globalisation on society, loss of public confidence of political processes and the holistic approach required to address sustainability. It argues that it is necessary to act locally but think globally, and that local planning is at the heart of sustainable development. Spatial planning is projected as a new integrative approach that is not constrained by 'artificial' administrative boundaries. In this new paradigm planning is viewed as no longer just a local authority activity and planning skills should be developed as a corporate management tool that looks at environmental impacts of business decisions.

All interests are to be integrated by the planning process although it accepts there will be trade offs balancing the costs and benefits of alternative decisions. It stresses the need therefore to promote compromise and mechanisms for collaboration rather than negotiation, and longer term goals rather than expediency. This vision sees all members of society as having an opportunity to participate in planning on an equal basis that respects differences but agrees to be bound by negotiated outcomes. To achieve these goals it argues that planning need to draw on a wide range of disciplines and cross-disciplinary activities.

Sustainable development is to be achieved by restrained economic growth, social justice, protection of the environment, prudent use of natural resources and integrative transport. It accepts that there is a tension between these different elements and that our society is, 'driven more powerfully by private sector led economic forces than by the political will of national or local communities' (RTPI, 2001: 7). Sustainable development policies are identified as taking a long term approach to development proposals which should 'relate to the need or demand for development to a clear context of planning horizons and markets' (RTPI, 2001: 7). In the medium term this means a 'prudential' approach to decisions based on a test of whether a development is appropriate for the need of a locality. Short-term actions centre on applying developers' obligations through planning agreements.

The document states that the need for visionary and effective planning has never been greater although it is seen as a framework for decision making. The key policy areas are identified as the quality of urban development, the delivery of sustainable urban settlement patterns (including a reappraisal of green belt policy), the quality of rural life, and the exploitation of natural resources.

The vision is a combination of aspiration, recruiting sergeant, call to arms, and the rudiments of normative planning practice. In the context of the arguments in this book there is only one reference to 'market' and only as an area. Spatial planning itself received legislative legitimacy in 2004 with the Planning and Compulsory Purchase Act for England and was subsequently incorporated in Planning Policy Statement 1 (CLG, 2006a). Nevertheless, spatial planning summarised succinctly as 'critical thinking about space and place as a basis for action or intervention' by the RTPI (2002) continues to be a fuzzy concept, although it was fleshed out by a study supported by the RTPI, CLG and other bodies that reported in 2007 (UCL Deloitte, 2007). This study defines and summarises spatial planning as:

> Spatial planning is the practice of place shaping and delivery at the local and regional levels that aims to:
>
> * Enable a vision for the future of regions and places that is based on evidence, local distinctiveness, and community derived objectives.
> * Translate the vision into as set of policies, priorities, programmes and land allocations together with the public sector resources to deliver them.
> * Create a framework for private investment and regeneration that promotes economic, environmental and social well being for the area.
> * Coordinate and deliver the public sector components of the vision with other agencies and processes (UCL Deloitte, 2007: 1).

This RTPI study is limited as its research method is simply for planners to interview planners about what they do. It does, however, illuminate the notion of the spatial planning revolution as primarily about proactive corporate planning within the wider public sector, and so its recommendations focus on improving this process by advising other public agencies to participate and improved education for planners in project and programme management. For spatial planning to succeed, the study argues, it needs enhanced skills in visioning, scenario building, scoping, networking, partnership working, facilitation, consultation technique, the collection and use of evidence and so on. It therefore recommends specialist MBAs for planners. It does discus planning as a facilitator and a need to focus on outcomes but curiously fails to consider the housing market except in the context of sustainable development and planning gain. There is one reference to the need for a transparent evidence base for land allocations and the use of functional market areas.

CLG has also funded a research project entitled Spatial Planning in Practice that has undertaken a number of longitudinal studies of change and sought to place spatial planning in a wider context of cultural change and its challenges. A number of working papers have been published as the project developed. The paper in this series by Nadin (2006) is of most significance here as it acknowledges that there is little evidence that planning has made use of formal analytical techniques of policy analysis and that most local plans do not demonstrate an understanding of the spatial development characteristics of their areas. He notes that:

> Few local plans go beyond a collection of policy criteria and decision rules for development control, and the formal procedures have turned on the defence of individual policies and land allocations. Important though that is, practice at the local level has undervalued an understanding of spatial development patterns and trends, and the generation of strategic options that might flow from that understanding (Nadin, 2006, para 2.9).

Nadin sees positive change in the growing collaboration between neighbouring local authorities to address this issue. This phenomenon is also noted by the final report of the study which also argues that the collection and use of evidence in local planning authorities has increased considerably (Baker Associates *et al.*, 2006). However, it too notes a weak skills base.

The aspiring planning revolution has only just begun and it is therefore difficult to be definitive on its likely outcomes. The short-term direction and emphasis is on a more proactive and corporate approach that suggests it wishes to be more evidence based with analytical support. There is considerable rhetoric on the reform of planning but very little of this zeal is directed toward the issue of the relationship between planning and the market. Economic growth is to be promoted. Economic forces rather than market forces are noted but there is no reference in any of these documents to market forces. The RTPI's vision makes no reference directly to the unaffordability problem in the housing market but does identify urban development as an important policy question. It is useful to compare the RTPI's response to the twin pillars of government planning policy over the last decade both inspired by government sponsored reports; the post-Barker agenda on increasing the responsiveness of planning to market pressures and the promotion of an urban design agenda stimulated by the Urban Task Force report of 1999.

The RTPI has set up a series of networks that include 'urban design' and 'room for all – the housing network' to share good practice. The urban design network promotes and campaigns for improvements in policy and practice, and since 1999 it has held an annual design conference. Urban design also features heavily at the annual current issues conference. The housing network's goals are more extensive and more diffuse, and the 2007 monitoring report makes very little reference to affordable housing. None of the events focused explicitly on expanding housing supply. The planning profession is curiously silent on advice for a more market-oriented planning system. It has chosen to interpret the need for greater market orientation as increasing the use of planning agreements and has accepted it needs to expand development appraisal and negotiation skills to do this. However, the use of planning agreements is about extracting benefits from the market for the community not the use of market signals to support planning. These are two distinctly different activities. The tone of attitudes is illustrated by the following study. A survey of skill gaps and training requirement for the planning profession requested views on 45 different competences but property market analysis was not on this apparently exhaustive list (Heriot-Watt University, 2007) The nearest competence offered for assessment was 'Housing – including affordable housing and housing needs assessment', but again a very different activity.

There is marked inaction by the RTPI to promote market-oriented planning other than the mechanics of the application of planning agreements, as demonstrated by its inability even to refer to it in its own policy documents and no apparent attempt to develop good practice and skills. There are expressed concerns about the understanding and extent of skills acquired by planners to extract developers' obligations within planning agreements but this is a narrow perspective. Overall the planning profession's attitude toward a central policy of governments in Britain to expand housing supply can be described at best as agnostic, if not hostile. The lack of positive buy-in to the policy by the profession is a barrier and has contributed to the slow progress toward the expansion of supply.

Part of the reason why the policy has been slow to progress can be traced to the contribution of economists (or more precisely academic economics). Economics has had relatively little to offer planning professionals (see Chapter 6). Cullingworth (1997: 951) comments that 'economic analysis plays a very modest role in land-use planning', and Evans (2003) bemoans the fact that planning has consistently ignored the work of urban economists. Yet it is not surprising that planners have not signed up to economic analysis when it is often based on highly aggregated econometric and simulation models (see Chapter 6 and Gibb, 2003, for a recent review) or highly simplified assumptions. The latter issue is exemplified by Lancaster (1966: 132):

> The theory of consumer behaviour...is a thing of great beauty, a jewel in a glass case. The product of a long process of refinement...it has been shorn of all irrelevant postulates so that it now stands as an example of how to extract the minimum of results from the minimum of assumptions.

The problem is compounded by the arrogance of economists who can proffer unrealistic advice that incorporates 'market' signals or adjustments ignoring the thin number of transactions and the operation of land and property markets.

The consequences are more than unsatisfactory for planning both in terms of meeting housing demand and understanding its impact on the market. There are some analogies – macroeconomic policy is often likened to driving a car with just a rear-view mirror. In the same vein, it can be argued, planning, as practiced, has no idea what controls the car's engine except the brake, most of the time driving with the clutch depressed in neutral wary of the accelerator, and the automatic choke in the form of social mix gradually bringing the car to a stop. This is evidently hyperbole but is indicative that planning needs a compass at least and it is hoped this book offers such a role.

A prerequisite is to be clear about what planning policy and the planning system are trying to achieve. The RTPI vision expresses this goal as sustainable development and this has been incorporated as the statutory objective of planning. Unfortunately, sustainable development is a very nebulous concept. Urban sustainability encroaches on a wide range of policy issues: social stability, environmental, ecological, commercial industrial and residential land use patterns and low transport use, urban sprawl and the compact city, housing and urban design, cultural identity and physical heritage and conservation, demographic change and energy efficiency of the built environment. There is therefore scope for misunderstandings partly arising from the disparate languages of its components and a laudable holistic vision is vulnerable to the criticism of vague idealism (Campbell, 1996).

The goal of sustainable development within the new spatial planning framework has been embedded in a corporate planning perspective for local government first promoted in the 1970s. Despite its evident ephemeral nature, the term has been applied to reinforce a view of planning based on a rational paradigm, implying planning based on scientifically inferable knowledge. This is very much in the traditional technocratic view of planning in the UK but such an approach is constrained by the level of knowledge (Low, 1991). A major issue is trade offs within this overarching goal.

Campbell (1996), in a very influential article, postulates sustainable development as the centre of the 'planners' triangle'. He argues that there is nothing inherent in the discipline that steers planners either toward environmental protection or toward economic development, or toward a third goal of planning: social equity. Instead, planners work within the tensions generated among these three fundamental aims that represent the triangle. He argues that for sustainable development to be effective it needs to act as a tool to focus on the conflicting economic environmental and social interests.

The problem in the UK is that sustainable development has not been taken as the basis of a debate but rather has become the umbrella term to represent a new planning orthodoxy that has emerged. This orthodoxy can be summarised as 'sustainable' containment through the compact city of high densities with the planner as the manager/coordinator that seeks partnership and the plan as a strategic framework (Roberts, 2002). As a result, Goodstadt (2005) bemoans the lack of academic and professional debate about planning and the focus of research on planning processes rather than outcomes, with new policies often bereft of an evidence base and with limited substantive reasoned justification. He asks whether sustainable development is really promoted by adding it as branding to planning documents.

Planning policy centring on sustainable development has been developed beyond the knowledge base (Jenks and Jones, 2009). The technocratic planning approach aimed at delivering sustainable development can be described almost as a collective bluff that obfuscates the real underlying issues and trade offs. Chapter 7 exposes the deficiencies in the 'sustainable' housing policies and highlights the trade off between the provision of 'affordable' housing and encouraging social mix. While a comprehensive view of sustainable development is beyond the scope of this book it follows Jones *et al.* (2009) who argue that there is an affordability constraint to sustainable urban form. In other words for the planning system to achieve sustainable development there needs to be a supply of housing at prices people can afford (this should be distinguished from 'affordable housing' defined by the UK government).

How can this be achieved? Planning policies must be designed to ensure that two market conditions hold: the market viability of new housing building and an adequate supply of houses that people can afford. There are alternative avenues by which this latter goal can be achieved. The current policy emphasis is on a private-led solution with a minor role for social housing funded by the state. An alternative would be a return to a greater role for the supply of new social housing. Planning could also actually zone land not just for housing but also for whether it should be affordable (social and subsidised) or market housing. A joint CIH/RTPI policy paper has argued for this approach (Simpson and MacDonald, 2003). In this way land values would be reduced for land zoned for affordable housing and this in turn would limit the need for the complexities associated with planning agreements. The logic of this approach fits well with a proactive spatial planning agenda and arguably gives planners more power, but there are likely to be problems undertaking the research required to identify these segments. As discussed in Chapter 6, planning forecasting techniques are not sufficiently developed to make meaningful estimates of demand in individual segments. In any case as discussed earlier the demand for affordable housing is a function of the number of houses provided so there is a clear endogeneity in the relationships. In practice, the amount of social housing (and affordable housing more generally) built is a political decision rather than simply the outcome of a forecasting demand model. The analysis therefore focuses on market housing.

Planning for a supply of affordable market housing is essentially a passive activity in the sense that it is dependent on a private sector response to economic conditions. Roberts (2002) outlines a series of guiding principles of planning that he calls the 'seven lamps'. His second is the lamp of reason, namely that policies cannot simply be advocated as 'good' in themselves but must be founded upon sound research and thorough analysis rather than assertion. The lamp of reason also incorporates an awareness of the consequences of planned actions. The current approach to meeting housing demand does not follow this principle. Instead there is a flawed approach incorporating a simplistic view of the housing market and complex bureaucratic decision structures. The outcome, a shortage of housing, is blamed by the planning profession almost entirely on the house builders failure to build on the land allocated (Macdonald and Kliman, 2007). In other words, the market supply has not followed the plan. Yet this argument is unsatisfactory as planning cannot avoid its duty to ensure sufficient houses are built. This means that planning needs to take into account the economics, and weaknesses, of the house building industry in its land allocation, just as it also argued earlier that it should interface with housing demand/market dynamics. In other words, it has to approach its task not by reference to normative statements about what builders could do or the type of housing that people should live in but by taking a more behavioural view to how the housing system works.

A central argument in this book is that the planning system will never be able to effectively plan for the housing market in its current form. There are several requirements for success. First, the inherent tensions between policy objectives can only be resolved if the prevailing holistic vagueness is replaced with a more honest statement of priorities and a clearer sense of the desired outcomes. This relates to planning theorists concern with the need for the development of a clear ethical framework within which to explore alternative courses of action (Khakee, 2007; Campbell, 2006). The priorities set should be sensitive to local issues. Second, there needs to be a willingness to engage with the market. This does not mean that planners should uncritically accept that markets are immutable. Rather there needs to be a detailed understanding of the way markets operate and how outcomes can be shaped by policy interventions. In the housing context, this means that planners need to develop a detailed understanding of the structure and dynamics of local markets. This, of course, will present particular challenges for the development of knowledge and skills. The techniques and competencies used in analysing housing markets at present are not fit for purpose.

The book recognises that both the planning policy environment and the operation of the housing market are complex. And, by extension, it recognises that the solutions to contemporary challenges in planning for housing are complex too. Politicians need to make difficult decisions, planning professionals need to embrace new competencies, and housing economists need to offer greater conceptual clarity and better analytical tools.

References

Adair, A.S., Berry, J. and McGreal, W.S. (1996) Hedonic modeling, housing submarkets, and residential valuation. *Journal of Property Research*, **13** (1), 67–84.

Adair, A.S., McGreal, W.S., Smyth, A., Cooper, J. and Ryley, T. (2000) House prices and accessibility: the testing of relationships within the Belfast area. *Housing Studies*, **15**, 199–215.

Adams, D. and Leishman, C. (2008) *Factors Affecting Build Out Rates.* Report to Department for Communities and Local Government, available www.henley.reading. ac.uk/nmsruntime/saveasdialog.asp?lID=22662&sID=77833. Accessed 25 March 2009.

Adams, D. and Watkins, C. (2002) *Greenfields, Brownfields and Housing Development*, Blackwell, Oxford.

Adams, D., Dunse, N. and White, M. (2005a) Conceptualising state-market relations in land and property: the growth of institutionalism – extension or challenge to mainstream economics. In: *Planning, Public Policy and Property Markets* (eds D. Adams, C. Watkins and M. White). Blackwell, Oxford.

Adams, D., Watkins, C. and White, M. (2005b) *Planning, Public Policy and Property Markets.* Blackwell, Oxford.

Adams, D., Payne, S. and Watkins, C. (2008a) Corporate social responsibility and the housebuilding Industry. In: *Corporate Social Responsibility and the Construction Industry* (eds A. Dainty, and M. Murray). Routledge, London.

Adams, D., Cartlidge, L., Leishman, C. and Watkins, C. (2008b) *Understanding Residential Land Transactions.* Report to Communities and Local Government, Universities of Sheffield and Glasgow.

Allen, C., Camina, M., Casey R., Coward, S. and Wood, M. (2005) *Nothing Out of the Ordinary: Mixed Tenure Twenty Years On.* Joseph Rowntree Foundation, York.

Allen, M.T., Springer, T.M. and Waller, N.G. (1995) Implicit pricing across residential submarkets. *Journal of Real Estate and Financial Economics*, **11** (2), 137–151.

Alliance and Leicester (2007) *Parents fork out more than £21K for children to fly the nest*, http://www.alliance-leicester-group.co.uk/html/media/non-indexed/release. aspx?txtcode=PR2208071. Accessed 5 March 2008.

Allinson, J. (1999) The 4.4 million households: do we really need them? *Planning Practice and Research*, **14**, 107–113

Alonso, W. (1964) *Location and Land Use.* Harvard University Press, Cambridge, MA.

Andrew, M. (2006) Housing tenure choices by young. *CML Housing Finance*, **7**, 1–12.

Armstrong, H. (1999) A new vision for housing. In: *Stakeholder Housing: A Third Way* (ed. T. Brown). Pluto Press, London.

Ashworth, J. and Parker, S.C. (1997) Modelling regional house prices in the UK. *Scottish Journal of Political Economy*, **44** (3), 225–246.

Atkinson, R. (2002) *Does Gentrification Help or Harm Urban Regeneration? An Asessment of the Evidence-Base in the Context of the New Urban Agenda.* Centre for Neighbourhood Research Paper No 5, http://www.neighbourhoodcentre.org.uk/ research/research.html. Accessed 25 March 2009.

Atkinson, R. (2006). Padding the bunker: strategies of middle-class disaffiliation and colonisation in the city. *Urban Studies*, **43**, 819–832.

Atkinson, R. and Kintrea, K. (2000) Owner occupation, social mix and neighbourhood impacts. *Policy and Politics*, **28**, 93–108.

Bailey, N., Haworth, A., Manzi, T., Paranagamage, P. and Roberts, M. (2006) *Creating and Sustaining Mixed Income Communities: A Good Practice Guide*. Chartered Institute of Housing/Joseph Rowntree Foundation, York.

Bajic, V. (1985) Housing-market segmentation and demand for housing attributes: some empirical findings. *AREUEA Journal*, **13**, 58–75.

Baker Associates, Terence O'Rourke, University of Liverpool, University of Manchester, University of the West of England (2006) *Final Report: Spatial Plans in Practice: Supporting the reform of local planning*, CLG, London.

Baker, M. and Wong, C. (1997) Planning for housing land in the English regions: a critique of household projections and Regional Planning Guidance mechanisms. *Environment and Planning C*, **15**, 73–87.

Balchin, P.N. and Rhoden, M. (2002) *Housing Policy: An Introduction*. Routledge, London.

Ball, M. (1983) *Housing Policy and Economic Power*. Methuen, London.

Ball, M. (1999) Chasing a snail: innovation and housebuilding firms' strategies. *Housing Studies*, **14**, 9–22.

Ball, M. (2002) Cultural explanations of regional property markets: a critique. *Urban Studies*, **39**, 1453–1469.

Ball, M. (2003) RICS European Housing Review. Royal Institution of Chartered Surveyors, London.

Ball, M. (2006) *Markets and Institutions in Real Estate and Construction*. Blackwell, Oxford.

Ball, M. and Kirwan, R. (1977) Accessibility and supply constraints in the urban housing market, *Urban Studies*, **14**, 11–32.

Barker, K. (2003) *Review of Housing Supply – Interim Report: Analysis*. HMSO, London.

Barker, K. (2004) *Review of Housing Supply: Delivering Stability – Securing Our Future Needs, Final Report – Recommendations*. HMSO, London.

Barker, K. (2006) *Barker Review of Land Use Planning: Final Report*. HMSO, London.

Barker, K. (2008) Planning policy, planning practice and housing supply. *Oxford Review of Economic Policy*, **24**, 1, 34–49.

Barlow, J. (1999) From craft production to mass customisation. Innovation requirements for the UK housebuilding industry. *Housing Studies*, **14**, 23–42.

Barlow, J. and Bhatti, M. (1997) Environmental performance as a competitive strategy? British speculative housebuilders in the 1990s. *Planning Practice and Research*, **12**, 33–44.

Bates, L.K. (2006) Does neighbourhood really matter? Comparing historically defined neighbourhood boundaries with housing submarkets. *Journal of Planning Education and Research*, **26**, 5–17.

Batty, S. (2001) The politics of sustainable development. In: *Planning for a Sustainable Future* (eds A. Layard, S. Davoudi, S. Batty), pp. 19–31. Spon, London.

Batty, S. (2006) Planning for sustainable development in Britain: a pragmatic approach. *Town Planning Review*, **77** (1), 25–40.

Berry, J. McGreal, S., Stevenson, S., Young, J. and Webb, J. (2003) Estimation of apartment submarkets in Dublin, Ireland. *Journal of Real Estate Research*, **25**, 159–170.

Berube, A. (2005) *Mixed Communities in England: A US Perspective on Evidence and Policy Prospects.* Joseph Rowntree Foundation, York.

Bianconi, M., Gallent, N. and Greatbach, I. (2006) The changing geography of subregional planning. *Environment and Planning C: Government and Policy*, **24**, 317–330.

Blackaby, B. (2000) *Understanding Local Housing Markets: Their Role in Local Housing Strategies.* CIH, Coventry and CML, London.

Bond, S. and Coombes, M. (2007) *2001-based Travel-to-Work Areas Methodology*, http://www.communities.gov.uk.

Bourassa, S., Hamelink, F., Hoesli, M. and MacGregor, B. (1999a) Defining housing submarkets. *Journal of Housing Economics*, **8**, 160–183.

Bourassa, S., Peng, V., Hoesli, M. and Forer, P. (1999b) *Defining Housing Submarkets Using Transactions Data.* Department of Urban and Public Affairs, University of Louisville, Louisville, KY.

Bourassa, S., Hoesli, M. and Peng, V. (2003) Do housing submarkets really matter? *Journal of Housing Economics*, **12**, 12–28.

Bourassa, S., Cantoni, E. and Hoesli, M. (2007) Spatial dependence, housing submarkets, and house price prediction. *Journal of Real Estate Finance and Economics*, **13**, 143–160.

Bover O., Muellbauer J. and Murphy, A. (1989) Housing, wages, and UK labour markets. *Oxford Bulletin of Economics and Statistics*, **51**, 2, 97–162.

Boyle, R. and Mohamed, R. (2007) State growth management: smart growth and urban containment: a review of the US and a study of the heartland. *Journal of Environmental Planning and Management*, **50**, 5, 677–697.

Bramley, G. (1993a) The impact of land use planning and tax subsidies on the supply and price of housing in Britain. *Urban Studies*, **30**, 5–30.

Bramley, G. (1993b) Land-use planning and the housing market in Britain: the impact on housebuilding and house prices. *Environment and Planning A*, **25**, 1021–1051.

Bramley, G. (1997) Housing policy: a case of terminal decline? *Policy and Politics*, **25**, 387–407.

Bramley, G. (2007) The sudden rediscovery of housing supply as a key policy challenge. *Housing Studies*, **22**, 221–242.

Bramley, G. and Kirk, K. (2005) Does planning make a difference to urban form? Recent evidence from central Scotland. *Environment and Planning C*, **37**, 355–78.

Bramley, G. and Leishman, C. (2005a) Modelling local housing market adjustment in England. In: *Planning, Public Policy and Property Markets* (eds D. Adams, C. Watkins, M. White). Blackwell Publishing, Oxford.

Bramley, G. and Leishman, C. (2005b) Planning and housing supply in two-speed Britain: modelling local market outcomes. *Urban Studies*, **42** (12), 2213–2244.

Bramley, G. and Leishman, C. (2005c) *Developing a system to measure and model housing demand.* Unpublished Report to ODPM, Heriot-Watt University, Edinburgh.

Bramley, G. and Watkins, C. (1995) *Circular Projections.* CPRE, London.

Bramley, G. and Watkins, C. (1996) *Steering the Housing Market.* Policy Press, Bristol.

Bramley, G., Munro, M. and Lancaster, S. (1997) *The economic determinants of household formation.* Report to DETR, Heriot-Watt University, Edinburgh.

Bramley, G., Rosenburg, L., Williams, A., Jones, C. and Leishman, C. (2001) *The Impact of Former Coal-Mineshafts on the Property Market in Stoke on Trent.* Department of Trade and Industry, London.

Bramley, G., Munro, M. and Pawson, H. (2004) *Key Issues in Housing: Policies and Markets in 21st-Century Britain.* Palgrave, London.

Bramley, G., Karley, N.K. and Watkins, D.S. (2006) *Local Housing Need and Affordability Model for Scotland – Update (2005 based).* Communities Scotland, Edinburgh.

Bramley, G., Leishman, C., Karley, N.K., Morgan, J. and Watkins, D. (2007) *Transforming Places: Housing Investment and Neighbourhood Market Change.* Joseph Rowntree Foundation, York.

Bramley, G., Leishman, C. and Watkins, D. (2008) Understanding neighbourhood housing market performance: untangling the regional, local and specific drivers of market outcomes, *Housing Studies,* **23** (2), 179–212.

Breheny, M. and Hall, P. (1996) National questions, regional answers. In: *The People – Where Will They Go?* (eds M. Breheny and P. Hall). TCPA, London.

Bridge, G. (2002) *Time-space Trajectories in Tentative Gentrification,* Centre for Neighbourhood Research Paper No 7, http://www.neighbourhoodcentre.org.uk/research/research.html.

Brindley, T., Rydin, Y. and Stoker, G. (1989) *Remaking Planning: The Politics of Urban Change in the Thatcher Years.* Unwin Hyman, London.

Brindley, T., Rydin, Y. and Stoker, G. (1996) *Remaking Planning.* Routledge, London.

Brown, P.J.B. and Hincks, S. (2008) A Framework for housing market area delineation: principles and application. *Urban Studies,* **45** (11), 2225–2247.

Burton, T. (2001) Vision for the future. *Roof,* **Jan/Feb,** 14–15.

Brueckner, J. (2000) Urban sprawl: diagnosis and remedies. *International Regional Science Review,* **23** (2), 160–171.

Burgess, G., Monk, S., Whitehead, C. and Crook, T. (2007) *The Provision of Affordable Housing through Section 106: An Update.* Report for the Joseph Rowntree Foundation, York.

Burrows, R. and Wilcox, S. (2000) *Half the Poor: Low Income Home Owners.* Council of Mortgage Lenders, London.

CABE (2004) *Housing Audit: The Design Quality of New Homes.* CABE, London.

Calcutt, J. (2007) *Review of Housebuilding Delivery.* CLG, London.

Cameron, S. (1992) Housing, gentrification and urban regeneration policies. *Urban Studies,* **29** (1), 3–14.

Cameron, S. (2002) Gentrification, housing redifferentation and urban regeneration: 'Going for Growth' in Newcastle Upon Tyne. *Urban Studies,* **40** (12), 2367–2382.

Campbell, S. (1996) Green cities, growing cities, just cities? Urban planning and the contradictions of sustainable development. *Journal of the American Planning Association,* **62** (3), 296–312.

Campbell, H. (2006) Just planning: the art of situated ethical judgement. *Journal of Planning Education and Research,* **26**, 92–106.

Campbell, H., Ellis, H., Henneberry, J. and Gladwell, C. (2000) Planning obligations, planning practice, and land-use outcomes. *Environment and Planning B: Planning and Design*, **27**, 759–775.

CEC Commission of the European Communities (1990) *Green Paper on the Urban Environment.* European Commission, Brussels.

Champion, A., Atkins, D., Coombes, M. and Fotheringham, S. (1998) *Urban Exodus.* CPRE, London.

Chaplin, R. and Freeman, A. (1999) Towards and accurate description of affordability. *Urban Studies*, **36**, 1949–1957.

Cherrett, T. (1993) *Affordable Housing in Rural Areas.* The Planner, London.

Cheshire, P. (2007) *Segregated Neighbourhoods and Mixed Communities: A Critical Analysis.* Joseph Rowntree Foundation, York.

Cheshire, P. and Sheppard, S. (1989) British planning policy and access to housing. *Urban Studies*, **26**, 469–485.

Cheshire, P. and Sheppard, S. (1996) On the price of land and the value of amenities. *Economica*, **62**, 247–267.

Cheshire, P. and Sheppard, S. (2004a) The price of access to better neighbourhoods. *Economic Journal*, **114**, F391-F396.

Cheshire, P. and Sheppard, S. (2004b) The introduction of price signals into land-use planning decision-making: a proposal, *Research Papers in Environmental and Spatial Analysis*, No 89, Department of Geography and Environment, London School of Economics, London.

Clapp, J.M. and Wang, Y. (2006) Defining neighbourhood boundaries: are census tracts obsolete? *Journal of Urban Economics*, **59**, 259–284.

Claydon, J. and Smith, B. (1997) Negotiating planning gains through the British Development Control System. *Urban Studies*, **34**, 12, 2003–2022.

CLG Department for Communities and Local Government (2006a) *Planning Policy Statement 1*, CLG, London.

CLG Department for Communities and Local Government (2006b) *Planning Policy Statement 3: Housing.* CLG, London.

CLG Department for Communities and Local Government (2006c) *Delivering Affordable Housing.* CLG, London.

CLG Department for Communities and Local Government (2006d) *Changes to Planning Obligations: A Planning-gain Supplement.* CLG, London.

CLG Department for Communities and Local Government (2007a) *Strategic Housing Land Availability Assessments: Practice Guidance*, CLG, London.

CLG Department for Communities and Local Government (2007b) *Strategic Housing Market Assessments: Practice Guidance.* CLG, London.

CLG Department for Communities and Local Government (2007c) *Housing Market Information Advice Note.* CLG, London.

CLG Department for Communities and Local Government (2008a) *New Projections Of Households For England and the Regions to 2029.* CLG, London.

CLG Department for Communities and Local Government (2008b) *2006 Housing Strategy Statistical Appendix (HSSA) data.* http://www.communities.gov.uk/documents/housing/xls/153008.xls.

Cobbold, C. (2007) *What is the Extent of Buy to Leave in England?* CLG Housing Markets and Planning Expert Panel Report, http://www.henley.reading.ac.uk/nmsruntime/saveasdialog.asp?lID=20285&sID=77833.

Coombes, M.G. (1997) Travel to Work Areas: frequently asked questions. In: *Travel-to-Work Areas and the Measurement of Unemployment: Conference Proceedings* (ed. I. Turok). Centre for Housing Research and Urban Studies, University of Glasgow.

Coombes, M.G., Dixon, J.S., Goddard, J.B., *et al.* (1979) Urban systems in Britain: from theory to practice. *Environment and Planning A*, **11**, 565–574.

Coombes, M.G., Green, A. and Openshaw, S. (1986) An efficient algorilthm to generate official statistical reporting areas: the case of the 1984 Travel to Work Areas: revision in Britain. *Journal of the Operations Research Society*, **37**, 943–953.

Coombes, M.G., Green, A.E. and Owen, D.W. (1988) Substantive issues in the definition of 'Localities': evidence from sub-group on local labour market areas in the West Midlands. *Regional Studies*, **22** (4), 303–318.

Coombes, M.G., Raybould, S. and Wymer, C. (2006) *Housing Market Areas across the North East Region: Draft Report, Centre for Urban and Regional Studies.* University of Newcastle, Newcastle Upon Tyne.

Costello, G. and Watkins, C. (2002) Towards a system of local house price indices. *Housing Studies*, **17**, 857–873.

CPRE (Campaign to Protect Rural England) (2006) *Compact Sustainable Communities*, CPRE, London.

Crook, A.D.H. and Whitehead, C.M.E. (2002) Social housing and planning gain: is this an appropriate way of providing affordable housing? *Environment & Planning A*, **34**, 1259–1279.

Crook, T., Henneberry, J., Tait, M. and Watkins, C. (2005) *Planning and market signals: a review.* Report to ODPM, University of Sheffield.

Crook, A.D.H., Monk, S., Rowley, S. and Whitehead, C.M.E. (2006) Planning gain and the supply of new affordable housing in England: understanding the numbers. *Town Planning Review*, **77** (3), 353–373.

Crook, A.D.H., Henneberry, J.M., Rowley, S., Smith, R. and Watkins, C.A. (2008) *Valuing Planning Obligations in England: Update Study of 2005-06*, Report to Department of Communities and Local Government, London.

Cullingworth, J.B. (1997) British land-use planning: a failure to cope with change? *Urban Studies*, **34** (5–6), 945–960.

Cullingworth, J.B. (1999) Postscript: British planning: positive or reluctant? In: *British Planning: Fifty Years of Urban and Regional Policy* (ed. B. Cullingworth). Athlone, London.

Dale-Johnson, D. (1982) An alternative approach to housing market segmentation using hedonic price data. *Journal of Urban Economics*, **11**, 311–332.

Davoudi, S. (2001) Planning and the twin discourses of sustainability. In: *Planning for a Sustainable Future* (eds A. Layard, S. Davoudi, S. Batty), pp. 81–93. Spon, London.

Dawkins, C.J. and Nelson, A.C. (2002) Urban containment policies and housing prices: an international comparison with implications for future research. *Land Use Policy*, **19**, 1–12.

Dawson, D., Jones, C., Maclennan D. and Wood, G. (1982) *The Cheaper End of the Owner Occupied Housing Market in Scottish Cities.* Scottish Development Department, Edinburgh.

Department of the Environment (1980a) *Development Control: Policy and Practice,* Circular 22/80. DoE, London.

Department of the Environment (1980b) *Land for Private Housebuilding,* Circular 9/80. DoE, London.

Department of the Environment for Northern Ireland (DoENI) (2002) *Modernising the Planning Process.* The Planning Service, Belfast.

Department for Environment Transport and the Regions (DETR) (2000a) *Planning Policy Guidance Note 3: Housing.* HMSO, London.

Department for the Environment, Transport and the Regions (DETR) (2000b) *Tapping the Potential: Assessing Urban Capacity – Towards Better Practice.* DETR, London.

Department for Environment Transport and the Regions (DETR) (2000c) *Our Towns and Cities: The Future – Delivering an Urban Renaissance.* DETR, London.

Department for the Environment, Transport and the Regions/Ministry for Agriculture, Fisheries and Food (DETR/MAFF) (2000) *Our Countryside: The Future. A Fair Deal for Rural England.* TSO, London.

Dixon, T., Pocock, Y. and Waters, M. (2006) An analysis of the UK development industry's role in brownfield regeneration. *Journal of Property Investment and Finance,* **24** (6), 521–541.

Downs, A. (2004) *Growth Management and Affordable Housing: Do they Conflict?* Brookings Institution, Washington, D.C.

Drake, L. (1995) Testing for convergence between UK regional house prices. *Regional Studies,* **29** (4), 357–366.

DTZ Pieda (2003) *Housing Market Areas in Scotland: Definition and Review.* Communities Scotland, Edinburgh.

DTZ Pieda (2004) *Housing Market Assessment Manual.* Office of the Deputy Prime Minister, London.

Dunse, N. and Jones, C. (2005) UK roads policy, accessibility and industrial property rents. In: *Planning, Public Policy and Property Markets* (eds D. Adams, C. Watkins and M. White), Blackwell, Oxford.

Evans, A.W. (1973) *The Economics of Residential Location.* Macmillan, London.

Evans, A.W. (1988) *No room! No room! The costs of the British Town and Country Planning System.* Occasional Paper No. 79, Institute of Economic Affairs, London.

Evans, A.W. (1990) A house price-based regional policy. *Regional Studies,* **24** (6), 559–567.

Evans, A.W. (1991) Rabbit hutches on postage stamps: planning, development and political economy. *Urban Studies,* **28**, 853–870.

Evans, A.W. (1995) The property market: ninety per cent efficient? *Urban Studies,* **32**, 5–29.

Evans, A.W. (1996) The impact of land use planning and tax subsidies on the supply and price of housing in Britain: a comment. *Urban Studies,* **33**, 3.

Evans, A.W. (2003) Shouting very loudly: economics, planning and politics. *Town Planning Review,* **74**, 195–212.

Evans, A.W. and Hartwich, O.M. (2005) *Unaffordable Housing: Fables and Myths.* Policy Exchange, London.

Farthing, S. and Ashley, K. (2002) Negotiations and the delivery of affordable housing through the English Planning System. *Planning, Practice and Research,* **17** (1), 45–58.

Fernie, J. (1995) The coming of the fourth wave: new forms of retail out-of-town development. *International Journal of Retail & Distribution Management,* **23** (1), 4–11.

Ferrari, E. (2008) Do planners need to understand housing markets? Paper presented at the ACSP/AESOP Conference, Chicago, June.

Field, B. and MacGregor, B. (1987) *Forecasting Techniques for Urban and Regional Planning.* Hutchinson, London.

Fik, T., Ling, D. and Mulligan, G. (2003) Modelling spatial variation in housing prices: a variable interactions approach. *Real Estate Economics,* **31** (4), 623–646.

Fingleton, B. (2008) Housing supply, housing demand, and affordability. *Urban Studies,* **45,** 1545–1563.

Fisher, E. M. and Fisher, R. (1954) *Urban Real Estate,* New York, Henry Holt.

Fisher E.M. and Winnick, L. (1951) Reformulation of the Filtering Concept. *Journal of Social Issues,* **7** (1–2), 47–85.

Fletcher, M., Gallimore, P. and Mangan, J. (2000) The modelling of housing submarkets. *Journal of Property Investment and Finance,* **4,** 473–487.

Fordham, R.C., Finlay, S., Muldoon, C., *et al.* (1998) *Housing Need and the Need for Housing.* Gower, Aldershot.

Fordham Research (2007) *Modelling Housing Markets in the PPS3 World.* Fordham Research, London.

Fraser-Andrews, J. (2004) Stock market outlook. In: *Private Housebuilding Annual 2004* (ed. F. Wellings), pp. 10–12. The Builder Group, London.

Gabriel, S. (1984) A note on housing market segmentation in an Israeli development town. *Urban Studies,* **21,** 189–194.

Gallent, N. and Tewdwr-Jones, M. (2007) *Decent Homes for All – Planning's Evolving Role in Housing Provision.* Routledge, London.

Gallet, C.A. (2004) Housing market segmentation: an application of convergence test to Los Angeles region housing. *Annals of Regional Science,* **38,** 551–561.

Galster, G.C. (1996) William Grigsby and the analysis of housing submarkets and filtering. *Urban Studies,* **33,** 1797–1806.

Galster, G.C. (2001) On the nature of neighbourhood. *Urban Studies,* **38,** 2111–2124.

Galster, G.C. (2003) Neighbourhood dynamics and housing markets. In: *Housing Economics and Public Policy* (eds T. O'Sullivan and K. Gibb), pp. 153–171. Blackwell, Oxford.

Galster G.C., Cutsinger, J. and Lim, U. (2007) Are neighbourhoods self-stabilising? Exploring endogenous dynamics. *Urban Studies,* **44** (1), 167–185.

Gibb, K. (2003) Urban housing models. In: *Housing Economics and Public Policy* (eds T. O'Sullivan and K. Gibb). Blackwell, Oxford.

Gibb, K., McGregor, A. and Munro, M. (1997) Housebuilding in recession: a regional case study. *Environment and Planning A,* **29,** 1739–1758.

Girouard, N., Kennedy, M., Van den Noord, P. and Andre, C. (2006) *Recent House Price Developments: The Role of Fundamentals.* Working Papers 475. OECD Economics Department, Paris.

Glasgow and the Clyde Valley Structure Plan Joint Committee (1999) *A Housing Market Area Framework for Glasgow and the Clyde Valley: Summary Technical Note.* Glasgow and the Clyde Valley Structure Plan Joint Committee, Glasgow.

Glass, R. (1964). *London: Aspects of Change.* MacGibbon & Kee, London.

Goodchild, B. (1997) *Housing and the Urban Environment: A Guide to Housing Design, Renewal and Urban Planning.* Blackwell, Oxford.

Goodchild, B. and Karn, V. (1997) Standards, quality control and housebuilding in the UK. In: *Directions in Housing Policy* (ed. P. Williams). Paul Chapman Publishing, London.

Goodlad, R. (2001) Housing and local government. In *Health of Scottish Housing* (eds C. Jones and P. Robson). Ashgate, Aldershot.

Goodman, A.C. (1978) Hedonic prices, price indices and housing markets. *Journal of Urban Economics*, **5**, 471–484.

Goodman, A.C. (1981) Housing submarkets within urban areas: definitions and evidence. *Journal of Regional Science*, **21**, 175–185.

Goodman, A.C. and Thibodeau, T. (1998) Housing market segmentation. *Journal of Housing Economics*, **7**, 121–143.

Goodman, A.C. and Thibodeau, T. (2003) Housing market segmentation and hedonic prediction accuracy. *Journal of Housing Economics*, **12**, 181–201.

Goodman, A.C. and Thibodeau, T. (2007) The spatial proximity of metropolitan are housing submarkets. *Real Estate Economics*, **35**, 209–232.

Goodstadt, V. (2005) Commentaries: rebuilding the planning community: questioning the orthodox and speaking the truth. *Planning Theory & Practice*, **6** (2), 247–249.

Gordon, P. and Richardson H.W. (1997) Are compact cities a desirable planning goal? *Journal of the American Planning Association*, **63** (1), 95–106.

Greater London Authority (2008) *The London Plan: Spatial Development Strategy for Greater London Consolidated with Alterations since 2004*, http://www.london.gov.uk/thelondonplan.

Green, B. (2008) *Housing Market Intelligence Report.* Bliss Books, Cheshire.

Grigsby, W.G. (1963) *Housing Markets and Public Policy.* University of Pennsylvania Press, Philadelphia, PA.

Grigsby, W.G. (1978) Response to Quigley. In: *Urban Housing Markets: Recent Directions in Housing Research* (eds L. Bourne and J. Hitchcock). University of Toronto Press, Toronto.

Grigsby, W.G. and Rosenburg, L. (1975) *Urban Housing Policy.* APS Publications, New York.

Grigsby, W., Baratz, M., Galster, G. and Maclennan, D. (1987) *The Dynamics of Neighbourhood Change and Decline.* Pergamon, London.

Gunn, S.C. (2007) Green belts: a review of the regions' response to a changing housing agenda. *Journal of Environmental Planning and Management*, **50** (5), 595–616.

Hague, C. (2002) Comment on Roberts, T., 'The seven lamps of planning. *Town Planning Review*, **73** (1), 9–11.

Hall, P. (1989) *Urban and Regional Planning*, 2nd edn. Unwin Hyman, Boston, MA.

Hall, P. (2001a) Sustainable cities or town cramming. In: *Planning for a Sustainable Future* (eds A. Layard, S. Davoudi and S. Batty), pp. 101–114. Spon, London.

Hall, P. (2001b) Global city-regions in the twenty-first century. In: *Global City-Regions: Trends, Theory, Policy* (ed. A.J. Scott), pp. 59–77. Oxford University Press, Oxford.

Hall, P., Gracey, H., Drewett, R. and Thomas, R. (1973) *The Containment of Urban England*. Allen and Unwin, London.

Hamilton, W.H. (1932) Institutions. *Encyclopedia of the Social Sciences*, Vol. 8, pp. 84–89.

Hamnett, C. (1991) The blind men and the elephant: the explanation of gentrification, *Transactions of the Institute of British Geographers*, **16**, 259–279.

Hancock, K. (1991) *The Determination of Housing Submarkets: Case Studies Using Scottish Data*, unpublished paper. Centre for Housing Research, University of Glasgow, Glasgow.

Hancock, K. (1993) Can pay? Won't pay? On economic principles of affordability. *Urban Studies*, **30**, 127–145.

Hancock, K. and Maclennan, D. (1989) *House price monitoring systems and housing planning in Scotland: a feasibility study. A Report for The Scottish Office*. Centre for Housing Research, Glasgow University, Glasgow.

Harrison, A.J. (1977) *Economics and Land Use Planning*. Croom Helm, London.

HBOS Halifax Bank of Scotland (2003) *Twenty Years of UK Housing*. HBOS, Edinburgh.

HBOS Halifax Bank of Scotland (2007a) *Halifax House Price Index, Regional House Prices Third Quarter 2007*, http://www.hbos.com.

HBOS Halifax Bank of Scotland (2007b) *Lowest number of first time buyers since 1980: FTB Annual Review*, http://www.hbos.com.

Henderson, W.O. (1967) *Engels: Selected Writings*. Penguin, Harmondsworth.

HM Government (2007) *Homes for the Future: More Affordable, More Sustainable*. CLG Command Paper 7191. TSO, London.

HM Treasury (2007) *Meeting the Aspirations of British People: 2007 Pre-Budget Report and Comprehensive Spending Review*. TSO, London.

Heriot-Watt University School of Built Environment (with Oxford Brookes University) (2007) *Scottish Planning Authorities Skills Assessment*. Improvement Service, Broxburn, Scotland.

Hodgson, G. (1999) *Economics and Utopia*. Routledge, London.

Holmans, A. (1995) What has happened to the north-south divide in house prices and the housing market? In: *Housing Finance Review 1995/96* (ed. S. Wilcox). The Joseph Rowntree Foundation, York.

Holmans, A. (2001) *Housing Demand and Need in England 1996–2016*. Town and Country Planning Association/National Housing Federation, London.

Holmans, A. (2007) *Higher household projections – but are the projections on track?* Town and Country Planning, London.

Holmes, M. J. and Grimes, A. (2008) Is there long-run convergence among regional house prices in the UK? *Urban Studies*, **45** (8), 1531–1544.

Hooper, A., Dunmore, K. and Hughes, M. (1998). *Home Alone: The Housing Preferences of One Person Households*. Report for The Housing Research Foundation. National House Building Confederation, Amersham.

House of Commons Environmental Select Committee (1998) *Inquiry on Housing*. TSO, London.

House of Commons Environmental Audit Committee (2005) *Building a Sustainable Future*. HMSO, London.

House of Commons ODPM Select Committee (2007) *Affordability and the Supply of Housing*, Third Report of Session 2005–06, Vol. 1: Report and Minutes. TSO, London.

Hoyt, H. (1939) *The Structure and Growth of Residential Neighbourhoods in American Cities.* Government Printing Office, Washington, D.C.

Hughes, G. and McCormick, B. (1981) Do council house policies reduce migration between regions? *Economic Journal*, **91** (4), 919–939.

Hulchanski, D. (1995) The concept of affordability: six contemporary uses of the housing expenditure to income ration. *Housing Studies*, **10**, 471–491.

Hull, A. (1997) Restructuring the debate on allocating land for housing. *Housing Studies*, **12**, 367–382.

Innes C (2007) *35% of city centre flats are empty*, Liverpool Daily Post, 24 April 2007. http://icliverpool.icnetwork.co.uk/0100news/0100regionalnews/tm_headline=35--of-city-centre-flats-are-empty&method=full&objectid=18953338&siteid=50061-name_page.html.

International Monetary Fund (IMF) (2008) *World Economic Outlook: Financial Stress, Downturns and Recoveries.* IMF, Washington, D.C.

Jackson, A., Morrison, N. and Royce, C. (1994) *The Supply of Land for Housing: Changing Local Authority Mechanisms*, Discussion Paper 42, Department of Land Economy, University of Cambridge, Cambridge.

Jarvis, H. and Russell, W. (1999) *The Use of Prices in Planning for Housing: A Review of Current Practice.* Discussion Paper 96, Department of Land Economy, University of Cambridge, Cambridge.

Jenks, M. and Jones, C. (2009) *Dimensions of the Sustainable City.* Springer, Rotterdam.

Jenks, M., Burton, E. and Williams, K. (eds) (1996) *The Compact City: A Sustainable Urban Form.* Spon, London.

Jones, C. (1978) Household movement, filtering and trading up within the owner occupied sector. *Regional Studies*, **12** (5), 551–561.

Jones, C. (1979a) Housing: the element of choice. *Urban Studies*, **16** (2), 197–204.

Jones, C. (1979b) Population decline in cities. In: *Urban Deprivation and the Inner City* (ed. C. Jones). Croom Helm, London.

Jones, C. (1981) Residential mobility: an economic model. *Scottish Journal of Political Economy*, **28** (1), 62–75.

Jones, C. (1996a) Urban regeneration, property development and the land market. *Environment and Planning Series C*, **14**, 269–279.

Jones, C. (1996b) Property-led local economic development policies: from advance factory to English partnerships and strategic property investment? *Regional Studies*, **30** (2), 200–206.

Jones, C. (2002) The definition of housing market areas and strategic planning. *Urban Studies*, **39** (3), 549–564.

Jones, C. (2003a) *Exploitation of the Right to Buy Scheme by Companies.* Office of the Deputy Prime Minister, London.

Jones, C. (2003b) *Devolution and Policies toward the Built Environment*, paper presented to the International Regional Science Association, St Andrews.

Jones, C. (2004) *House Prices, Housing Market Trends, and Housing Supply issues in Scotland.* Chartered Institute of Housing Scotland, Edinburgh.

Jones, C. (2007) Private investment in rented housing and the role of REITS. *European Journal of Housing Policy*, **7** (4), 383–400.

Jones, C. (2009a) The right to buy. In: *Housing Markets and Policy: Change and Transformation* (eds P. Malpass and R. Rowlands). Routledge, London.

Jones, C. (2009b) *Government Review of Regulation and Redress in the UK Housing Market*. Department of Business Enterprise Regulation and Reform/ DCLG, London.

Jones, C. and Brown, J. (2002) The establishment of markets for owner occupation within public sector communities. *European Journal of Housing Policy*, **2** (3), 265–292.

Jones, C. and Leishman, C. (2006) Spatial dynamics of the housing market: an inter-urban perspective. *Urban Studies*, **43**, 1041–1059.

Jones, C. and Maclennan, D. (1987) Building societies and credit rationing: an empirical examination of redlining. *Urban Studies*, **24** (3), 205–216.

Jones, C. and Maclennan, D. (1991) Urban growth and housing market change: Aberdeen 1968–1978. *Environment and Planning A*, **23**, 571–590.

Jones, C. and Murie, A. (2006) *The Right to Buy*. Blackwell, Oxford.

Jones, C. and Orr, A. (1999) Local commercial and industrial rental trends and property market constraints. *Urban Studies*, **36** (2), 215–229.

Jones, C. and Patrick, J. (1992) The merchant city as an example of housing led urban regeneration. In: *Rebuilding the City: Property Led Urban Regeneration* (eds P. Healey *et al.*). E&FN Spon, London.

Jones, C. and Watkins, C. (1996) Urban regeneration and sustainable markets. *Urban Studies*, **33** (7), 1129–1140.

Jones, C. and Watkins, C. (1999) Planning for housing. In: *Planning Beyond 2000* (eds P. Allmendinger and M. Chapman). John Wiley & Sons, Chichester.

Jones, C., Leishman, C. and Watkins, C. (2003) Structural change in a local urban housing market. *Environment and Planning A*, **35**, 1315–1326.

Jones, C., Leishman, C. and Watkins, C. (2004) Intra-urban migration and housing Submarkets: theory and evidence. *Housing Studies*, **19** (2), 269–283.

Jones, C., Leishman, C. and Watkins, C. (2005a) Housing market processes, urban housing submarkets and planning policy. *Town Planning Review*, **76** (2), 33–52.

Jones, C., Leishman, C. and MacDonald, C. (2005b) *Urban Form and Local Housing Markets*, paper presented at the European Real Estate Society Conference, Dublin.

Jones, C., Leishman, C., MacDonald, C., Orr, A. and Watkins, D. (2009) Economic viability. In: *Dimensions of the Sustainable City* (eds M. Jenks and C. Jones). Springer, Rotterdam.

Joseph Rowntree Foundation (1994) *Inquiry into Planning for Housing*. Joseph Rowntree Foundation, York.

Joseph Rowntree Foundation (2007) *JRF Submission to Green Paper*. Joseph Rowntree Foundation, York.

Kain, J.F. (1961) *The Journey to Work as a Determinant of Residential Location*. Rand Corporation, P-2489, Santa Monica, CA.

Kauko, T. (2001) Combining theoretical approaches; the case of urban land value and housing market dynamics. *Housing Theory and Society*, **17**, 875–894.

Kauko, T. (2004) A Comparative perspective on urban spatial housing market structure: some more evidence of local submarkets based on a neural networks classification of Amsterdam. *Urban Studies*, **41**, 2555–2579.

Khakee, A. (2007) From Olympic Village to middle-class waterfront housing project: ethics in Stockholm's development planning. *Planning Practice and Research*, **22** (2) 235–251.

Keskin, B. (2009) *Alternative approaches to modelling housing market segmentation: evidence From Istanbul*. PhD Thesis. University of Sheffield.

Lambert, C. and Boddy, M. (2002) *Transforming the city: post-recession gentrification and re-urbanisation*, paper presented at the Conference on Upward Neighbourhood Trajectories: Gentrification in the New Century, 26–27 September, University of Glasgow; copy available from the Faculty of the Built Environment, University of the West of England, Bristol.

Lancaster, K.J. (1966) A new approach to consumer theory. *Journal of Political Economy*, **74** (2), 132–157.

Lee, P. and Nevin, B. (2003) Changing demand for housing: restructuring markets and the public policy framework. *Housing Studies*, **18**, 65–85.

Leishman, C. (2007) *Hedonic methods and the housing market as a multi-level spatial system*, Paper presented at the American Real Estate Society Conference, San Francisco, April.

Leishman, C. and Watkins, C. (2002) Estimating repeat sales house price indices for British cities. *Journal of Property Investment and Finance*, **20** (1), 36–58.

Leishman, C., Jones, C. and Fraser, W. (2000) The influence of uncertainty on house builder behaviour and residential land values. *Journal of Property Research*, **17**, 147–168.

Leishman, C., Gibb, K., Meen, G., *et al.* (2008) *Scottish Model of Housing Supply and Affordability*. Scottish Government, Edinburgh.

Lloyd, M.G. and Peel, D. (2007) Green belts in Scotland: towards the modernisation of a traditional concept? *Journal of Environmental Planning and Management*, **50** (5), 639–656.

Low, N.P. (1991) *Planning, Politics and the State: Political Foundations of Planning Thought*. Unwin Hyman, London.

Lowry, I. (1960) Filtering and housing standards: a conceptual analysis. *Land Economics*, **56**, 362–370.

Macalister, T and Kollewe, J. (2008) Construction: Taylor Wimpey wipes £660m from land and building site values. *The Guardian*, Tuesday 1 July 2008. http://www.guardian.co.uk/business/2008/jul/01/constructionindustry.

MacDonald, K. and Kliman, A. (2007) *Opening up the Debate: Exploring Housing Land Supply Myths*. RTPI, London.

Maclennan, D. (1976) Some thoughts on the nature and purpose of house price studies. *Urban Studies*, **14**, 59–71.

Maclennan, D. (1982) *Housing Economics: An Applied Approach*. Longman, London.

Maclennan, D. (1986) *The Demand for Housing: An Economic Perspective*. Scottish Development Department, Edinburgh.

Maclennan, D. (1987) *The efficient market framework and real estate economics* [mimeo]. University of Glasgow, Glasgow.

Maclennan, D. (1992) *Housing Search and Choice in a Regional Housing System: New Housing in Strathclyde.* A report to the Housing Research Foundation for the Scottish House Builders Federation, University of Glasgow, Glasgow.

Maclennan, D. and Bannister, J. (1995) Housing research: building the connections. *Urban Studies*, **32** (10), 1581–1585.

Maclennan, D. and Pryce, G. (1998) *Missing Links: The Economy, Cities and Housing.* National Housing Federation, London.

Maclennan, D. and Tu, Y. (1996) Economic perspectives on the structure of local housing markets. *Housing Studies*, **11**, 387–406.

Maclennan, D. and Whitehead, C. (1996) Housing economics – an evolving agenda. *Housing Studies*, **11** (3), 341–344.

Maclennan, D., Munro, M. and Wood, G. (1987) Housing choice and the structure of urban housing markets. In: *Between State and Market Housing in the Post-Industrial Era* (eds B. Turner, J. Kemeny and L. Lundquist). Almquist and Hicksell, Gothenburg.

Maclennan, D., Gibb, K. and More, A. (1990) *Paying for Britain's Housing.* Joseph Rowntree Foundation, York.

Maclennan, D., More, A., O'Sullivan, A. and Young, G. (1998) *Local Housing Systems Analysis: Best Practice Guide.* Scottish Homes, Edinburgh.

Maclennan, D., Gibb, K., McLaren, J., *et al.* (2004) *Local Housing Systems Analysis: Good Practice Guide.* Communities Scotland, Edinburgh.

Malpass, P. (1999) Housing policy: does it have a future. *Policy and Politics*, **27**, 217–228.

Malpass, P. and Murie, A. (1994) *Housing Policy and Practice.* Macmillan, London.

McGreal, W.S., Adair, A.S., Smyth, A., Cooper, J. and Ryley, T. (2000) House prices and accessibility: the testing of relationships within Belfast area. *Housing Studies*, **15**, 699–716.

McMaster, R. and Watkins, C. (2006) Economics and underdetermination: a case study of urban land and housing economics. *Cambridge Journal of Economics*, **30** (6), 901–922.

McMaster, R., U'ren, G., Carnie, J., Strang, G. and Cooper, S. (2008) *An Assessment of the Value of Planning Agreements in Scotland.* Scottish Government, Edinburgh.

Meen, G. (1999) Regional house prices and the ripple effect: a new interpretation. *Housing Studies*, **14** (6), 733–753.

Meen, G. (2001) *Modelling Spatial Housing Markets.* Kluwer Academic Press, New York.

Meen, G. and Andrew, M. (2008) Planning for housing in the post-Barker era: affordability, household formation and tenure choice. *Oxford Review of Economic Policy*, **24** (1), 79–98.

Meen, G., Allmendinger, P., Andrew, M., *et al.* (2005a) *Affordability Targets: Implications for Housing Supply in 2005.* CLG and Office of the Deputy Prime Minister, London.

Meen, G., Gibb, K., Goody, J., McGrath, T. and Mackinnon, J. (2005b) *Economic Segregation in Britain: Causes, Consequences and Policy.* Policy Press, Bristol.

Michaels, R. and Smith, V.K. (1990) Market segmentation and valuing amenities with hedonic models: the case of hazardous waste sites. *Journal of Urban Economics*, **28**, 223–242.

Minford, P., Ashton, P. and Peel, M. (1988) The effects of housing distortions on unemployment. *Oxford Economic Papers*, **40** (2), 322–345.

Monk, S. (1999) *The Use of Price in Planning for Housing: a Literature Review*. DP105, Department of Land Economy, University of Cambridge, Cambridge.

Monk, S. and Whitehead, C. (1996) Land supply and housing: a case study. *Housing Studies*, **11**, 407–423.

Monk, S. and Whitehead, C. (1999) Evaluating the impact of planning controls in the United Kingdom: some implications for planning. *Land Economics*, **75** (1), 74–93.

Monk, S., Short, C. and Whitehead, C. (2005) Planning obligations and affordable housing. In: *Planning, Public Policy and Property Markets* (eds D. Adams, C. Watkins and M. White). Blackwell, Oxford.

Monk, S., Crook, T., Lister, D., *et al.* (2006) *Delivering Affordable Housing through Section 106 Agreements*. Joseph Rowntree Foundation, York.

Monk, S., Whitehead, C. and Martindale, K. (2008) *Increasing Housing Supply CLG Housing Markets and Planning Analysis Expert Panel Paper 2/08*. Cambridge Centre for Housing and Planning Research, University of Cambridge, Cambridge.

Moore, V. (1995) *Planning Law*, 5th edn. Blackstone Press, Oxford.

Mullins, D.W. and Malpass, P. (2002) Local authority housing stock transfer in the UK: from local initiative to national policy. *Housing Studies*, **17** (4), 673–686.

Munro, M. (1986) *Testing for segmentation in the private housing market in Glasgow*. Centre for Housing Research, Discussion Paper No. 8, University of Glasgow, Glasgow.

Munro, M. and Lamont, D. (1985) Neighbourhood perception, preference and mobility in the Glasgow private housing market. *Environment and Planning A*, **17**, 1330–1351.

Munro, M., Ford, J., Leishman, C. and Karley, N.K. (2005) *Lending to Higher Risk Borrowers: Sub-prime Credit and Sustainable Home Ownership*. Joseph Rowntree Foundation, York.

Muth, R. (1969) *Cities and Housing*. University of Chicago Press, Chicago, IL.

Myers, D. (1975) Housing allowances, housing submarkets and the filtering process. *Urban Affairs Quarterly*, **11**, 215–240.

Nadin, V. (2006) *The Role and Scope of Spatial Planning: Literature Review – Spatial Plans in Practice: Supporting the Review of Spatial Planning*. CLG, London.

National Audit Office (NAO) (2007) *Department for Communities and Local Government: Housing Market Renewal*. HMSO, London.

Nationwide Building Society (2007) *FTB Affordability Indices*, http://www.nationwide.com.

Nevin Leather Associates, Manchester Geomatics, University of Sheffield and Inner City Solutions (2008) *Strategic Housing Market Assessments for the North West*. 4NW, Wigan.

Newhaven Research (2008) *All Pain, No Gain? Finding the Balance Delivering Affordable Housing Through the Planning System in Scotland*. Chartered Institute of Housing, Edinburgh.

National Housing and Planning Advice Unit (NHPAU) (2007) *Affordability Matters*. DCLG, London.

O'Sullivan, A. (2003) Economics and housing planning. In: *Housing Economics and Public Policy* (eds A. O'Sullivan and Gibb, K.). Blackwell, Oxford.

Office of National Statistics (ONS) (2007) UK population set to increase to 65 million over the next ten years [Press Release] 23 October.

Office of the Deputy Prime Minster (2000) *Planning Policy Statement 3: Housing*. ODPM, London.

Office of the Deputy Prime Minister (2003) *Sustainable Communities: Building for the Future*. ODPM, London.

Office of the Deputy Prime Minister (2004) *The Egan Review: Skills for Sustainable Communities*. ODPM, London.

Office of the Deputy Prime Minister (2005a) *Planning Policy Statement 1: Delivering Sustainable Development*. ODPM, London.

Office of the Deputy Prime Minister (2005b) *Planning Policy Statement 11: Regional Spatial Strategies*. ODPM, London.

Office of the Deputy Prime Minister (2005c) *Housing Market Assessments: Draft Guidance*. ODPM, London.

Office of the Deputy Prime Minister (2005d) *Planning: Consultation Paper on PPS3 – Housing*. ODPM, London.

Office of Fair Trading (OFT) (2008) *Homebuilding in the UK: A Market Study*. Office of Fair Trading, London.

Pace, R.K. and Lesage, J.P. (2004) Spatial statistics and real estate. *Journal of Real Estate Finance and Economics*, **29**, 147–148.

Palm, R. (1978) Spatial segmentation of the urban housing market. *Economic Geography*, **54**, 210–221.

Parr, J.B. and Jones, C. (1983) City size distributions and urban density functions: some inter-relationships. *Journal of Regional Science*, **23** (3), 283–307.

Pavlov, A. (2000) Space-varying regression coefficients: a semi-parametric approach applied to real estate markets. *Real Estate Economics*, **28**, 249–283.

Payne, S. (2008) *The institutional capacity of the UK speculative housebuilding industry*. Unpublished PhD thesis, University of Glasgow, Glasgow.

Pearce, B. and Wenban-Smith, A. (1998) *Planning Gains – Negotiating with Planning Authorities*. Estates Gazette, Hampshire.

Power, A. (1999) *Estates on the Edge*. MacMillan, Basingstoke.

Prescott, J. (2000) *Statement on PPG 3 by the Deputy Prime Minister*. DETR, London, 7 March.

Prest. A.R. (1981) *The Taxation of Urban Land*. Manchester University Press, Manchester.

Prior, A. (2005) UK planning reform: a Regulationist interpretation. *Planning Theory and Practice*, **6** (4), 465–484.

Prior. A. and Raemaekers, J. (2007) Is Green Belt fit for purpose in a post-Fordist landscape? *Planning, Practice & Research*, **22** (4), 579–599.

Pryce, G. (2004) *Micro and Macro Effects of the Location of New Housing*. Report to ODPM, University of Glasgow, Glasgow.

Pryce, G. and Evans, G. (2007) Is it possible to identify housing submarkets? Testing a new approach. RICS FiBRE Series, June.

Quercia, R.G. and Galster, G.C. (2000) Threshold effects and neighbourhood change. *Journal of Planning Education and Research*, **20**, 145–162.

Quigley, J.M. (1979) What have we learned about urban housing markets? In: *Current Issues in Urban Economics* (eds M. Straszheim and P. Mieszkowski). pp. 391–429. Johns Hopkins University Press, Baltimore, MD.

Rapkin, W., Winnick, L. and Blank, D. (1953) *Housing Market Analysis.* US Housing Home and Finance Agency, Washington, D.C.

Ratcliff, R. (1949) *Urban Land Economics.* McGraw Hill, New York.

Richardson, H.W. and Gordon, P. (1993) Market planning: oxymoron or common sense? *Journal of the American Planning Association,* **59** (3), 347–352.

Roberts, T. (2002) The seven lamps of planning. *Town Planning Review,* **73** (1), 1–9.

Robson, B., Parkinson, M., Boddy, M. and Maclennan, D. (2000) *The State of English Cities.* Department of Environment, Transport and the Regions, London.

Rosen, S. (1974) Hedonic prices and implicit markets: product differentiation in pure competition. *Journal of Political Economy,* **82**, 34–55.

Rothenberg, J., Galster, G., Butler, R. and Pitkin, J. (1991) *The Maze of Urban Housing Markets: Theory, Evidence and Policy.* University of Chicago Press, Chicago.

Rowlands, R., Murie, A. and Tice, A. (2006) *More than Tenure Mix: Developer and Purchaser Attitudes to New Housing Estates.* Chartered Institute of Housing/Joseph Rowntree Foundation, York.

Royal Town Planning Institute (RTPI) (2001) *A New Vision for Planning: Delivering Sustainable Communities, An Agenda for Action.* RTPI, London.

Royal Town Planning Institute (RTPI) (2002) *Education Commission Report.* RTPI, London.

Royal Town Planning Institute (RTPI) (2007) *Planning Together: Local Strategic Partnerships and Spatial Planning: A Practical Guide.* RTPI, London.

Royal Town Planning Institute (RTPI) (2008) http://www.rtpi.org.uk.

Schelling, T.C. (1971) Dynamic models of segregation. *Journal of Mathematical Sociology,* **1**, 143–186.

Schelling, T.C. (1972) The process of residential segregation: neighbourhood tipping. In: *Racial Discrimination in Economic Life* (ed. A.H. Pascal), pp. 157–184. DC Heath and Co., Lexington, MA.

Schnare, A. and Struyk, R. (1976) Segmentation in urban housing markets. *Journal of Urban Economics,* **3**, 146–166.

School of Planning and Housing (2001) *The Role of the Planning System in the Provision of Housing.* Scottish Executive, Edinburgh.

Scottish Executive (2003) *Planning Advice Note 38: Housing Land.* Scottish Executive, Edinburgh.

Scottish Executive Development Department (2004) *Making Development Plans Deliver: A Consultation Paper.* Scottish Executive, Edinburgh.

Scottish Executive (2005) *Planning Advice Note: PAN 74 Affordable Housing.* Scottish Executive, Edinburgh.

Scottish Government (2008a) *Scottish Planning Policy SPP3: Planning for Housing.* Scottish Government, Edinburgh.

Scottish Government (2008b) Affordable Housing Securing Planning Consent Bulletin 2005–2007 [Online] http://www.scotland.gov.uk/Resource/Doc/221329/0059514.pdf.

Shaw, C. (2007) Fifty years of UK National Population Projections: how accurate have they been? *Population Trends*, 128.

Simpson, M. and MacDonald, K. (2003) *Planning for Housing – The Potential for Sustainable Communities*. CIH/RTPI, London.

Smith, L.B. (1978) Comment on Quigley and Grigsby. In: *Urban Housing Markets: Recent Directions in Housing Research* (eds L. Bourne and J. Hitchcock). University of Toronto Press, Toronto.

Smith, L.B., Rosen, K.T. and Fallis, G. (1988) Recent developments in economic models of housing markets. *Journal of Economic Literature*, **26**, 29–64.

Smith, N. (1996) *New Urban Frontier: Gentrification and the Revanchist City*. Routledge, London.

Smith, N. and Williams, P. (eds) (1986) *Gentrification of the City*. Unwin Hyman, London.

Smith, S.J. and Munro, M. (2008) The microstructures of housing markets. *Housing Studies*, **23** (2), 159–162.

Smith, S.J., Munro, M. and Christie, H. (2006) Performing (housing) markets. *Urban Studies*, **43**, 81–98.

Smith, T.R. and Mertz, F. (1980) An analysis of the effects of information revision on the outcome of housing market search with special reference to the influence of reality agents. *Environment and Planning A*, **12**, 155–174.

Smith, T.R. and Clark, W.A.V. (1982a) Housing market search behaviour and expected utility theory: 1. Measuring preferences for housing. *Environment and Planning A*, **14**, 681–698.

Smith, T.R. and Clark, W.A.V. (1982b) Housing market search behaviour and expected utility theory: 2. The process of search. *Environment and Planning A*, **14**, 717–737.

Smyth, H. (1984) *Land Supply, Housebuilders and Government Policy*. Working Paper 43, School for Advanced Urban Studies, University of Bristol, Bristol.

Sonstelie, J.C. and Portney, P.R. (1980) Gross rents and market values: testing the implications of Tiebout's hypothesis. *Journal of Urban Economics*, **7**, 102–118.

Stigler, G. and Sherwin, R.A. (1985) The extent of the market. *Journal of Law and Economics*, **28**, 555–585.

Stone, M. (2006) A housing affordability standard for the UK. *Housing Studies*, **21** (4), 453–476.

Straszheim, M. (1975) *An Econometric Analysis of the Urban Housing Market*. National Bureau of Economic Research, New York.

Strathclyde Regional Council (1994) *Structure Plan Review: Consultative Draft*. Department of Physical Planning, Glasgow.

Thomas, R. (2006) The Growth of Buy to Let. *CML Housing Finance*, **9**, 1–13.

Thornley, A. (1991) *Urban Planning under Thatcherism*. Routledge, London.

Thornley, A. (1996) Planning policy and the market. In: *British Planning Policy in Transition: Planning in the 1990s* (ed. M. Tewdwr-Jones). UCL Press, London.

Tu, Y., Sun, H. and Yu, S-M. (2007) Spatial autocorrelation and urban housing market segmentation. *Journal of Real Estate Finance and Economics*, **34**, 385–406.

University College London Deloitte (2007) *Shaping and Delivering Tomorrow's Places: Effective Practice in Spatial Planning*. RTPI, London.

Urban Task Force (1999) *Towards an Urban Renaissance*. E&FN Spon, London.

Vigar, G., Healey, P., Hull, A. and Davoudi, S. (2000) *Planning, Governance and Spatial Strategy in Britain: An Institutional Analysis*. MacMillan, Basingstoke.

Von Boventer, E. (1978) Bandwagon effects and product cycles in urban dynamics. *Urban Studies*, **15**, 261–272.

Watkins, C. (1999) Property valuation and the structure of urban housing markets. *Journal of Property Investment and Finance*, **17**, 157–175.

Watkins, C. (2001) The definition and identification of housing submarkets. *Environment and Planning A*, **33**, 2235–2253.

Watkins, C. (2005) *Planning and price signals*. Paper presented to the ERSC Planning and Development Seminar Group, University of Cardiff, Cardiff.

Watkins, C. (2008) Microeconomic perspectives on the structure and operation of local housing markets. *Housing Studies*, **23**,163–178.

Watson, C.J. (1973) *Household Movement in West Central Scotland: A Study of Housing Chains and Filtering*. Occasional Paper No 26. Centre for Urban and Regional Studies, University of Birmingham, Birmingham.

Watson, J. (2006) *Understanding Planning Gain: What Works*. Joseph Rowntree Foundation, York.

Wellings, F. (2005) *The rise of the national housebuilder – A history of British housebuilders through the twentieth century*. Unpublished PhD thesis, University of Liverpool.

Wellings, F. (2006) *Private Housebuilding Annual 2006*. Troubador Publishing, Leicester.

Welsh Assembly Government (2002) *Planning: Delivering for Wales – A Consultation Paper*. WAG, Cardiff.

Whitehead, C. (1997) Changing needs, changing incentives. In: *Directions in Housing Policy* (ed. P. Williams). Paul Chapman Press, London.

Whitehead, C. (1999) Urban housing markets: theory and policy. In: *Handbook of Regional and Urban Economics* (eds P. Chesire and E.S. Mills), Vol. 3. Elsevier, Amsterdam.

Wingo, L. (1961) *Transportation and Urban Land*. Resources for the Future, Washington, D.C.

Wilcox, S. (2006) *UK Housing Review 2005/2006*. CIH/CML, London.

Wong, C. and Watkins, C. (2009) Measuring the outcomes of spatial planning: conceptual and methodological challenges. *Town Planning Review*, in press.

Wong, C., Baker, M., Hincks, S., Rae, A., Ferrari, E. and Watkins, C. (2008) *Measuring the Outcomes of Spatial Planning in England*. Final Report to CLG and RTPI. Universities of Manchester and Sheffield.

Index